FERMENTING

WARDEE HARMON

T0054577

Publisher: Mike Sanders
Editor: Christopher Stolle
Book Designer: William Thomas
Cover Designer: Lindsay Dobbs
Compositor: Ayanna Lacey
Proofreader: Chrissy Guthrie
Indexer: Jessica McCurdy Crooks

First American Edition, 2021
Published in the United States by DK Publishing
6081 E. 82nd Street, Suite 400, Indianapolis, IN 46250

Copyright © 2021 by Wardee Harmon

21 22 23 24 25 10 9 8 7 6 5 4 3 2 1
001-322092-JUN2021

All rights reserved.
Without limiting the rights under the copyright reserved above, no part of this publication
may be reproduced, stored in or introduced into a retrieval system, or transmitted, in any form,
or by any means (electronic, mechanical, photocopying, recording, or otherwise),
without the prior written permission of the copyright owner.
Published in Great Britain by Dorling Kindersley Limited.

Library of Congress Catalog Number: 2020950766
ISBN 978-1-61564-990-7

Note: This publication contains the opinions and ideas of its author. It is intended to provide helpful and informative material on the subject matter covered. It is sold with the understanding that the author and publisher are not engaged in rendering professional services in the book. If the reader requires personal assistance or advice, a competent professional should be consulted. The author and publisher specifically disclaim any responsibility for any liability, loss, or risk, personal or otherwise, which is incurred as a consequence, directly or indirectly, of the use and application of any of the contents of this book.

Trademarks: All terms mentioned in this book that are known to be or are suspected of being trademarks or service marks have been appropriately capitalized. Alpha Books, DK, and Penguin Random House LLC cannot attest to the accuracy of this information. Use of a term in this book should not be regarded as affecting the validity of any trademark or service mark.

DK books are available at special discounts when purchased in bulk for
sales promotions, premiums, fund-raising, or educational use. For details, contact:
DK Publishing Special Markets, 1450 Broadway, Suite 801, New York, NY 10018
SpecialSales@dk.com

Printed and bound in the United States of America

Reprinted and updated from
The Complete Idiot's Guide® to Fermenting Foods

For the curious
www.dk.com

Contents

I dedicate this book to my parents, Ibrahim and Martha Bisharat, who filled my childhood with yogurt, cheese, olives, and pickles and who gave me my love for cultured foods.

Introduction

I grew up appreciating and enjoying a select few fermented foods, mostly Middle Eastern: goat cheese, yogurt, and olives. But I never learned to make anything fermented until I grew up and had a family of my own. I embraced fermentation for many reasons—all intertwined. Some of our health challenges were resolved by eating regular servings of fermented, cultured foods. I saw that fermentation meets a need for preservation—without modern refrigeration, freezing, or high-pressure canning. Keeping our own family milk cow means we have gallons upon gallons of creamy Jersey milk to turn into cheese or other cultured dairy foods. I already loved sour, complex flavors, but I got ridiculously excited about being able to ferment foods myself. And perhaps most importantly, I saw God's hand in creating the wild, beneficial organisms we simply put to work for us in smart (not hard) ways.

We might never know all the differences fermented foods make in our bodies (but I share known health benefits in Chapter 2). Some changes are imperceptible or could be attributed to many factors and some things we just can't know this side of Heaven. But what we do know is so very encouraging. I feel privileged to be able to share the skills of fermenting foods with you.

I got my experience in fermentation a bit haphazardly. I did a little dabbling here and there before I got serious and then I tackled fermentation by food type. I created simple beverages, then krauts and pickles, then dairy and sourdough. Here and there, I added experiments with chutneys and meats and fish. My family and I liked some of what I made and hated other things. Fermented foods and their complex, sour flavors take some adjustment for most modern folks and we were no exception. I had more than a few flops. I made crumbly, dry, tasteless cheese. I made bitter sauerkraut. I made mushy pickles. Experience is a wonderful teacher, as they say. I think I got a great education.

Along the way, I improved my fermentation skills and got into a groove. I learned what was happening during fermentation and why it was happening. The more I experienced it through bubbling jars and crocks on my countertop, the more I could adapt and adjust and even break rules—and succeed. I learned what were the rules and what were not. These are important nuances born of trial and error.

I'm beyond excited about fermenting foods. I love to do it and I love that fermenting is a traditional, sustainable, low-tech method of preserving food with incredible health benefits. This book (and the recipes it contains) barely scratches the surface. Our world has a rich history of fermentation, with thousands upon thousands of recipes and techniques from all parts of the world. Since the beginning of history, people with varying levels of scientific knowledge combined the principles of fermentation (whether merely observed or known) uniquely to produce the world's best cheeses, pickles, krauts, beverages (alcoholic and otherwise), sourdough breads, sausages, and more.

On your fermentation journey, please start at the beginning of this book and work your way to the end. I can't promise you'll have a flawless journey, but I can assure you that you'll get a better start than I did. I devote the entirety of Part 1 to giving you an understanding of fermenting foods—from history to health benefits and the science of it as well as a consideration of the tools and equipment. You shouldn't move on to the recipes (organized by food type) until you know what's going on. The recipes (Parts 2 and 3) are necessarily brief because they build on the principles that were shared before. Some breakfast, side dish, main dish, dessert, and snack recipes are included to give you uses for the fermented foods you create.

Whether your interest in fermenting foods is to get an intellectual understanding or to practice the art of fermenting foods (or both), this book will get you well on your way. If you're looking for a particular recipe and don't find it here, you'll learn enough about the methodology and principles to make it yourself or recognize it when you see it elsewhere.

How This Book Is Organized

Successfully fermenting foods builds on knowledge gained from others as well as practice, practice, practice. In this book, I'll help you understand fermentation—from the terminology and tools to the processes. Then you can put it all into practice through more than 150 recipes—most of which are simple and a few of which require more equipment or skill. But nothing is beyond your reach.

Part 1: The Fermentation Story

You'll learn some of the history of fermented foods, the health benefits of eating fermented foods, the types of fermentation and how each works, and the essentials of fermentation (tools, equipment, and signs of good fermenting).

Part 2: Fermenting the Fruits of the Vine

You'll get to practice fermentation through fermenting plant foods: turning vegetables into pickles, krauts, relishes, and salsas; changing fruits into chutneys and relishes; creating condiments like cultured ketchup and mustard; making beverages, like nonalcoholic natural sodas and health tonics as well as alcoholic and old-fashioned herbal beers; transforming beans into hummus, tempeh, and miso; and souring grains into sourdough breads and cultured baked goods.

Part 3: Surf to Turf Fermenting

You'll learn how to ferment the milk and meat of animals and fish. You'll culture dairy into basic foods, like sour cream, butter, and yogurt, and then create simple cultured and raw cheeses. Finally, you'll learn to ferment meats and fish through brining, open-air fermentation, and smoking.

Acknowledgments

I want to thank my dear, dear family—my husband, Jeff, and our children, Haniya (with her husband and two boys), Naomi, and Mikah—for supporting my endeavors and giving me extra time and space to complete this book. Our already-busy life barely had room, but you helped make it happen.

Some parts of this book came together thanks to generous friends who shared recipes and techniques, listed here in alphabetical order:

- Donielle Baker (www.NaturalFertilityandWellness.com)
- Marillyn Beard (www.Just-Making-Noise.blogspot.com)
- Jerri Beddell (www.HomesteaderSupply.com)
- Sylvia Britton (www.ChristianHomeKeeper.org)
- Michael Bunker
- Haniya Cherry (www.twitter.com/haniyajenan)
- Annette Cottrell
- Amy Davis
- Christina Dickson
- Lindsey Dietz (www.AllTheNourishingThings.com)

- Jami Ellis

- Kresha Faber (www.NourishingJoy.com)

- Julie Feickert (www.CulturesForHealth.com)

- Andrea Sabean (www.ArtisanInTheWoods.com)

- Katie Mae Stanley (www.NourishingSimplicity.org)

- Megan Stevens (www.EatBeautiful.net)

- Gerard Van Assche and the Umpqua Valley Brewer's Guild (www.UmpquaValleyBrewersGuild.com)

- Erin Vander Lugt

- Emily Sunwell-Vidaurri (www.RecipesToNourish.com)

- Tracey Vierra

- Dawn Yoder (www.OhSweetMercy.com)

A special thank-you to friends and students in my online classes who tested recipes and shared impressions: Connie Burt, Kimarie Card, Buffi Frazier, Nikki Hughes, Deborah Ledet, and Elisabeth Tull.

Thank you to Stanley Marianski and Adam Marianski (www.meatsandsausages.com), authors of *The Art of Making Fermented Sausages*, who graciously allowed me to include four of their fermented sausage recipes in this book.

Thank you to friends Rand Dickson, Sonya Hemmings, and Shannon Stonger as well as the editing team at DK Publishing and Alpha Books for reviewing my work for accuracy and clarity.

And my utmost and grateful thanks go to my God and Savior, who has blessed my life abundantly with purpose, joy, and good gifts.

The Complete Idiot's Guide to Fermenting Foods was tech-reviewed by Shannon Stonger, who double-checked the accuracy of what you'll learn here to help us ensure this book gives you everything you need to know about fermenting foods.

Fermentation Basics

To ferment foods, you need to understand what fermentation is. This section covers several introductory topics to help you get started with fermenting. You'll learn about the history of fermented foods and contrast traditional fermentation with methods employed by today's food producers. You'll discover the incredible health benefits of consuming fermented foods. You'll also read about the various types of fermentation, fermenting organisms, and how fermentation works. That includes ideal conditions, vessels, tools, and ingredients—all part of a fermenter's toolbox.

A First Look at Fermentation

Almost every society has eaten and enjoyed fermented foods. This preservation technique gradually led to the development of regional flavors and techniques. In this chapter, I'll explain how fermentation got its name and we'll explore the first fermented foods of civilization, including the first attempts at sauerkraut and cheese. You'll learn what happened to traditional fermentation when large-scale food production appeared on the scene. And finally, you'll find out how you can preserve practically every food through fermentation.

Fermentation Throughout History

Fermentation—the traditional methods of preserving and improving foods—gave us our first breads, wines, and cheeses. As early as 4000 BCE, Egyptians likely discovered *grain fermentation*, also known as *sourdough leavening*, by accident. After leaving a bundle of dough in a warm place for a little too long, they saw that the dough had risen. They couldn't know what had happened though: Beneficial yeasts and bacteria consumed sugars in the flour, giving off gases that caused the dough to rise. When they baked the puffy, warm lump of dough, they probably enjoyed the pleasant sour flavor or noticed how their bodies digested the bread.

Fermentation occurs when microorganisms break down food, giving off gases and producing beneficial acids and/or alcohol. This and other happy accidents like it led ancient cultures to learn how to control fermentation. As people experimented, they created and nurtured regional and cultural varieties of ales, wines, beers, sausages, breads, yogurt, cheeses, sauerkrauts, pickles, and more.

The word "ferment" comes from the Latin root *fervere*, which means "to boil." Fermenting foods can indeed appear to be boiling. Not only does the action of fermentation heat up the food, but an effervescence also builds up from the gases given off by fermenting organisms. Perhaps you've seen bubbly or fizzy sourdough starter, sauerkraut, or champagne. Now you know how fermentation got its name.

Sourdough Bread

Traditional Fermented Foods

Besides bread, wine, and cheese, most of us know about sauerkraut, or fermented cabbage. Although its name comes from the German words *sauer* (meaning sour) and *kraut* (meaning vegetable), sauerkraut is surprisingly *not* of German origin. Legend tells us that more than 2,000 years ago, fermented cabbage was a staple food for the workers constructing the Great Wall of China, who packed all their food, including cabbage, in big crocks. Fermentation began within a few days and the people noticed the delicious flavor change.

One thousand years later, Genghis Khan brought sauerkraut to Eastern Europe during an invasion. Many elite Europeans shunned this crunchy, sour, fermented cabbage dish, but the peasants loved it and kept making it. Sailors took barrels and barrels of kraut on long sea voyages because its high vitamin C levels saved them from scurvy, or vitamin C deficiency. Eventually, sauerkraut came to the Americas. It became a traditional part of American farm life, as homesteaders turned large crops of cabbage into sauerkraut, effectively preserving the cabbage to feed their families all winter.

Preserved milk (in the form of cheese) is yet another fermented food of history. A couple legends tell how the first cheese was made. Usually, the stories include a traveling nomad with a primitive canteen (made of repurposed animal stomach) full of milk. Animal stomachs contain an enzyme called rennin, which we now know coagulates, or curdles, milk. When this nomad arrived at his destination and untied his canteen, he would have found coagulated milk, or cheese, because of the milk being curdled from the rennin. It's also possible that milk acids coagulated the milk during the long, bumpy journey. Either way, milk was turned into cheese and people soon learned how to repeat the process.

We have records of cow and goat cheese being eaten in ancient Sumaria as early as 4000 BCE. Tomb murals in ancient Egypt, dated 2000 BCE, show cheese and butter being made. In the 300s BCE, Aristotle praised cheese. Zoroaster, a Persian prophet from around the sixth century BCE, was said to live on cheese alone for 20 years. The Holy Bible mentions David, a future king of Israel, who as a boy carried 10 cheeses as a gift to a captain in Israel's army (1 Samuel 17:18).

Goat Cheese

Almost every country in the world boasts unique varieties of cheese—processes developed and perfected by their people for hundreds or thousands of years. Think of France's Camembert; England's Cheddar, Gloucester, Roquefort, and Cheshire cheeses; Greece's feta; Switzerland's aptly named Swiss cheese; or Italy's mozzarella, traditionally made from the milk of water buffalo.

Sausage and salami come from the Latin word *sal* for salt. Indeed, the first preserved meats (from before 2200 BCE and later) were pounded, salted, and dried into nutritious salamis that kept well for a long time and were a staple food for Roman soldiers. However, these salamis, or sausages, weren't fermented.

Later on, butchers around the world created extraordinary, high-quality fermented sausages by cultivating the growth of local microorganisms while meat aged. But while the particular microorganisms of a locale have particular effects on fermentation, so does a region's climate. Cool temperatures and mild humidity are favorable conditions for meat fermentation. On the other hand, higher temperatures and lower humidity don't favor fermentation. To account for climate and seasonal differences while yielding the best results, people learned to combine unique methods of smoking and drying with long or short periods of fermenting. This is why specialty sausages vary from region to region: smoked, smoked and dried, air-dried, fast-fermented, or slow-fermented.

Further discussions of fermented foods around the world could take up this entire book, but I'll conclude this section by giving you a brief list of other fermented foods in history. East Asian food culture was largely founded on fermented foods, such as miso, soy sauce, soy nuggets, rice vinegar, and *sake* (a Japanese alcoholic drink made from fermented rice that's traditionally drunk warm in small porcelain cups). Interestingly, whereas much of Western fermentation is accomplished through beneficial yeasts and bacteria, the good guys of Asian fermentation are actually various molds.

Villages in Northern Europe had their own breweries with their own styles of beers, ales, ciders, and meads. In South and Latin Americas, you'll find *chicha*, an all-encompassing label for the many varieties of fermented corn beverages. Mayans created *pozol*, a fermented corn dough, and Ecuadorans enjoyed a fermented rice dish called *Sierra rice*. A Russian staple is *kvass*, a drink consumed daily that's easily made in just a few days from stale bread or beets. Finally, early Americans fermented countless varieties of relishes from corn, cucumbers, carrots, and other abundant garden produce.

Modern Pickling Methods

In the early 1900s, the practice of food fermentation declined. The most significant factor in its decline? Food fermentation isn't suited for an industrialized food system. Because fermentation is an often-variable process where results can't be guaranteed nor flavors consistent from batch to batch, it became impossible for food manufacturers to produce safe, good-tasting food on a large scale while still using old-fashioned fermenting methods. With the pressure of built-up gases in fermented foods, food producers also had trouble preventing some fermented foods from exploding on grocery store shelves.

So they turned to methods that were suited to large-scale food production, such as vinegar pickling, high-heat or pressure processing (canning), pasteurizing, and using increased levels of salt. These methods made food "safe" in the sense that they'd be shelf-stable, travel far, and taste the same from batch to batch. However, the downsides aren't insignificant: Modern pickled foods are less nutritious and impart less complex and pleasing flavors.

Pasteurization is the process of heating foods to kill disease-causing bacteria or microorganisms. However, it also kills beneficial organisms, destroys heat-sensitive vitamins, and denatures fragile proteins. As you'll learn in Chapter 2, traditional fermentation yields extremely nutritious foods. In contrast, modern pickled foods are essentially dead. No time or organisms are allowed to work on the food to yield beneficial acids, to create more nutrients, or to break down hard-to-digest food substances. When subjected to high-heat canning or pasteurization, beneficial organisms, vitamins, and enzymesare lost. White vinegar, used in modern pickling, is an overly acidic food with no nutritional benefits. By contrast, the acids produced by traditional fermentation are nutritious.

Comparing Pickles

You can see the reality of the decrease in nutrition with modern methods when reading food labels. Let's consider pickles and sauerkraut. There's a company selling delicious old-fashioned pickles and sauerkraut in the refrigerated section of your health food store, specialty grocer, and even many conventional grocery stores. Their old-fashioned pure kosher dills contain cucumbers, artesian well water, garlic, salt, dill, and spices.

For contrast, check out the ingredients listed on a jar of conventional kosher dill whole pickles: fresh cucumbers, water, distilled vinegar, salt, and less than 2% of high-fructose corn syrup, dried garlic, spices, calcium chloride, sodium benzoate (to preserve flavor), dried red peppers, natural flavors, and polysorbate 80. Notice that the second type of pickles lists distilled, or white, vinegar as an ingredient, while the first doesn't. Fermentation gives the old-fashioned pickles naturally occurring acids that not only preserve them but also produce probiotics—similar to the familiar yogurt. But distilled vinegar simply preserves a food that has had all potential nutrients stripped through the pasteurization process.

The old-fashioned pickles contain no added preservatives, while the modern pickles contain the preservative sodium benzoate, widely used in acidic foods to lengthen shelf life. Although there's no evidence of its being harmful on its own, there's reason to believe it changes into a proven carcinogen—benzene—in the presence of vitamin C. (Carcinogens are substances capable of causing cancer in living tissue.)

The modern pickles also contain polysorbate 80, a common additive used to prevent food separation. You'll find it in ice cream, whipped cream, nondairy creamers, chewing gum, condiments, and more. Side effects of consuming it range from mild to severe, including various allergic reactions, digestive upset, infertility, or heart problems.

And although it's not mentioned, today's pickles are canned with high heat—and here's why: to seal the jar, to kill any microorganisms (whether beneficial or of the spoiling kind), and to make the pickles last on the shelf a long time. This heat destroys vitamins and enzymes and would be unnecessary if the pickles were made through traditional fermentation, distributed locally, and stored in cool storage rather than on an open-air grocery store shelf.

Comparing Sauerkraut

In modern food culture, old-fashioned sauerkraut experienced a demise similar to that of traditional pickles. Prior to 1940, each autumn, American families turned cabbage into sauerkraut to preserve it through the winter. Basic cookbooks contained traditional, healthful recipes calling for cabbage and salt. The simple fermentation produced acids and organisms to preserve the kraut through the winter and increase the nutrition of the cabbage.

Then in the 1940s, ready-to-go sauerkraut appeared on grocery store shelves. Over time, people stopped making their own and bought the ready-made kind instead. Was it the same quality food? Hardly. The new kraut, like pickles, was processed at high temperatures to prolong its shelf life. It also contained chemical preservatives and much more salt—again, to help it last longer on the shelf. Vitamin C was destroyed through the high-heat canning process. Ready to compare labels again?

Here are the ingredients for homemade sauerkraut: cabbage and salt. That's it.

Here are the ingredients in a comparable, although conventional, brand of shredded sauerkraut: cabbage, water, salt, caraway, sodium benzoate (preservative), and sodium bisulfite (to promote color retention).

Can you see the difference? The old-fashioned fermented sauerkraut is free of preservatives. Acids aren't mentioned, but we know that fermentation produces beneficial acids. You can preserve this old-fashioned kraut long term in cool storage. The modern kraut contains preservatives for shelf stability and another additive to maintain color. Also, the modern kraut is subjected to high heat, which causes vitamins, enzymes, and organisms (beneficial or otherwise) to perish.

Return to Tradition

Whether by accident or by applying what they observed in similar fermentations, old societies learned to preserve and improve the nutrition of a multitude of foods. Modern food methods have undone these thousands of years of traditions, but all is not lost.

If you look hard, you can find traditionally fermented foods from artisan food producers. Your neighborhood deli, health food store, or cultural market might have old-fashioned pickles or kraut; a microbrewery might produce traditional beers and ales; a baker might sell authentic sourdough; and an artisan cheese-maker might offer aged, cultured cheeses.

Or you can learn to make fermented foods yourself. That's why this book is primarily a cookbook. In Parts 2 and 3, I share many recipes and techniques so you can learn to ferment almost every food group.

What Can You Ferment?

The number of foods you can ferment might astound you. I'll give you a glimpse here at the possibilities (but check Parts 2 and 3 for the recipes).

Vegetables become sauerkraut and pickles—but even more besides. You can make pickles out of carrots, asparagus, green beans, beets, spinach stalks, radishes, peppers, and more. Imagine flavorful, diverse salsas and relishes. You can ferment fruits, transforming them into wines and ciders as well as jams, chutneys, relishes, salsas, and sauces. Ferment beans into soy sauce, miso, natto, and tempeh (all nutritious transformations of soy beans) as well as hummus or other bean pastes.

Sourdough is the art of fermenting grains. The organisms involved cause dough to rise and contribute marvelously complex sour flavors. In Part 3, I share myriad useful sourdough recipes with you—from breads to biscuits and crêpes to muffins. What's exciting is you can ferment many grains besides wheat. For example, *injera* is a flatbread made by Ethiopians after fermenting teff, a grain.

Turning to the foods produced by animals, you can ferment (or culture) dairy into sour cream, yogurt, kefir, buttermilk, all kinds of cheeses, and more. You can create pickled fish condiments, corned beef, and delicious sausages and salamis.

For long-term use and greater nutrition, you can ferment other condiments, such as mayonnaise, ketchup, mustard, horseradish, guacamole, or pickled eggs. You can also create natural sodas and traditional alcoholic beverages from roots, weeds, flowers, and honey.

What's in It for You?

In this chapter, we'll dig into the remarkable nutritional benefits of fermented foods. Fermentation makes foods more nutritious and digestible: Vitamin and enzyme levels increase, and beneficial acids are produced while fermentation neutralizes problematic nutrients of food. The beneficial organisms in fermented foods then populate your gut to restore and improve your digestive and immune systems.

A Nutrition Boost

Fermenting involves beneficial organisms. (We'll talk more about them and the major fermentation types in Chapter 3). In the most healthful kind of fermentation—and to some degree in other forms—those organisms do amazing things:

- They make minerals in certain foods more easily absorbed.
- They manufacture vitamins and enzymes, increasing the amounts above and beyond what the food contained originally.
- They produce beneficial acids, such as lactic acid in yogurt.
- They predigest the food and neutralize harmful food components

Let's take a look at each of these nutritional benefits to uncover their potential.

Vitamins & Minerals

Vitamins and minerals are essential for good health and nutrition. Our bodies need them in small quantities. Because we can't make them ourselves, we must get them through our diet. When we don't get enough, we suffer from nutritional deficiencies. Which vitamins and minerals are increased or made available in fermented foods depends on which organisms are fermenting a food.

In almost all foods, fermentation increases the amount of B and C vitamins exponentially because these vitamins are produced when organisms ferment. When dairy ferments, the fermenting organisms help make the calcium more absorbable. When soy ferments, the fermenting bacteria manufacture vitamin K2.

How important are vitamins and minerals to our health? Very. We need vitamins for metabolism and cell and tissue growth. Vitamin C is especially crucial for tissue growth and connectivity and is extremely important during pregnancy. Your body uses B vitamins to make energy from food and to make red blood cells. Because vitamins B and C aren't stored by the body, they must be replenished on a regular basic. Vitamin K2—found in the fermented soy food called *natto* and in the fat of animals—is key to strong bones and good cardiovascular health.

Minerals are also essential for good health. One of the most important—calcium—is critical for strong bones and teeth, heart, nervous system, and muscle growth and contraction. Fermented dairy is one of the best sources of usable calcium.

Enzymes

Enzymes are substances (usually proteins) that act as catalysts to bring about specific actions in the body, such as the digestion of particular nutrients. Thousands of enzymes exist, but our bodies run on two major types: digestive and metabolic. *Digestive enzymes*, provided through food or manufactured by the body, help your body efficiently break down proteins, fats, and carbohydrates. *Metabolic enzymes*, which must be made by the body and can't come from anywhere else, are involved in countless body functions, such as proper gland functioning, removing toxins, producing energy, delivering oxygen to organs and cells, repairing damaged tissue, and purifying blood. Interestingly, vitamins are called "cofactors" of enzymes, which means they function as helpers for the enzymes—yet another reason vitamins are essential.

In a lifetime, our bodies produce only a finite amount of enzymes. Overall enzyme production slows down with aging, and additionally, the body prioritizes making digestive enzymes over metabolic enzymes. Do you see the problem here? If our bodies must make digestive enzymes (that could be provided through food instead), we make fewer of the metabolic enzymes that keep our bodies functioning optimally. The smartest thing for us to do is to eat more foods rich in digestive enzymes.

So what are those foods? The answer might surprise you. Most people think raw, fresh foods provide an abundance of enzymes. Yes, they do provide some enzymes—but not that many. On the other hand, fermented foods provide digestive enzymes in abundance. (Cooked foods provide none.)

Enzymes in fermented foods come about in three possible ways: They're already present in the food, they're produced by the microorganisms doing the fermentation, or they're produced by microorganisms that are around but not involved in the primary fermentation. Thus, a fermented food usually contains more enzymes after being fermented than it did before.

Interestingly, fermented foods can provide the very enzymes required to digest that particular food best. For example, fermented dairy is abundant in lactase, the enzyme required to digest the milk sugar lactose. This happens because the fermenting organisms produce the enzymes they need to consume the food. Keep in mind that enzymes don't get "used up," which means they can perform over and over again, but they'll expire if heated. So unless the fermented food is heated, the enzymes are still present when we eat it. Pretty amazing, isn't it?

Predigestion

Fermentation involves encouraging beneficial organisms to grow and proliferate as they feast on sugars and starches in the fermenting food. This results in a partial to complete breakdown of proteins, carbohydrates, and fats in the foods before you eat them!

For example, the fermentation of grains—known as sourdough—accomplishes a predigestion of gluten. When dairy is fermented, such as in the making of yogurt, the organisms consume lactose. This is why many lactose-intolerant people can eat fermented dairy foods, such as yogurt, kefir, or aged cheeses. In the fermentation of beans, you'll see a breakdown of complex carbohydrates into simple carbohydrates. And as we know, beans can be very hard to digest.

Finally, all starchy foods, including grains, beans, fruits, and vegetables, contain much less sugar when fermentation is complete. This is good news for anyone who's following a low-carb or low-glycemic diet. The organisms eat up the sugar, leaving behind beneficial acids.

The main beneficial acid produced in the most healthful food fermentation (called "lacto-fermentation," which is discussed in depth in Chapter 3) is lactic acid. Lactic acid is a natural food preserver—it makes food too acidic for spoiling organisms.

But beneficial organisms love its acidity and exist quite happily in its presence—whether in the food or when entering the digestive system. In the stomach, lactic acid acts like a key, opening and closing the glands that secrete digestive juices for a perfect balance.

Antinutrients

The work of fermentation neutralizes food components known as "antinutrients." *Antinutrients* are natural or synthetic substances that interfere with the absorption of nutrients. One of these is phytic acid, which is found in all seeds, including grains, beans, nuts, and what we normally think of as seeds (such as sesame seeds). If left intact, the phytic acid binds with minerals in our digestive tract, prevents effective mineral absorption, and leads to mineral deficiencies. Most modern recipes involve quick-cooking or the immediate consumption of seeds—whether they're grains, nuts, seeds, or beans—while traditional societies employed more careful methods of preparation, including fermentation. Today's high incidence of mineral deficiencies (as well as other ailments) could be related to the fact we no longer take care to ferment or otherwise prepare seeds before consumption.

Other antinutrients neutralized by fermentation include tannins in tea, oxalic acid in leafy green vegetables or those in the cabbage family, and phytoestrogens in soybeans. In Part 2 of this book, we'll discuss each food group's antinutrients more specifically as well as how fermentation deactivates those antinutrients.

Great for Your Gut

We've been discussing how fermentation increases vitamins and enzymes, makes minerals more digestible, predigests our food, and also neutralizes antinutrients. Those are great benefits, but I think it's time for us to investigate how fermented foods and the beneficial organisms they contain help with practically every system in our bodies by supporting gut health.

In a moment, you'll see that the gut isn't simply a place where food is digested. Rather, when we're healthy, it's where beneficial organisms act on our behalf to facilitate pulling nutrients from food and defending our bodies against infection, disease, toxins, and other stressors. Let's talk about how the presence of or a lack of beneficial organisms in our guts determines more than what vitamins we absorb.

Probiotics

Probiotics are microorganisms consumed by the body for their beneficial qualities. Probiotics go by other names, such as beneficial organisms, beneficial bacteria, beneficial microbes, beneficial yeasts, or beneficial bacteria. Probiotics—the good guys of fermented foods—are arguably the most acclaimed heroes of fermented foods. Why? Our *gut* health—and, in turn, our overall health—relies on whether our guts make a cozy home for an estimated 100 trillion beneficial microbes. (When discussing nutrition, *gut* is a casual term referring to the intestines. *Gut flora* refers to the colony of microscopic organisms living within the intestines.) Ideally, we enter the world having acquired a healthy *gut flora* from our mothers. Then we maintain that balance throughout our lives by following a nutrient-dense diet and, of course, through living a life of ease without any stress whatsoever.

I don't know about you, but that's not my life! The ideal I just mentioned is far from the norm in modern society. Instead, most people in civilized countries have poor gut flora. This can be attributed to many causes—early and later in life—including being born via C-section instead of through a microbe-rich birth canal, being born through a mother's birth canal that lacks a proper balance of beneficial organisms, consuming infant formula rather than breast milk, consuming a high-sugar and high-starch processed food diet, keeping a stressful lifestyle, living in a toxic environment, or experiencing liberal or even occasional use of antibiotics.

But take heart. Many of us are in the same boat. Here's the hope we can all share: Whether or not your gut got a good start in life, the future of your gut health can be impacted by what you eat and do each day from here on out. Fermented foods to the rescue! They're rich in beneficial microbes to help restore healthy gut flora. For example, kefir—a yogurt-like fermented dairy food—can contain up to 50 beneficial organism strains.

Immune System

A layer of bacteria protects the gut wall, also known as the digestive tract. In a healthy adult, that bacteria weighs between 3 and 4½ pounds (1.4 to 2 kilograms)! This is the heart of the immune system. Think of the digestive tract like a pasture. The gut wall is the soil. The beneficial bacteria that reside there are the various grasses, herbs, and legumes covering the soil. These plants—a highly organized system—act as protection against invasion and erosion. Some opportunistic plants are also in the pasture as well as various passersby floating on the wind, but the healthy plants keep everything else away and tightly regulated by outcompeting it.

However, if the beneficial plants in this pasture are damaged, the soil will be exposed to anything else that comes along and takes root, such as a virus, fungus, pathogen, or toxin. Over time, further erosion and stripping occurs. Eventually, the enemy invaders might take over completely. They'll continue damaging the soil, sucking up nutrients and spreading disease.

Remember, this analogy is about the gut and the microbial population. But don't think for a second that what happens there is isolated. No, our overall health is intimately tied to this balance of organisms. When the good guys are in charge, they facilitate the efficient absorption of nutrients from food. They neutralize potential toxins and antinutrients. They produce antibiotic, antitumor, antiviral, and antifungal substances. And certainly not last *or* least, the acids they give off make the gut wall an uncomfortably acidic place for pathogens.

Evidence even suggests that compromised gut health leads to the development of food allergies, sensitivities, and intolerances. Conversely, some researchers believe that good gut health can improve these conditions as well as reverse or significantly improve such conditions as autism, dyslexia, depression, and schizophrenia. Even though those subjects are beyond the scope of this book, they're worth mentioning.

Eating fermented foods is a way to supply beneficial organisms to keep your gut functioning well. When the gut works well, it nourishes the rest of the body, including the immune system. Thus, the health of your immune system depends on the health of your gut.

Benefits Beyond Nutrition

We've covered the nutritional benefits of fermented foods and now we can move on to the positive qualities that tug at the heart and the purse strings. In other words, the fun stuff.

Flavor & Texture

Crispy and crunchy sauerkraut, with a sour bite and sometimes hot-pepper spicy, is arguably the world's signature fermented food. And with good reason. Whether fruit, vegetable, or meat, fermentation develops, deepens, and improves flavor. Can you think of anything more scrumptious than a sharp cheddar or a crunchy dill pickle pulled from a cloudy brine? I can't.

Perhaps adults and children of the modern age with little exposure to fermented foods don't love fermented foods as well as others. I think we can chalk that up to lack of exposure. I grew up on Middle Eastern pickled foods, tangy raw cheese, and salty-sour plain yogurt. On the other hand, because my husband grew up on almost no fermented foods, he has had to come around. And come around he has.

Go Low-Tech

One of the most joyful aspects of fermenting foods is that it's incredibly simple—almost hands off. Sure, you and I are a part of the process, but we're not the principal actors. Nor are we forced to watch a canning pot in a stifling summer kitchen. Our role is as facilitators of a divine culturing process that's bigger and more creative than we are. Thank God for that!

You see, the beneficial organisms do the real work, the real magic, of transforming foods into tasty, nutritional powerhouses while we happily witness and help them along. These are our jobs: Burp jars, give a stir here and there, skim off the top, change containers, feed the starter, transfer curdled milk to a cheesecloth, and add more fruit to a bubbling soda. Talk about easy and satisfying. There's not much easier than doing some chopping, mixing, packing food down into a crock or jar, and waiting. In fact, the waiting is the hardest work.

When you begin fermenting foods, it might seem daunting. This isn't because it's hard—it's because you haven't done it before. Your head doesn't yet know what fermented foods look, act, or taste like.

You'll read my words—and perhaps the words of other fermenting guides—and I'll tell you what the fermenting process should look like and what's normal. I'll also tell you what you'll see if something's gone wrong. But you won't *really* know any of this until you experience it or see it for yourself.

Then, after you make your first dilly beans (and I'll be so proud of you!), you might say to yourself: "Now I know what fermenting bubbles look like!" You'll take your first bite and reflect with satisfaction on how much time you did *not* spend in a hot room with a whistling, boiling pressure canner. Then you can tackle the next fermentation with more confidence.

Let's say you make the clabber cheese in Chapter 13. Take milk fresh from the morning milking—when it's the perfect temperature for culturing—or use unpasteurized milk from the fridge. (Don't worry too much about figuring out what milk you'd use. I'll cover your milk options in Chapter 12.) Leave it at room temperature for a day or two. Then take the milk, which is now curdled and set up like yogurt, and transfer it into a cheesecloth-lined colander. Tie the ends of the cheesecloth and hang up that bag of curds for yet another day. The third morning, open up the bag and transfer the ball of curds to a bowl. Season with a little sea salt or perhaps with fresh or dried herbs to eat with crackers or toast. You could even hang the cheese longer to dry it out more. Then, after a few more days, you can salt it and shape it into balls, then plop the balls in a jar of olive oil and finally store them in your pantry or cellar. You just made soft cheese—one of the simplest and most ancient cultured foods. And you spent no more than 20 minutes on it!

Low-Tech Middle Eastern Cheese

With fermenting, you're working smarter, not harder. You're saving your appliances, resources, and money. Fermented food recipes don't require much cooking—if any at all. You certainly won't be pressure-canning or boiling anything to death! This means you'll use very little gas or electricity to fire up the range, much less the range itself. Most fermented foods need a cool location for storage, and while many folks' modern homes offer only a fridge for that purpose, those whose houses boast a cellar can save even more resources.

Fermentation is totally sustainable. It requires no fancy equipment and no repurchasing of canning lids, and you can accomplish this year after year by filling jars with your backyard harvest.

How is this all possible? How can fermentation be so low-tech and sustainable? I'll tell you more about the science behind it in Chapter 3, but here's the gist of it: The "cooking" is done by the organisms as they eat the food. They give off acids that change the texture of the food, add flavor, and acidify the food sufficiently to preserve it and protect it from putrefaction. The presence of the colony of beneficial organisms themselves in the food provides a deterrent to spoilage microbes. What bad guys would be able to take up residence with all those good guys around? With this innate protection, you don't need to apply high heat or pressure in an attempt to sterilize a food for protection.

So we spend less time cooking while we save time, money, and resources. Sometimes, when you put less into a project, you get less out of it. Not so with fermented foods. Relatively simple and traditional fermentation methods give us great-tasting foods with supreme nutrition.

Embrace the Seasons

If you've done any amount of canning or putting up your own produce or making wine from the annual grape harvest, then you know about seasonal eating.

If you wait with bated breath for the opening day of farmers markets and keep your eyes peeled for the first strawberries of the season, then you know about seasonal eating.

If you know that nothing beats vine-ripened, juicy heirloom tomatoes or sweet U-pick cherries, then you know about seasonal eating.

Fermenting foods is seasonal eating and then some. Because it embraces what the seasons produce, it nurtures those foods to last beyond their seasons while deepening and developing flavor, texture, and nutrition.

There's an art to fermenting food—but also a flexibility. The traditional practice has only a few rules (which you'll learn in chapters 3 and 4). The history of cultured foods is bound together with artisan home-and-hearth cooks who explored the boundaries of fermentation to extend the flavors and bounty of the seasonal harvests. Generation to generation passed down traditions and recipes we can master and morph into creations of our own.

How Much to Eat?

We can learn much from traditional societies that consumed probiotic, fermented foods on a daily basis. Except for the occasional drunkard at a tavern, known to many of us through the fantasies and legends of older times, the common person ate small amounts of fermented foods and beverages with practically every meal. The cultured foods aided digestion and continually repopulated the gut with beneficial organisms.

Of course, these people didn't know the specifics of how it worked and we still have much to learn ourselves. But through years of raising families and treating diseases, the wise healers and elders learned through observation the healing properties of fermented foods. When a woman was trying to conceive or became pregnant, women of an entire tribe contributed a special conception diet rich in fermented foods and other foods containing significant essential nutrients. Throughout history, people believed that consuming a few tablespoons of sauerkraut each day could be a powerful defender against disease and illness.

My family's strategy is to learn from and follow the example of the people who came before us. For the most part, they were relatively free of modern diseases, lived healthy and vigorous lives, and possessed strong bones and teeth. What did they do differently from people in modern society? Among other things, they ate small amounts of unheated fermented foods daily—if not with every meal. We try to do the same. It isn't hard—the many recipes in this book show you the options. With all the fantastic and varied fermented foods available, each meal you'll find at least something fermented to add to a salad, spread on a sandwich, or pour into a glass.

Why unheated fermented foods? Cooking undoes many benefits of fermented foods: Vitamins, enzymes, and probiotics expire when heated. But don't be scared of this. It isn't a hard-and-fast rule and it isn't all or nothing.

If to date you consume very few fermented foods and you start eating more, your body might have difficulty adjusting. As the organism balance shifts in the digestive system, people experience mild to severe symptoms that are generally called die-off or detoxing symptoms. When pathogenic bacteria, virus, and fungi in the gut are crowded out and killed, they release more toxins. The toxins make you feel ill or tired or even experience more severe conditions, such as rashes, headaches, or more. These are temporary and might last a few days to a few weeks depending on the person.

If you experience die-off symptoms, you don't necessarily need to stop eating the fermented foods. They're doing good work after all. But your body needs time to adjust and flush out all the pathogens. If your symptoms are very severe, cut back on the amount of fermented foods you're eating to a tolerable amount and then increase from there.

How Fermentation Works

Fermentation is a story of heroes and villains—each with a role to play. Because this is a story played out at the microscopic level, that's where we'll go: deep into a crock of bubbling sauerkraut or jug of fermenting cider. We're going to find out just who's inside, what they're doing in there, and what makes them tick. We'll also explore how to ensure that fermentation is successful. Once you get this down pat, you'll be able to navigate the world of fermented foods like a pro.

Three Kinds of Fermentation

We're concerned with three types of beneficial food fermentation—each classified mainly through the major by-product: lactic acid, ethyl alcohol, or acetic acid.

Lactic Acid

This acid gives sauerkraut, other natural pickled foods, and San Francisco sourdough their distinctly sour tastes. This manner of fermentation is called "lacto-fermentation." Lacto-fermentation is the type of fermentation that occurs when yeasts and bacteria convert starches and sugars in foods into lactic acid. Because lacto-fermented foods tend to be more nutritious than other fermented foods as well as easier to make in many cases, this book contains a great deal more lacto-fermented recipes than any other type.

What's so great about lactic acid? It's the most healthful of all the acids we'll discuss and a main reason why lacto-fermentation is healthier than the other forms of fermentation we're also covering. Lactic acid helps with blood circulation, prevents constipation, balances digestive acids, and encourages good pancreatic function. Finally, rather than asking anything of our digestive systems, the presence of lactic acid makes lacto-fermented foods easy on the digestive system.

Ethyl Alcohol

Ethyl alcohol is the intoxicating component of wine, beer, and other alcoholic beverages. It's also known as "ethanol" or simply as alcohol. It's produced when fermenting organisms convert carbohydrates in grains or fruit into wine, beer, mead, or other alcoholic beverages. These beverages have varying levels of intoxicating capacity as well as a diverse range of flavors. Traditional alcoholic beverages contained lower levels of alcohol. They were also more nutritious because of the presence of beneficial organisms and other beneficial compounds in addition to lower alcohol and sugar levels.

Acetic Acid

When you expose that alcohol to oxygen, you get this third kind of fermentation. Fermenting organisms in the air—a group known as "acetobacter bacteria"—convert alcohol to acetic acid, or vinegar. Take apple cider vinegar. What began as apples is fermented sans oxygen into apple cider—an alcoholic beverage—and then makes a final transformation to apple cider vinegar when exposed to the air. This is the basic process by which all vinegars are made. Each started with a different alcoholic beverage and ended up as a particular variety of vinegar through fermentation by acetobacter bacteria, which produce acetic acid.

The Players

The microscopic players in fermentation are various yeasts, bacteria, and molds. *Yeasts* are single-celled microscopic fungi that convert sugar into water, alcohol, acids, and carbon dioxide. Scientists know of about 1,500 species of yeasts. *Bacteria* are single-celled microscopic organisms with a cell wall but lacking organelles and an organized nucleus. They eat starches and sugars in foods. *Molds* are multicellular fungi that grow in moist environments, such as on food. They produce enzymes that break down food for them to eat.

Within those categories are countless different strains. There are three main groups you need to know about. Let's call the first group "beneficial organisms," and from here on out, I'll lump the other two groups into what I call "spoiling organisms." Beneficial and spoiling organisms are capable of fermenting foods. But for best taste and nutrition, we're obviously most interested in eating foods fermented by beneficial organisms. Equally apparent yet worth stating, spoiling organisms produce fermented foods fit for the compost or the garbage—not us.

Heroes

The heroes of fermentation are beneficial yeasts, bacteria, and molds. If it weren't for these microscopic helpers, we wouldn't have healthy fermented foods—period.

Beneficial Yeasts

Yeasts are probably the earliest cultivated organisms of fermentation and most often are used for fermenting alcoholic beverages and breads. The word "yeast" comes from combining the Old English "gist" or "gyst" with the Indo-European root "yes," meaning "boil," "foam," or "bubble." That's definitely appropriate when you think of a bubbly sourdough starter or foamy champagne.

Beneficial yeasts convert simple sugars in foods to some or all of the following: water, ethyl alcohol, lactic acid, and carbon dioxide. What they produce depends on the fermentation stage. If the food being fermented contains complex sugars, the yeasts produce enzymes to break those sugars down into a simpler form. Here's an example: We keep a sourdough starter—an active colony of wild yeasts and bacteria—alive through regular feedings of flour. This flour provides food for the organisms as they multiply, filling the starter with fresh organisms. In the flour are simple and complex sugars. The simple sugars provide instant food, or fuel, for the yeasts while they produce enzymes to break down the complex sugars to more easily consumed simple sugars. The cycle repeats through regular feedings.

Some beneficial yeasts need oxygen to do their thing and some don't. For example, the yeasts involved in sourdough need oxygen, which is why I tell students to mix their sourdough starter well to incorporate lots of air. This is called "aerobic fermentation." The yeasts that make wine are different—they don't require oxygen and their fermentation is considered "anaerobic." Yeasts don't require sunlight to grow. Various strains have their own ideal temperatures for optimum growth, ranging from just below freezing to well over 100°F/38°C. You can rely on a recipe's instructions to let you know the right temperature.

Yeasts work as a leavening agent in bread. But there's a difference between the wild yeasts used in traditional sourdough bread and the quick-acting yeast that makes most grocery store breads. In true sourdough-leavened bread, wild yeasts give off carbon dioxide that raises the bread, while beneficial bacteria contribute delicious sour flavors. In other breads available, the yeast type at work is a single factory-isolated strain that scientists and food producers have identified as quick-acting and efficient as well as a good producer at ideal temperatures. This bread isn't as nutritious, but it's easier and quicker way to get a good result.

Why is sourdough bread more nutritious than modern bread? When dough is fermented, the fermenting organisms in the sourdough starter neutralize antinutrients, such as phytic acid and enzyme inhibitors, and they predigest the starches and gluten in grains (all of which is discussed in more detail in Chapter 2). This helps our digestion and ultimately boosts the nutrition we get from the grains. Modern breads can't offer these benefits because they don't get fermented.

Yeasts are key players in alcohol fermentation, where they produce ethanol from sugars or starches. This is the fermentation process that makes beer, wine, cider, mead, and liquors. Old-fashioned alcoholic beverages were made by wild yeasts kept alive year to year in the family home (a beer starter, if you will) or from wild yeasts captured and cultivated on the spot. By contrast, beer-making today relies on cultivated and isolated strains of yeast sold in packets, which increase our chances of success, consistency, and desired end flavors. Excitingly, some laboratories are devoted to keeping alive traditional yeast strains, providing us with a mix of tradition and modern convenience.

Beneficial Bacteria

Here we're talking about the broader category of bacteria called "lactobacillus," of which there are currently 125 identified species as well as other beneficial strains. Contrary to what the name *lactobacilli* implies (lactose, or milk sugar), they ferment much more than dairy. Certain strains handle dairy and other strains are involved in the fermentation of fruits, vegetables, beverages, beans, grains, fish, meat, and other foods. Sometimes, *lactobacilli* work alone or in a symbiotic relationship with beneficial yeasts, such as in a sourdough starter.

Just like the beneficial yeasts, these bacteria eat simple sugars and starches in many foods: fruits, vegetables, grains, beans, nuts, other seeds, dairy, and meats. They don't need oxygen to thrive, making their fermentation anaerobic in all cases. Their by-products include lactic acid, some ethanol, and carbon dioxide.

Lactic acid is a natural antibiotic that keeps spoiling organisms away from the naturally preserved foods that contain it. And on the taste side of the equation, the lactic acid contributes wonderfully sour and complex flavors to vats of deli pickles, sauerkraut, old-fashioned fermented sausages, and sourdough bread as well as many other fermented foods. The ethanol isn't a primary by-product of these beneficial bacteria and contributes more to taste than anything else. The carbon dioxide production can be quite significant in certain bacteria-fermented foods—it's responsible for the bubbles in natural sodas, other fermented beverages, effervescent dairy kefir, and fermented salsa.

Beneficial Molds

Thousands of strains of molds exist, although only a handful are involved in food production. Rather than spreading and growing throughout a food, mold tends to grow right on the surface of a food. What also makes molds different from beneficial yeasts and bacteria is they can survive colder temperatures.

To get nourishment from a food source, molds secrete enzymes that break down the starches in food, making them easily absorbable. Molds multiply through small spores and over time will spread over the food's surface. They produce compounds that inhibit the growth of competing organisms.

Special molds are cultivated to produce particular flavors in cheese, fermented soy foods (such as tempeh and soy sauce), the Japanese wine *sake*, and cured meat. Molds have been used in Asia for centuries. The Western world uses primarily beneficial bacteria and yeasts for fermenting foods.

Villains

I won't spend a lot of time on spoiling organisms, but it's important you know they're there. However, if you grasp and implement the methods of successful fermentation I'm teaching, you won't need to worry about the spoiling organisms.

When you began forming in your mother's womb, your gut was a blank slate. The good guys or the bad guys could populate it. All the factors I listed in Chapter 2 contributed to which set of organisms took and maintained control. One set must come out on top—they don't share very well.

With fresh foods, you've got the same deal. A food—whether just picked from a tree or a fresh piece of meat—is ripe for fermentation. Either the good guys or the bad guys can do the job—and they're both eager to do that. As fermenters, our job is to come in with various protections and methods of fermentation to control the end result. We'll talk more about those protections later in this chapter and also in Chapter 4. As you'll see in the next section, the most important actions we take when fermenting foods is with this goal in mind: to help the good guys flourish and to suppress any spoiling organisms. To do it well, you need to understand how to create the best environment to ensure successful and tasty fermentations.

Setting the Stage

To create tasty and healthful fermented foods, you must create the right conditions for the beneficial organisms. If you can get the conditions right, you can get the fermentation right. This isn't hard, but it's important. Now let's get specific with their four needs:

- **Protection:** They need protection from spoiling organisms, especially at the beginning of a fermentation when they're most vulnerable because they've not yet established dominance.

- **Right temperature:** Which temperature is needed varies, but right around room temperature is a common fermentation temperature. When fermentation is complete, nearly all fermented foods require cool temperatures for aging and long-term stability.

- **Food:** The organisms get their food from the carbohydrates (sugars and starches) in the food being fermented or through the addition of special food. Most fermentations fall into the first category, with meat fermentation being one notable exception—we add sugar to provide the organisms with food because the meat doesn't provide it.

- **Time:** Once we've got all the other conditions right, only time is needed for the organisms to undergo and complete fermentation. They need time to transform the food to the right texture, which is a matter of taste, and to multiply into sufficient numbers for effective preservation of the food.

If we can optimize all these conditions, the fermenting organisms will be happy. They'll eat, give off gases, produce acids and/or alcohol, multiply, and thrive. This is the fermentation cycle. When it proceeds unhindered and the food is stored properly, we end up with marvelous, nutritious fermented foods that are protected against spoiling.

Protecting the Good Guys

Protection for the beneficial fermenting organisms and their work is essential to successful fermentation. Fermenters employ various methods of protection—some depending on personal preference and some determined by the food itself and what's actually possible to implement.

Salt

Of all protective fermenting ingredients, salt is the most common and most traditional. For thousands of years, meat preservation was carried out simply and effectively through salting and drying. Because most foods have high water content, including meat, they're susceptible to spoiling—and spoiling organisms thrive in moist conditions. To make the water content unavailable to spoiling organisms, you have three salting options: Add salt to a food mixture, salt the surface of a food, or pour salt brine over the food. You see, spoiling organisms thrive in free water or purified water, but they can't use or abide salty water. The salt makes the water unavailable to them. It effectively ties it up—just as if it had evaporated. On the other hand, beneficial organisms have no difficulty surviving in reasonably salty conditions. If we go too salty, though, even the good guys can't survive, not to mention that we humans don't enjoy oversalted foods.

Starter Cultures

Another protective measure employed by fermenters is to add a starter culture to the food being fermented. This is a set of living beneficial organisms in wet or dry form that gives the food an active colony of organisms from the beginning. Not only does this increase the likelihood that a healthy colony of organisms will get established, but these beneficial organisms also go to work right away repelling spoiling organisms. Beer, wine, yogurt, or cheese starter cultures are just a few examples of specialty starters. Keep in mind that certain ferments, such as those with fruit or pasteurized dairy, require a starter culture for success, while most vegetable ferments, such as sauerkraut or pickles, don't. I'll share specifics about starter cultures in Chapter 4 as well as in individual recipes.

Limit Oxygen

The fact that a lot of fermentation occurs best without oxygen suggests yet another fermentation protection: removal or restriction of oxygen from fermenting foods. This helps in two ways:

- It provides optimum conditions for our beneficial organisms to establish a strong colony.

- It limits foods' exposure to spoiling organisms in the air.

Beer-makers use a special fermentation device called an "airlock." When placed on the top of fermenting jugs, this special tool employs a water barrier that lets fermenting gases escape while preventing outside air and, therefore, spoiling organisms contained in it from accessing the fermenting food. Because it works so well, many in recent times are using modified jars and jugs with airlocks for fermenting fruits, vegetables, meats, and other foods. You also have other options for fermenting vessels. We'll talk about them in Chapter 4. I should point out that this protection only suits anaerobic fermentations. It doesn't work for sourdough.

Increase Acidity

As mentioned already, because spoiling organisms can't abide acidity, upping these levels in fermenting foods is a no-brainer way to ensure good results. However, this isn't always a preferred method because fermenters sometimes desire other flavors to be prominent. But for beginners, this strategy helps you ensure success while getting your fermenting feet wet. What acids can you add? As mentioned before, whey is acidic and used quite often. A small amount of lemon juice, vinegar, or other acidic ingredients are frequently included in recipes. In fruit ferments, whether chutneys, relishes, jams, or wine, recipes usually call for at least one of the following: additional acid, salt, or a starter culture. The high sugar content of fruits makes them especially susceptible to spoiling. Also remember that fermenting organisms often produce acids. So whether or not acids are added at the beginning, the production of acids during fermentation is essential to successful long-term protection against spoiling organisms.

Strength in Numbers

Much like the late acid production just mentioned, our final protection enters the scene after the fermenting organisms establish themselves. Their very colony, their very presence in the food, is a deterrent to spoiling organisms. With all the good guys present, spoiling organisms can't get a leg up. Whether or not you add a starter culture at the beginning, you can bet that by the time you're done, a successful ferment contains an army of beneficial organisms prepared to wage war against any invaders.

You now have a good understanding of the types of fermentation as well as the players involved: who they are, what they do, and what protections you can leverage to help them work their magic. It's time to open the fermenter's toolbox and equip yourself for successful home fermentation.

The Fermenter's Toolbox

In this chapter, we'll discuss what tools, equipment, and ingredients are best suited for fermentation. We'll go over how to make the best choices when purchasing raw food ingredients. I'll share common methods of fermentation to help you get a good understanding of the overall process. We'll talk about what a good fermentation looks, smells, and tastes like. Sadly, but rarely, some ferments don't turn out and I'll also help you recognize those signs.

Equipment & Tools

People employ a wide variety of equipment and tools for fermentation. Some scour yard sales, estate sales, or thrift stores for suitable vessels. Some buy commercial fermenting vessels, which are fine-tuned for a high success rate. Sometimes, people just plain make do with what they have. Which type are you?

Few hard-and-fast rules exist when it comes to fermenting tools, equipment, and ingredients, but in this chapter, I share important options to consider. The goal? To set you up for successful fermentation with minimal expense or inconvenience. I suppose if you want to break the bank, you can. But there's really no need.

Cleanliness & Sanitation

Food fermentation is the art of nurturing and growing beneficial strains of organisms in foods, right? These foods are contained in various vessels and touched by utensils in our kitchens. The organisms we encourage to thrive will produce the most consistent flavors and results if not impeded by competing organisms on equipment, tools, vessels, or utensils.

From countertops, food processors, utensils, jars, or vessels, keep anything that touches or contains fermenting foods clean. However, there's a difference between complete sterility and keeping a sanitary working environment.

A sterile environment is one completely free of living organisms of any kind. Sterility is hard to achieve outside of a bubble, which is why you don't need to stress over it. Rather, sanitary or generally clean conditions should be our goal with most fermentation. However, alcoholic and meat fermentation benefit from more stringent efforts and I'll discuss those in chapters 9 and 14, respectively.

Before employing fermenting vessels or utensils, wash them in a dishwasher or by hand with hot, soapy water. You can also boil these items for two minutes to eliminate competing organisms. Let them air-dry (or heat-dry in the automatic dishwasher). Because towels and cloths might harbor competing organisms, it's best not to use them for drying—just let the air do the job. My friend Sylvia takes another step of rinsing all vessels and utensils in white vinegar (which is inexpensive and doesn't bring other microorganisms into the ferment) because vinegar's antibacterial properties can reduce or eliminate spoiling organisms.

Vessels & Utensils

You have many choices for fermenting vessels: jars, crocks, bowls, barrels, buckets, and more. They come in all shapes and sizes, and after you've fermented a few times, you'll get a better feel for what you prefer and what works well with what you're fermenting. Glass or canning jars—from 1-pint (½-liter) to 1-gallon (4-liter) sizes—are the most versatile when it comes to fermenting most simple foods.

When choosing what you'll use, keep a few things in mind. If you're using plastic, choose food-grade (and preferably BPA-free) plastic and don't use a plastic container that's held some caustic or toxic material previously. BPA-free products (such as plastic containers and metal cans) don't contain bisphenol A, or BPA. BPA is a chemical compound linked to such health conditions as infertility, cardiovascular problems, and diabetes. Avoid corrosive or reactive metals, such as aluminum, tin, or copper. Even stainless steel is minimally reactive to the acids in fermenting foods. Although you can use stainless steel to stir, mix, strain, or funnel your ferment, it's best to avoid sustained contact. Your best materials are glass, ceramic, and wood (although not the strong-smelling fir or pine, which easily transfers odors to foods).

Thrift stores, estate sales, flea markets, and auctions might yield useful surprises. I've found a few smaller crocks and a friend found a 5-gallon (18-liter) crock! Sometimes, people donate their old fermenting vessels because they're cracked or otherwise flawed—you don't want those. Whatever you find, examine it closely for cracks or leaks. If a manufacturer's name is stamped on the crock, it might be worth your time to do some research to find out whether lead or cadmium was used in the glaze. Unfortunately, many colored glazes do contain unsafe metals. I mention a resource for learning more about this in Appendix B.

An Ohio Stoneware 1-Gallon (4-Liter) Crock With a Lid

If you have some cash to burn and really want a great fermenting vessel, you have several good options. Online merchants and some hardware stores stock or will special-order reasonably priced, lead-free Ohio Stoneware crocks in 1-, 2-, 3-, 4-, 5-, and 10-gallon (4-, 8-, 12-, 15-, 18-, and 38-liter) sizes. These crocks often include weights and lids. Our family owns several 1- and 3-gallon (4- and 12-liter) crocks from Ohio Stoneware. I especially love my 3-gallon (12-liter) crock with a water gutter. While some crocks (as pictured) come with a weight and lid, other crocks are designed with a water gutter. This offers additional protection because the water gutter lets fermenting gases escape while preventing outside air from touching the food. A frequent concern with fermentation is that certain yeasts in the air thrive right at the top of a ferment. This yeast isn't harmful, but it can contribute "off" flavors and must be skimmed off frequently. Using a crock with a water barrier eliminates this hurdle.

The German company Harsch also makes cream-of-the-crop fermenting crocks with a water gutter. They're more expensive—from $100 to more than $500. These crocks include weight stones to press down and protect food from spoilage. And like some of the Ohio Stoneware crocks I just mentioned, these are also designed with a water gutter.

What if you have or acquire a crock without weights or a lid? Then you get creative. I'll give more information later on in this chapter.

You can also use glass jars or canning jar lids modified with airlocks, such as for fermenting alcoholic beverages. They go by various names because several online merchants carry their own versions. You can even make these yourself. (See Appendix B for sources and for online instructions to make them yourself.) The airlock on the lid performs the same function as the Ohio Stoneware or Harsch crock's water gutter. These range in price but are the least expensive of the available fermenting vessels. Some brands come with weights for the food, but some don't.

Utensils and bowls for chopping, stirring, and shredding should be glass, wood, ceramic, food-grade plastic, or nonreactive metal.

Fermentations of certain food groups will differ from the norm, such as when fermenting sourdough or dairy. Read more about those particulars in chapters 11, 12, and 13.

Jar With a Modified Airlock Lid

Weights

Fermentation in most cases is anaerobic, so it's essential we get the fermenting food away from oxygen and packed down well under the cover of brine or fermenting juices. Some foods—such as green beans, mushrooms, eggs, and radishes—are naturally buoyant and bob up at the top surface. Even nonbuoyant foods remain at the top surface. Sometimes, it can be quite comical trying to get all the food submerged.

But for successful fermentation without "off" flavors or spoilage, we've got to keep all the food down. This is where weights come in. Commercial fermentation vessels might include weights that fit right in the container. Various online merchants offer glass weights that fit right inside regular or wide-mouth canning jars and work great. (See Appendix B.) If you're using odds and ends for fermenting, you can get creative with weights without spending much, if any, money. Choose large stones; bags, smaller jars, or jugs full of water; or other heavy objects. It all works like a puzzle. Scrounge around in your house and see what you can put together.

But before you place weight on the food, you might need a base to spread the weight over all the food rather than letting it settle in one place. Here are some ideas for weight bases. If you're fermenting in a bowl, an open crock, or a large barrel, plates or wood boards make good bases to place weights on. Select one that fits well or even use a few to make sure all the food is covered. Again, don't choose pine or fir wood. If your fermenting vessel is a jar, a lid of a smaller diameter might fit just inside.

Weights and weight bases should be as clean as your fermenting vessels. Many people scrub and then boil these items to avoid introducing competing or spoiling organisms. You can also add a vinegar rinse.

Whether or not the fermenting vessel is sealed off from the air, you want the food to be under cover. When fermenting beverages, dairy, or sourdough as well as other exceptions, you might not need a weight system. Those particulars will be covered in their respective chapters and/or recipes.

Bottles

If you'd like, you can bottle naturally fermented sodas and alcoholic beverages. But you can't use just any kind of bottle and here's why: Fermented beverages can build up more pressure than commercial beverages because of the living organisms that might continue to give off gases. For this reason, I recommend the strong and traditional Grolsch or Grolsch-style bottles. Some stores offer knockoffs that are weaker and explode easily. See Appendix B for my recommended merchants or visit a local shop that sells beer-making supplies. And here's a less expensive option: I've heard that store-bought kombucha bottles are also pretty sturdy (and less expensive than Grolsch-style bottles).

Grolsch-Style Bottles With Rubber Stoppers

Storage

Fermented foods vary in their ideal storage temperatures and humidity levels. As a general rule and unless you're making a food where the recipe tells you something different (such as fermented meats, alcoholic beverages, or cheeses), fermented foods store best in cool storage that maintains a temperature between 32°F (0°C) and 50°F (10°C). At this temperature, the active colony of fermenting organisms remains stable and strong, and the food can continue to age and develop flavor.

You can also freeze some fermented foods, but they won't age or continue to develop flavor in the freezer. Also, your foods might develop freezer burn. And perhaps the most serious concern is that beneficial organisms die over time when frozen: The longer the food is frozen, the more probiotic benefits are lost.

You might want to transfer your fermented foods, including their juices, to other containers for storage. But then again you might not—it all depends. Big crocks or barrels are great to dip into from storage. Often, people unpack the container, transfer what they need for one week or so to a canning jar, and carefully repack the crock. On the other hand, if you've used a modified jar with an airlock sticking out of the lid, transferring the food to another jar enables you to use the airlock jar for fermenting something else. Within the recipes of this book, I specify when you need to do something special for storage.

Other Equipment

In the recipes, I mention other equipment, such as rubber bands to secure a cloth to a jar lid, cheesecloth, food processor, food chopper, blender, whisk, etc. While some are necessary, some aren't essential but simply make kitchen work easier. I write recipes around the least expensive, most versatile tools, avoiding specialty equipment as much as possible. Feel free to adapt or substitute any equipment of your own as you see fit.

Ingredients

You're going to be picking and choosing through many food groups to make and practice the fermenting recipes in this book. Here are general guidelines for choosing the best ingredients for fermentation.

Foods

We start with whole foods—ones that are in their natural forms. We want to use them before they've been processed significantly. Keep in mind that fermentation is one food-processing choice among many. We can cook, dehydrate, can, pressure-can, or ferment, among other options. By beginning our fermentation with whole foods, we ensure that additives, preservatives, or other ingredients don't interfere with the fermentation. I'm not referring here to starter cultures or other special ingredients that I'll ask you to get from time to time.

Whole foods possess distinct shapes, colors, and textures. A whole food is easily recognized and distinguished. Processing hasn't changed it into another form, except for simple changes, such as grinding grains into flour, chopping apples, or slicing pears.

With fruits, vegetables, nuts, seeds, grains, and beans, more important than any other consideration is that you grow or purchase foods that weren't sprayed with pesticides, herbicides, or other chemicals. These foods carry residues that can harm the beneficial organisms of fermentation. We don't want that!

Ideally, you should choose organic foods grown with a focus on soil health. Foods grown in healthy soils contain more nutrients, especially minerals. Fermenting organisms love minerals, as do our own bodies. Because fermentation is a means of preservation, choose fresh produce before it's started to decay and preferably within a few days of harvest or purchase.

Meats and eggs to be fermented should come from animals that weren't medicated or given hormones. Animals raised under natural conditions, such as on a pasture with fresh air and sunshine or on a natural diet, are less likely to be carriers of pathogens that can affect or spoil fermentation. Fish should be wild-caught or naturally and sustainably farmed. The bottom line is this: The more naturally the animal is raised, the healthier it is. The healthier the animal, the better suited it is for tasty and healthy fermented foods.

There are two parts to choosing your dairy foods: how the dairy animal is raised and how the dairy is processed. Quality fermented dairy comes from dairy animals fed and kept primarily on quality pasture (or good hay during the off-season) and also from minimally processed milk. Pasteurization and homogenization affect the fermentation process for the worse. Please get the best milk and cream you can find. Most of the time, ultra-pasteurized dairy (sometimes labeled on grocery store shelves as UHT) doesn't ferment well because this high-temperature processing renders the dairy unsuitable to support living cultures. For more information on the best choices of milk, see Chapter 12.

Water

Many fermentations call for water. Please don't use straight city tap water, which might contain chlorine, chloramine, fluoride, or other chemicals that can negatively interfere with fermentation. Don't use water contaminated with nitrites/nitrates, lead, or pathogens. If your water isn't clean and free of chemicals or other contaminants, consider purchasing spring water or filtered water or use an in-house filter to remove all traces of these chemicals.

Concerned about your water? Fill a glass and give the water a minute or so to resolve any cloudiness from oxygenation. Look at it for discoloration or sediment. Smell it. Chlorine will be evident in a pool-like smell, while smells such as rotten eggs suggest other impurities that should be checked out. To pursue testing, check for testing kits at a hardware store or ask your health department or extension office for a lab recommendation. A general water quality test that includes checking for pH, coliforms (bacteria), nitrates, metals, minerals, and TDS (total dissolved solids) will tell you whether you need to pursue filtering or alternative water options.

Because most water filter systems remove minerals (Radiant Life or Berkey filters being notable exceptions; see Appendix B for information), you can consider fortifying filtered water with natural mineral drops (see Appendix B for sources). Because water filters differ in what they remove, check with the filter manufacturer to find out the particulars.

Salt

Salt is the most common and most important fermenting ingredient. It's possible to make salt-free ferments, but they're more tricky and lack flavor. So what salt do you use? Actually, I should tell you what salt you *shouldn't* use. Table salt and iodized salt get a big no-no from me. Table salt includes anticaking ingredients and iodized salt contains iodine—both of which wreak havoc on or ruin fermentation.

Choose less-refined salt, also known as sea salt. Even within that category you'll find completely unrefined sea salts from various companies and areas of the world as well as lightly refined, less-expensive sea salts. Any of these will work. You'll know the unrefined sea salts because they're gray, brown, or pink in color, while the lightly refined is white. The benefit of using an unrefined variety is that it contains trace minerals, which are good for us and good for the fermenting organisms. Any size grain is fine, but the recipes in this book are written for fine-grain sea salt. If you're using coarse grain, you need to use about 50% more salt. In some recipes, such as cultured dairy, cheese, or sourdough, coarse-grain salt in such big chunks in the food isn't as pleasant as fine salts spread throughout.

Interested in making a low-salt vegetable ferment? If you use a starter culture in your ferment (discussed next), you can reduce the amount of salt in the brine or the recipe by half.

While mineral-rich seaweeds can't fill the same vital role as salt, consider adding seaweed as a flavor enhancer and for minerals. Some people reduce the salt when adding seaweed, but surface mold is more prevalent in those ferments.

Frequently, I'll have you using a premixed salt brine to cover fermenting foods. You'll find that recipe later in this chapter.

Starter Cultures

As we've discussed, one way to kick-start a fermentation from the beginning is to add a starter culture of desirable fermenting organisms. Some recipes in this book rely on starter cultures to get a desired result or to help beginning fermenters make successful fermentations.

While vegetable ferments often turn out great without a starter culture (fermenting with salt alone), certain other ferments, such as pasteurized dairy and fruits, require a starter culture to be successful. Here are options for starter cultures—my recipes will specify whether it's optional.

Most often, the best choice for fruit and vegetable fermenting is a powdered starter culture. I recommend the single- or double-strength "Fermenting Starter Culture" from Homesteader Supply (see Appendix B). If you're using the single-strength starter culture, add this to your ferments at the rate of $\frac{1}{16}$ teaspoon per 1 quart (1 liter) of ferment. Mix the powdered culture with ¼ cup of water and add it to your ferment as a liquid starter culture.

You can also use water kefir, a bubbly fermented beverage you'll learn about in Chapter 8. You can use this water kefir—containing an active population of lactic acid-producing organisms—as a direct substitution for whey (mentioned next).

Many people also use whey at the rate of ¼ cup per 1 quart (1 liter) of ferment. I refer not to the highly processed protein powder kind of whey but rather the "Little Miss Muffet sat on a tuffet eating her curds and whey" variety. Miss Muffet's whey is the liquid that naturally spills out of cheese or yogurt or other fermented dairy. Because we use whey as a starter culture in fermentation, we obviously need it to contain living beneficial organisms. This means it should come from cultured dairy whose temperature during the fermentation didn't exceed much more than 100°F (38°C). Higher temperatures kill the sensitive beneficial organisms.

Researchers differ in their opinions about the exact temperature at which most organisms perish, and indeed, different organisms perish at different temperatures. I prefer to keep things simple and make sure my whey wasn't heated much beyond 102°F to 105°F (39°C to 41°C).

Some people report that using whey as a starter culture makes their vegetable ferments, such as sauerkraut or pickles, "slimy" instead of crunchy. I've not experienced this personally, but if you have or are fearful of this, ferment your vegetables with salt alone or with salt and a powdered starter culture. Here's a recipe for uncooked Basic Whey.

Basic Whey

Yield:	Prep time:	Ferment time:	Ferment type:
2 cups	4 hours	none	lacto

1 quart (1 liter) plain yogurt, Kefir
(page 250), Clabber (page 246),
or another low-temperature
fermented dairy

1. Line a colander with two pieces of 90-thread-count cheesecloth. Place the colander in a pot or bowl that fits it. Pour the plain yogurt, kefir, clabber, or fermented dairy into the cheesecloth. Tie the ends.

2. Let the whey drip for about 1 day or find a place to hang the bag over the colander so gravity can speed up the process. (I don't recommend hanging your bag of dripping whey on a cupboard door because it can warp door hinges over time.) Store in an airtight jar in the fridge for up to 2 weeks.

If you notice any moldy bits, strain the whey, discarding the spoiled bits. If the strained whey smells spoiled, toss it. You can also freeze whey for several months—but not indefinitely because organisms perish over time when frozen.

Distancing Your Ferments

Different types of ferments using different starter cultures should ideally not be very close to each other. Organisms might pop out of one jar, and being close to the other, they decide to visit and stay for a while. This can alter the end result—sometimes without us noticing and sometimes causing complete failure. Ideally, keep different types of ferments more than five feet apart.

You can also get very creative! Some people save sauerkraut or pickle juice from a previous batch and use that to ferment the next batch, which could be carrots or asparagus. Remember, we want the organisms in the saved juice. If the flavor is a good match, the trick works. In the fermented dairy chapters, I talk more about the cultures and additional ingredients particular to that fermentation. For now, know that saving yogurt or sour cream from batch to batch is another extension of this frugal and inventive technique of keeping your own starters going indefinitely.

Methods of a Good Fermentation

Here's the part of this book where I tell you how fermentation is supposed to go—except that fermentation isn't always the same and people do things differently. So what I'm going to do is share with you the common threads in all fermentations. Things might look different when we get to fermenting things in the recipes and I'll let you know then if you should do something differently.

Right now, what I want you to understand is the overall process of fermentation so you can recognize when it's going well and when it's gone awry.

Methods of Fermentation

Really, the methods of fermentation are similar. Which way you go depends on the food you're fermenting and what form it takes—whether whole or chopped. For ease and simplicity, let's not talk about fermented dairy, beverages, or sourdough right now. Here are two scenarios when fermenting most other foods:

- **Whole or large pieces of food:** These are carrot sticks, sliced cucumbers, whole green beans, asparagus spears, chunks of fish, quartered radishes, or a mixture of any of these or similar-sized foods. These are separate pieces of food. They don't make a mixture and mash together nor do they produce enough juice to cover themselves.

- **Mixture of chopped or shredded foods:** These are smaller pieces of food that make a mash or mixture, such as a jam, paste, relish, salsa, chutney, or kraut. These foods are usually mashed, shredded, chopped, blended, or puréed. With the addition of salt or simply through the process of creating small pieces, they release enough juice to submerge themselves.

Whether your ferment is of the former or latter type of mixture, you must get it into a jar or container and provide the fermenting organisms with all the conditions they require for good fermentation. Remember those? Protection, the right temperature, food, and time. As you'll recall, protection can include adding salt, starter cultures, or acidity as well as eliminating oxygen.

The major difference between the two types of mixtures is that the second has a head start on protection because you can press this mixture into a jar to create a relatively air-free zone. If pressed down in a jar, the other mixture will have gaping holes where air surrounds the pieces of food.

Vegetables Covered With Brine

Basic Brine

Right away, we know we must submerge a mixture of whole or large pieces of food. The best cover is a brine—a salt and water solution. Use the following recipe any time you see "Basic Brine" listed in a recipe's ingredients.

Basic Brine

Yield:	Prep time:	Ferment time:	Ferment type:
½ gallon (2 liters)	5 minutes	none	lacto

6 tbsp fine-grain sea salt or 9 tbsp coarse-grain sea salt

8 cups water

1. In a ½-gallon (2-liter) jar, combine the salt and water. Stir until the salt dissolves. Store indefinitely at room temperature, but the glass might crack if the jar is stored for more than 1 week. Scale this recipe up or down to have about the amount you need.

Recipe Notes: If you need the brine right away, you can dissolve the salt in a few cups of water over low heat, then add cold water to reach the yield. Recipes will either call for Basic Brine or a special brine suited for a recipe's particular needs.

You can scale this brine recipe as needed. Add the brine to the jar that contains the whole or large pieces of food. This gives the separate pieces of food ample protection to achieve a good fermentation. You can use Basic Brine to top off shredded or chopped ferments. While adding salt to the chopped foods will draw out liquid, sometimes it's not enough to fully cover the food. Topping off with this brine will let your ferment be fully submerged for its anaerobic fermentation.

Fruit ferments would be way too salty if we used the same amount of brine or salt as a vegetable ferment (preserved lemons in Chapter 6 excepted). Generally, I use 1 to 1½ teaspoons of sea salt and ¼ cup of liquid starter culture per 1 quart (1 liter) of fruit ferment, plus any additional liquid as needed for consistency.

So now we've got our mixtures in the jar, along with any spices, herbs, or other flavors. To each quart (liter), you can also add ¼ cup of liquid starter culture. The entire mixture should stop 1 inch (2.5cm) from the fermenting vessel's rim to let liquids and gases be released.

Protecting Your Fermentation

- Weigh down the mixture if it needs it.

- Seal the jar or crock if you can seal it. As long as the mixture is submerged below the brine or its own juices, the container doesn't have to be sealed. However, ferments are generally more successful and results are more consistent if they're made in an airtight container.

- Place the container in a room temperature location and let the organisms do their thing.

- You might want to place the vessels on a towel to catch liquids that might bubble out. (It happens!)

- Check the mixture daily and skim away any mold or yeast that grows on top. Anything that grows at the top of a ferment is called "bloom." Most are quite normal. These organisms, usually yeasts and molds, aren't beneficial organisms—but they're not harmful either. Because they can affect the flavor of food, it's best to check and skim them off daily. Usually, this growth stays right at the top and doesn't go into the food.

- Daily burp a sealed container by opening it to release pent-up gases, then close it again. (With mixtures such as krauts or relishes, I also suggest pushing the mixture back down because the fermenting gases will be continually lifting it up.) A special fermenting crock or jar modified with an airlock won't need burping because these let fermenting gases escape continually. The gases released from a completely sealed container might be stinky. This is normal and not harmful. What's not normal are repulsive-smelling released gases that indicate rotting.

- When the texture and flavor are pleasing to you (see the next section), transfer your fermented food to cold storage as described earlier. Fermentation time ranges are generally provided with the recipes. When you're ready to branch out on your own, remember this general rule: Large and hard pieces of food take longer to ferment than small and soft. For example, a whole cucumber will take longer to ferment than mashed-up berries.

Now you know the most general of fermentation methods. Dairy, beverages, and sourdough have similarities and differences to these. Again, I'll share those with you in the appropriate chapters. But let's talk about the signs of a good fermentation.

All Is Well

When a ferment is going well, you might see all or some of the following signs: bubbles; sour and fresh but pleasant smell; increase in liquid content; cloudy brine; dimming of color; and softening texture. Not all these will be true in all fermented foods. Fermenting a thick paste, such as Fig Butter (page 98), won't bubble up or produce liquids—it's too thick. Some foods bubble up quite a bit and others not so much. Bubbles are quite common in vegetable ferments as well as natural sodas. What tends to happen is you'll see a few bubbles when the ferment gets going. As the organisms increase in numbers, because there are more of them to produce gases, you'll see more bubbles. As the food runs lower for the organisms, the fermentation nears its finish and the bubbles taper off. Usually, I transfer my ferments to cold storage at this point, but I also combine the visual signs with taste tests to determine when something is done.

When a food ferments, the texture usually softens and the food develops a tart yet pleasantly fresh taste. Granted, we don't all have the same feelings about sour foods—some of us like them more than others. Don't confuse sour with spoiled—they're two different things. And also keep in mind that while many foods soften when fermented, a soft texture isn't desirable for pickles we want to stay crunchy.

Let's say you decide you're happy with a ferment and call it done, then later eat it and discover it gives you digestive upset (otherwise known as gas). This is a sign it hasn't fermented long enough in the jar. You eat the food and it continues to be fermented in the gut, producing gas and other unpleasant symptoms. Before eating any more, pull the ferment out of cold storage and let it finish the fermentation. Or give it a few weeks in cold storage to continue fermenting. Even at cool temperatures, the organisms are alive and working, although more slowly.

Done for you? Done for me? Fermentation times vary, not only by what food is being fermented, the strength of the organisms, and the room temperature but also by the preferences of the fermenter. All other signs being good, consider the fermentation done when you're happy with the taste and texture.

A lot of factors contribute to a fermentation being done. When temperatures are cooler, organisms are slower to get established and slower to ferment the food. On the other hand, if temperatures are warmer, fermentation proceeds more quickly. This is why fermenting recipes give you ranges of time and leave the rest up to you. If you know your climate is cooler, always add time. If your climate is warmer, reduce the time. Additionally, you might learn over time to play with your fermentation temperature. Experienced kraut and cheese-makers often prefer a slower fermentation at lower temperatures because they say it yields better, more complex flavors.

Signs of Trouble

If you don't see bubbles or the flavor isn't getting sour, these aren't signs in and of themselves that a fermentation has gone awry. Some fermented foods don't bubble much and some don't get that sour.

To tell when a fermentation is in trouble, your only true sign is smell. And taste, of course—but usually none of us will get past a bad smell to actually put that questionable something in our mouths. At least I don't!

Please remember there's a difference between sour and spoiled or sour and rotting. A ferment gone wrong will smell repulsive, disgusting, and rotting—it's unmistakable. You might not know what I'm talking about now, but should you smell a spoiled fermenting food in the future, you'll know then. You'll have no doubt. Spoiled fermented foods shouldn't be eaten. Toss any such foods in the compost pile or in the garbage.

Fermenting the Fruits of the Vine

Now that you know how to ferment almost any food, this section of the book focuses on fermenting all the fruits of the vine. No, this doesn't mean just grapes. It includes anything a plant produces: fruits and vegetables, beans and grains, and beverages and condiments. Each chapter will help you understand the particulars of fermenting each food group. You'll also find recipes for fermenting foods as well as recipes to help you incorporate fermented foods into other dishes.

Vegetables

With this chapter, we enter the practical world of fermentation, focusing on vegetables. Vegetable fermentation is classic lactic-acid fermentation that's accomplished with a brine. I'll explain a little about that and then we'll dive into the delicious recipes for fermenting garden produce.

Two Ways to Brine

We'll be following in the footsteps of the legendary workers of the Great Wall of China, who it's said packed their vegetables in a crock and found the mixture happily fermented after a few days. But while their discovery was probably an accident, you and I will purposely duplicate their actions as we culture and create krauts, dips, chutneys, pickles, relishes, salsas, and more.

Fermenting vegetables doesn't differ significantly from the fermentation processes and guidelines I outlined in chapters 3 and 4. As in most fermentation, vegetable fermenting happens under the protective cover of brine, where beneficial organisms are protected from spoiling organisms. Let's talk a little bit more about brine, which can come into play in vegetable fermentation in one of two ways:

- You can add brine in the form of a saltwater solution that covers a vegetable or a mixture of vegetables, such as when making pickles.

- You can draw a brine out of the vegetables themselves: by pounding, from a spontaneous release of juices when the vegetables are cut, or by mixing cut-up vegetables with salt, which helps draw out their juices. This is the case with sauerkrauts, chutneys, relishes, salsas, and other juicy mixtures.

All the recipes in this book are one or the other of these brine types. How can you tell the difference? Easily. If the recipe calls for Basic Brine (page 41) or a higher salt concentration brine, then it's a recipe that must be covered in brine. If the recipe calls for salt to be mixed together with the other ingredients, then it doesn't require an added salt brine.

As a general rule, I call for about ½ tablespoon of salt per quart (liter) of vegetable ferment when a starter culture is also used. If you want to omit the starter culture, double the amount of salt. While you can ferment vegetables without salt, most fermenters choose to use it. Salt improves flavor and texture, and it protects the fermenting organisms and their work. If the recipe includes a sweetener (such as for sweet pickles), I don't recommend omitting the starter culture.

You might wonder what fermenting organisms are at work in vegetable fermentation and what they produce. Although yeasts are often present, vegetable fermentation is primarily the work of the beneficial *lactobacilli* bacteria living on vegetables in significant numbers. As the bacteria consume the starches and sugars in vegetables, they multiply and establish a colony, producing lactic acid and carbon dioxide as well as enzymes and vitamins. Most vegetable fermentation is lactic-acid fermentation. You can read more details about this type of fermentation in Chapter 3.

Source the highest-quality vegetables you can, opting for unsprayed to avoid pesticide residues that can interfere with fermentation. You can judge whether a vegetable ferment is done by the guidelines shared in Chapter 4. When you think it's finished fermenting, move it to cold storage—also outlined in Chapter 4.

The methods of pickling vegetables include fermentation (such as you'll see in this chapter) as well as two other significantly different pickling methods. You already know the first: canning. You also know what's inferior about this from our discussion in Chapter 1. The other method worth noting causes much confusion because it's appealingly traditional and decidedly nonindustrial. I refer to the practice of making fresh pickles by covering vegetables in vinegar and storing them in the fridge. Such recipes abound—they're often called "refrigerator pickles" or "fresh pickles." These pickles aren't canned and they're refreshingly crunchy, but the virtues end there. Using vinegar completely suppresses fermentation. Thus, those pickles aren't considered fermented and don't convey the incredible nutritional benefits of fermented foods.

Keep in mind that salsas, relishes, and krauts can get quite bubbly. If you're using canning jars, burp them once a day by opening the jar band enough to release the pent-up gases. When it comes time to open the jars fully, do it in the sink or with a towel underneath. Happy ferments have a habit of bubbling out all over the place.

The recipes in this chapter are organized this way: krauts, pickles, relishes, salsas, and other miscellaneous pickled vegetables.

Sauerkraut Recipes

- All krauts get better with age. If you don't like your kraut after its first week of fermentation, chances are you'll like it much more after six months.

- If you make a large quantity of any kind of sauerkraut, store the big crock or barrel in your cellar, only bringing up into the house what you'd eat in about one week. Make sure to repack the crock well in storage to protect the kraut from spoiling.

- After you make kraut a few times, you might find you no longer need a recipe. Just chop, shred, and combine what looks and sounds good. Add ½ tablespoon of sea salt and ¼ cup of starter culture (optional; see Appendix B) per quart (liter) and you're good to go for the fermentation.

- You can double the amount of salt in these krauts and omit the starter culture entirely. Because the *lactobacilli* are abundant on vegetables, you can easily leave out the starter culture. In fact, some fermenters prefer the crisper, cleaner texture of kraut without the starter culture. They say they can also taste the difference. Like with many ferments, the right way is the way that works best for you.

Garlic Sauerkraut

We're skipping basic sauerkraut and going for the garlic. You'll get the unbeatable sour crispness you really want—and just a little bit more.

Yield:	Prep time:	Ferment time:	Ferment type:
1 quart (1 liter)	40 minutes	3 to 7 days	lacto

1 medium head of cabbage,
    cored and shredded

3 garlic cloves, crushed

½ tbsp sea salt

¼ cup starter culture
    (see Appendix B)

1. In a medium bowl, combine the cabbage, garlic, salt, and starter culture. Cover with a tea towel and leave at room temperature for 30 minutes while the salt pulls the juices out of the vegetables. Remove the towel about halfway through and pound the mixture a few times with a potato masher to make sure it's getting juicy.

2. Transfer the mixture to a wide-mouth quart (liter) jar or another fermenting container. Press down firmly to bring liquid to the top of the mixture. Leave 1 inch (2.5cm) from the container's rim. Cover tightly with a lid or an airlock.

3. Leave at room temperature for 3 to 7 days. In the first 24 hours, open the jar and press down firmly on the ingredients a few times to make sure the liquid fully covers the mixture. Store in cool storage for up to 1 year.

High Vitamin C Sauerkraut

It's tangy and delicious—but that's not all. This recipe for homemade sauerkraut developed by my friend Megan also boosts the immune system and provides EMF (electromagnetic field) protection: It pairs probiotic (and vitamin C–rich) sauerkraut with an herb (rose hips) renowned as a high vitamin C food.

Yield:	Prep time:	Ferment time:	Ferment type:
1 quart (1 liter)	40 minutes	3 to 7 days	lacto

1 medium head of cabbage, cored and shredded

2 cups purified water

2 tbsp sea salt

¼ cup rose hips

1. In a large bowl, combine the cabbage, water, and salt. Stir slightly. Cover with a tea towel and leave at room temperature for 30 minutes while the salt pulls juices out of the vegetables. Remove the towel and toss the cabbage again. Re-cover and set aside for 30 minutes more.

2. Use a coffee or spice grinder to pulverize the rose hips until the largest pieces are about the size of peppercorns. Into a wide-mouth quart (liter) jar or fermenting crock, pack the cabbage mixture, layering the rose hips as you go. Add any remaining salted water to the jar or crock. Press down firmly to tightly pack and remove air bubbles. Seal according to crock instructions or use pickling weights and fermentation lids.

3. Leave at room temperature for 7 days. After 12 to 24 hours, pack down the cabbage again to make sure it's below the brine. Store in cold storage for up to 1 year, where flavors will continue to develop.

Tsukemono

A Japanese-style sauerkraut flavored with lemon and soy sauce, *tsukemono* is definitely my favorite kraut. I love to eat it with eggs for breakfast.

Yield:	Prep time:	Ferment time:	Ferment type:
1 quart (1 liter)	40 minutes	3 to 7 days	lacto

1 medium head of cabbage, cored and shredded

1 bunch of green onions (about 8), bulbs and stalks, chopped

2 tbsp store-bought traditional, aged, or fermented soy sauce

2 tbsp freshly squeezed lemon juice

½ tbsp sea salt

¼ cup starter culture (Appendix B)

1. In a medium bowl, combine the cabbage, green onions, soy sauce, lemon juice, salt, and starter culture. Cover with a tea towel and leave at room temperature for 30 minutes while the salt pulls juices out of the vegetables. Remove the towel about halfway through and pound the mixture a few times with a potato masher to make sure it's getting juicy.

2. Transfer the mixture to a wide-mouth quart (liter) jar or another fermenting container. Press down firmly to bring liquid to the top of the mixture. Leave 1 inch (2.5cm) from the container's rim. Cover tightly with a lid or an airlock.

3. Leave at room temperature for 3 to 7 days. In the first 24 hours, open the jar and press down firmly on the ingredients a few times to make sure the liquid fully covers the mixture. Store in cool storage for up to 1 year.

Kimchi

If you like some heat, try this Korean sauerkraut.

Yield:	Prep time:	Ferment time:	Ferment type:
1 quart (1 liter)	40 minutes	3 to 7 days	lacto

1 medium head of cabbage, cored and shredded

1 bunch of green onions (about 8 to 10), bulbs and stalks, chopped

1 cup shredded carrots

1 tbsp grated ginger

3 garlic cloves, crushed

½ tsp dried red pepper flakes

½ tbsp sea salt

¼ cup starter culture (Appendix B)

1. In a medium bowl, combine the cabbage, green onions, carrots, ginger, garlic, red pepper flakes, salt, and starter culture. Cover with a tea towel and leave at room temperature for 30 minutes while the salt pulls juices out of the vegetables. Remove the towel about halfway through and pound the mixture a few times with a potato masher to make sure it's getting juicy.

2. Transfer the mixture to a wide-mouth quart (liter) jar or another fermenting container. Press down firmly to bring liquid to the top of the mixture. Leave 1 inch (2.5cm) from the container's rim. Cover tightly with a lid or an airlock.

3. Leave at room temperature for 3 to 7 days. In the first 24 hours, open the jar and press down firmly on the ingredients a few times to make sure the liquid fully covers the mixture. Store in cool storage for up to 1 year.

Cortido

This is a spicy Latin American kraut that goes perfectly with just about all Mexican and Latin American foods. Traditional *cortido* is vinegar-pickled through the use of pineapple vinegar, but this more healthful version—from my friend Marillyn, a missionary in Honduras—is lacto-fermented through the use of salt and a starter culture.

Yield:	Prep time:	Ferment time:	Ferment type:
2 quarts (2 liters)	40 minutes	3 to 7 days	lacto

1 medium head of cabbage, cored and shredded

1 small head of red cabbage, cored and shredded

2 cups grated carrots

2 medium onions (red recommended), finely sliced

5 garlic cloves, crushed

1 tbsp dried oregano or 3 tbsp fresh oregano, chopped

¼ to 1 tsp red pepper flakes

1 tbsp sea salt

½ cup starter culture (Appendix B)

1. In a large bowl, combine the cabbages, carrots, onions, garlic, oregano, red pepper flakes, salt, and starter culture. Cover with a tea towel and leave at room temperature for 30 minutes while the salt pulls juices out of the vegetables. Remove the towel about halfway through and pound the mixture a few times with a potato masher to make sure it's getting juicy.

2. Transfer to 2 wide-mouth quart (liter) jars, a ½-gallon (2-liter) jar, or another fermenting container. Press down firmly to bring liquid to the top of the mixture. Leave 1 inch (2.5cm) from each container's rim. Cover tightly with lids or airlocks.

3. Leave at room temperature for 3 to 7 days. In the first 24 hours, open the containers and press down firmly on the ingredients a few times to make sure the liquid fully covers the mixture. Store in cool storage for up to 1 year.

Carrot Kraut

Carrots add sweetness and color to a basic sauerkraut. This is a mild kraut for more tentative eaters.

Yield:	Prep time:	Ferment time:	Ferment type:
1 quart (1 liter)	40 minutes	3 to 7 days	lacto

1 medium head of cabbage, shredded

2 medium carrots, shredded

½ tbsp sea salt

¼ cup starter culture (Appendix B)

1. In a medium bowl, combine the cabbage, carrots, salt, and starter culture. Cover with a tea towel and leave at room temperature for 30 minutes while the salt pulls juices out of the vegetables. Remove the towel about halfway through and pound the mixture a few times with a potato masher to make sure it's getting juicy.

2. Transfer to a wide-mouth quart (liter) jar or another fermenting container. Press down firmly to bring liquid to the top of the mixture. Leave 1 inch (2.5cm) from the container's rim. Cover tightly with a lid or an airlock.

3. Leave at room temperature for 3 to 7 days. In the first 24 hours, open the jar and press down firmly on the ingredients a few times to make sure the liquid fully covers the mixture. Store in cool storage for up to 1 year.

Spinach Kraut

Turn an abundance of garden spinach into a lemony, unique sauerkraut.

Yield:	Prep time:	Ferment time:	Ferment type:
1 quart (1 liter)	10 minutes	2 to 3 days	lacto

15 cups fresh spinach, washed and tightly packed

4 garlic cloves, crushed

½ tbsp sea salt

¼ cup starter culture (Appendix B)

1 lemon wedge

1. Chop the spinach into ½-inch-wide (1.25cm) strips. In a large bowl, combine the spinach, garlic, salt, and starter culture. Cover with a tea towel and leave at room temperature for 30 minutes while the salt pulls juices out of the spinach. Remove the towel about halfway through and pound the mixture a few times with a potato masher to make sure it's getting juicy.

2. Transfer to a wide-mouth quart (liter) jar or another fermenting container. Place the lemon wedge somewhere in the middle. Press down firmly to bring liquid to the top of the mixture. Leave 1 inch (2.5cm) from the container's rim. Cover tightly with a lid or an airlock.

4. Leave at room temperature for 2 to 3 days. In the first 24 hours, open the jar and press down firmly on the ingredients a few times to make sure the liquid fully covers the mixture. Store in cool storage for up to 1 year.

Variation: Use any dark, leafy green in place of the spinach.

Pickle Recipes

To ensure crispy pickles, you should do three things:

- Add something containing tannins to the pickle mixture—a clean oak or grape leaf or black tea.

- Cut off the blossom end of the cucumber, which contains an enzyme that interferes with crispness.

- Use fresh-picked cucumbers or crisp up your cucumbers in ice water for 30 minutes prior to pickling.

When fermenting pickles in warm weather, check them frequently. Your nose will let you know of any issues. When they're ready, get them in cool storage promptly.

Garlic Dill Pickles

These are pretty basic dill pickles—except they're kicked up with garlic.

Yield:	Prep time:	Ferment time:	Ferment type:
½ gallon (2 liters)	10 minutes	3 to 7 days	lacto

7¾ cups 3- to 4-inch (7.5 to 10cm) whole pickling cucumbers, ends trimmed

6 garlic cloves

2 tsp dill seeds or 2 to 3 fresh dill heads

¼ tsp black tea

4 cups Basic Brine (page 41), plus more

1. If you're not using just-picked cucumbers, submerge the cucumbers in ice-cold water for 30 minutes.

2. In a wide-mouth ½-gallon (2-liter) jar or another fermenting container, combine the cucumbers, garlic, dill, and tea. Add the brine, including more as needed to cover the ingredients, but stop 1 inch (2.5cm) from the container's rim. Place a regular-mouth lid on top to hold the ingredients below the brine. Cover tightly with a lid or an airlock.

3. Leave at room temperature for 3 to 7 days. Store in the fridge for up to 1 year.

Sweet Pickle Slices

These are mustardy and sweet—tuck some into your next juicy burger. Cucumbers that are about 3 to 4 inches (7.5 to 10cm) in length make the best pickles. Even so, I've made delicious pickles with larger pickling cucumbers and even fresh-eating cucumbers. I ferment fresh-eating cucumbers about 1 day less because they can get mushy quickly.

Yield:	Prep time:	Ferment time:	Ferment type:
1 quart (1 liter)	10 minutes	3 days	lacto

3 medium cucumbers, ends trimmed

⅓ medium onion (any type), thinly sliced

½ cup maple syrup or raw honey

¼ cup starter culture (Appendix B)

½ tbsp celery seeds

½ tbsp mustard seeds

½ tsp dill seeds

1 tsp ground turmeric

2 cups Basic Brine (page 41), divided, plus more

1. If you're not using just-picked cucumbers, submerge the cucumbers in ice-cold water for 30 minutes.

2. Slice the cucumbers into ⅜-inch (1cm) slices. In a wide-mouth quart (liter) jar or fermenting container, combine the cucumber slices and onion.

3. In a medium bowl, combine the maple syrup or honey, starter culture, celery seeds, mustard seeds, dill seeds, turmeric, and 1 cup of brine. Stir until the maple syrup or honey is completely mixed in. Pour the mixture over the cucumbers and onion.

4. Add the brine, including more as needed to cover the ingredients, but stop 1 inch (2.5cm) from the container's rim. Place a regular-mouth lid on top to hold the vegetables below the brine. Cover tightly with a lid or an airlock.

5. Leave at room temperature for 3 days. Store in cool storage for up to 1 year.

Bread & Butter Pickles

Yes, you can also make fermented bread and butter pickles! Adding raw vinegar to a ferment is usually a no-no to avoid introducing competing acetic acid–producing organisms. However, I find that a small amount of raw vinegar doesn't detrimentally effect my lactic-acid fermentations.

Yield:	Prep time:	Ferment time:	Ferment type:
1 quart (1 liter)	10 minutes	3 days	lacto

3 medium cucumbers, ends trimmed

1 tbsp pickling spice

¼ tsp celery seeds

½ cup maple syrup or raw honey

¼ cup starter culture (Appendix B)

2 tbsp apple cider vinegar

¾ cup water, plus more

1. If you're not using just-picked cucumbers, submerge the cucumbers in ice-cold water for 30 minutes.

2. Slice the cucumbers into ⅜-inch (1cm) slices. Into a wide-mouth quart (liter) jar or another fermenting container, pack the slices.

3. In a small bowl, combine the pickling spice, celery seeds, maple syrup or honey, starter culture, and apple cider vinegar until the maple syrup or honey is completely mixed in. Pour the mixture over the cucumbers.

4. Add the water, including more as needed to cover the ingredients, but stop 1 inch (2.5cm) from the container's rim. Place a regular-mouth lid on top to hold the cucumbers below the brine. Cover tightly with a lid or an airlock.

5. Leave at room temperature for 3 days. Store in cool storage for up to 1 year.

Spicy Cucumber Pickle Slices

Add a few of these to the sandwich or burger of the person who likes a little spice. They'll be thanking you!

Yield:	Prep time:	Ferment time:	Ferment type:
1 quart (1 liter)	10 minutes	3 days	lacto

3 medium cucumbers, ends trimmed

⅓ medium onion (any type), thinly sliced

4 garlic cloves, cut into thirds

5 peppercorns

¼ tsp red pepper flakes

½ tsp mustard seeds

¼ tsp celery seeds

1 tbsp grated fresh ginger

2 cups Basic Brine (page 41), plus more

1. If you're not using just-picked cucumbers, submerge the cucumbers in ice-cold water for 30 minutes.

2. Slice the cucumbers into ⅜-inch (1cm) slices. Into a wide-mouth quart (liter) jar or another fermenting container, pack the cucumbers and onion. Add the garlic, peppercorns, red pepper flakes, mustard seeds, celery seeds, and ginger.

3. Add the brine, including more as needed to cover the ingredients, but stop 1 inch (2.5cm) from the container's rim. Place a regular-mouth lid on top to hold the vegetables below the brine. Cover tightly with a lid or an airlock.

4. Leave at room temperature for 3 days. Store in cool storage for up to 1 year.

Relish Recipes

If your pickles have turned out mushy but are otherwise good (not spoiled), you can make a quick pickle relish by pulsing the contents of the jar in a food processor until you get a nice relish consistency. Store your new relish in an airtight jar in cold storage. You can make a relish out of endless combinations of vegetables or fruits. Try combining corn kernels with colorful bell peppers and onions, and add cilantro and lemon juice. Whatever you'd mix together for a salad or slaw—try fermenting into a relish. Or if you'd like to create a chunkier texture, try dicing ingredients instead of shredding them.

Cucumber Relish

Toasted sandwiches, hot dogs, and hamburgers—everything's better with some of this flavorful, universally liked fermented relish!

Yield:	Prep time:	Ferment time:	Ferment type:
1 quart (1 liter)	20 minutes	2 to 3 days	lacto

3½ cups coarsely chopped cucumbers

½ cup coarsely chopped red or yellow bell peppers

½ cup diced onions (any type)

½ tbsp sea salt

1 tsp ground turmeric

½ tsp mustard seeds

1 tsp dill seeds

¼ cup starter culture (Appendix B)

1. In a medium bowl, combine the cucumbers, bell peppers, onions, salt, turmeric, mustard seeds, dill seeds, and starter culture.

2. Into a wide-mouth quart (liter) jar or another fermenting container, pack the mixture 1 inch (2.5cm) from the container's rim. Cover tightly with a lid or an airlock.

3. Leave at room temperature for 2 to 3 days. Store in the fridge for up to 1 year.

Spicy Cucumber Relish

Serrano peppers and ginger make a nicely spiced—not too hot; not too mild—relish for those who like a little heat but not too much. Chunky or smooth? You can ensure the right texture of relish by the way you chop it. Finely hand-dicing the vegetables will give you a chunky relish, while using a food processor will yield a juicier, finer mash. If using a food processor, I recommend pulsing to avoid overchopping.

Yield:	Prep time:	Ferment time:	Ferment type:
1 quart (1 liter)	10 minutes	2 to 3 days	lacto

3½ cups coarsely chopped cucumbers

½ cup coarsely chopped red or yellow bell peppers

1 serrano or jalapeño pepper, diced, with seeds

½ cup diced onions (any type)

½ tbsp sea salt

2 tbsp grated fresh ginger

3 garlic cloves, crushed or minced

¼ cup starter culture (Appendix B)

1. In a medium bowl, combine the cucumbers, peppers, onions, salt, ginger, garlic, and starter culture.

2. Into a wide-mouth quart (liter) jar or another fermenting container, pack the mixture 1 inch (2.5cm) from the container's rim. Cover tightly with a lid or an airlock.

3. Leave at room temperature for 2 to 3 days. Store in the fridge for up to 1 year.

Variation: To reduce the spice, omit the serrano seeds. I find that just one serrano adds just enough heat. Of course, you can add more if you want it super spicy. When handling hot peppers, you might want to use gloves and avoid touching your face, eyes, or any other part of your body. When you're done, wash well with soapy water to remove all traces of the hot pepper oils.

Ginger & Zucchini Relish

Combining shredded zucchini with a generous amount of ginger, this relish is quite gingery and absolutely delicious mixed into a chicken salad.

Yield:	Prep time:	Ferment time:	Ferment type:
1 quart (1 liter)	10 minutes	2 to 3 days	lacto

4 cups shredded zucchini

¼ cup grated fresh ginger

½ cup diced onions (any type)

½ tbsp sea salt

½ tsp ground turmeric

½ tsp mustard seeds

¼ cup starter culture (Appendix B)

1. In a medium bowl, combine the zucchini, ginger, onions, salt, turmeric, mustard seeds, and starter culture.

2. Into a wide-mouth quart (liter) jar or another fermenting container, pack the mixture 1 inch (2.5cm) from the container's rim. Cover tightly with a lid or an airlock.

3. Leave at room temperature for 2 to 3 days. Store in the fridge for up to 1 year.

Spicy Zucchini Relish

Use up your summer zucchini bounty by making yet another relish. This one also gets its spice from serrano peppers.

Yield:	Prep time:	Ferment time:	Ferment type:
1 quart (1 liter)	10 minutes	2 to 3 days	lacto

3½ cups shredded zucchini

½ cup diced onions (any type)

1 serrano or jalapeño pepper, diced, with seeds

½ cup coarsely chopped red or yellow bell peppers

3 garlic cloves, crushed or minced

¼ tsp red pepper flakes

½ tbsp sea salt

¼ cup starter culture (Appendix B)

1. In a medium bowl, combine the zucchini, onions, peppers, garlic, red pepper flakes, salt, and starter culture.

2. Into a wide-mouth quart (liter) jar or another fermenting container, pack the mixture 1 inch (2.5cm) from the container's rim. Cover tightly with a lid or an airlock.

3. Leave at room temperature for 2 to 3 days. Store in the fridge for up to 1 year..

Corn Relish

Sweet corn combines with summer vegetables in a colorful, tasty relish with a kick.

Yield:	Prep time:	Ferment time:	Ferment type:
1 quart (1 liter)	10 minutes	2 to 3 days	lacto

3¼ cups fresh corn kernels

½ cup diced onions (any type)

½ cup diced Roma tomatoes

1 serrano pepper, diced, with seeds

¼ cup chopped fresh cilantro leaves

½ tbsp sea salt

¼ cup starter culture (Appendix B)

1. In a medium bowl, combine the corn, onions, tomatoes, pepper, cilantro leaves, salt, and starter culture.

2. Into a wide-mouth quart (liter) jar or another fermenting container, pack the mixture 1 inch (2.5cm) from the container's rim. Cover tightly with a lid or an airlock.

3. Leave at room temperature for 2 to 3 days. Transfer to cool storage. Leave for 2 weeks more in cold storage before eating. Store in cool storage for up to 1 year.

Salsa Recipes

Texture is everything when it comes to salsa. I like a salsa that's a little bit soupy. For my husband, that's a big no-no. A food processor is very handy to chop all the ingredients, but you risk making a soupier salsa. So if you like really chunky salsa, you might skip the food processor and opt for a knife and cutting board instead.

Cherry Tomato Salsa

The sweet flavor of cherry tomatoes is a great combination with the spices of salsa. Use the jalapeño pepper seeds if you like your salsa spicy.

Yield:	Prep time:	Ferment time:	Ferment type:
1 quart (1 liter)	10 minutes	1 to 2 days	lacto

5 cups cherry tomatoes, chopped

1 small to medium onion (red recommended), chopped

3 to 5 jalapeño peppers, seeds removed, chopped

1 garlic clove, minced

¼ to ½ tsp red pepper flakes

½ tbsp sea salt

¼ tsp ground black pepper

¼ cup starter culture (Appendix B)

1. In a medium bowl, combine the tomatoes, onion, peppers, garlic, red pepper flakes, salt, black pepper, and starter culture.

2. Into a wide-mouth quart (liter) jar or another fermenting container, pack the mixture 1 inch (2.5cm) from the container's rim. Cover tightly with a lid or an airlock.

3. Leave at room temperature for 1 to 2 days. Store in the fridge for up to 1 year.

Mild Salsa

Everyone needs a go-to basic salsa recipe. This one can't be beat. And here's an idea: Add fermented salsa to your favorite chicken salad and make it not only probiotic but also very tasty!

Yield:	Prep time:	Ferment time:	Ferment type:
1 quart (1 liter)	10 minutes	2 to 3 days	lacto

4 medium slicing tomatoes or 8 Roma tomatoes, quartered and cored

1 medium onion (any type), peeled and quartered

1 medium green bell pepper, halved, cored, and seeded

1 serrano pepper, seeded

1 garlic clove

½ cup packed fresh cilantro leaves

½ tbsp sea salt

¼ cup starter culture (Appendix B)

juice from 2 lemons or limes

1. In a food processor, combine the tomatoes, onion, peppers, garlic, cilantro leaves, salt, starter culture, and lemon or lime juice. Pulse to chop to your desired chunkiness.

2. Into a wide-mouth quart (liter) jar or another fermenting container, pack the mixture 1 inch (2.5cm) from the container's rim. Cover tightly with a lid or an airlock.

3. Leave at room temperature for 2 to 3 days. Store in the fridge for up to 1 year.

Spicy Salsa

The jalapeño heat is balanced with sweetness from tomatoes, peppers, and lemons for a fantastic spicy salsa.

Yield:	Prep time:	Ferment time:	Ferment type:
1 quart (1 liter)	10 minutes	2 to 3 days	lacto

4 medium slicing tomatoes or 8 Roma tomatoes, quartered and cored

1 medium onion (any type), peeled and quartered

1 medium green bell pepper, halved, cored, and seeded

1 jalapeño pepper, seeded

1 garlic clove

½ tbsp sea salt

¼ cup starter culture (Appendix B)

juice from 2 lemons or limes

1. In a food processor, combine the tomatoes, onion, peppers, garlic, salt, starter culture, and lemon or lime juice. Pulse to chop to your desired chunkiness.

2. Into a wide-mouth quart (liter) jar or another fermenting container, pack the mixture 1 inch (2.5cm) from the container's rim. Cover tightly with a lid or an airlock.

3. Leave at room temperature for 2 to 3 days. Store in the fridge for up to 1 year.

Rhubarb Salsa

This. Is. Scrumptious. Tart, spicy, sweet, and addictive. Make sure you don't skimp on the ginger or the honey in this recipe created by my friend Kresha. They make the rhubarb flavor shine.

Yield:	Prep time:	Ferment time:	Ferment type:
2½ cups	30 minutes	1 to 2 days	lacto

7 to 8 rhubarb stalks, coarsely chopped (about 2 cups)

2 to 3 tbsp water

1 tbsp orange zest, from approximately 1 orange

2 to 3 inches (5cm to 7.5cm) fresh ginger, peeled and finely grated

½ small yellow onion, finely diced

½ small red onion, finely diced

1 to 2 jalapeño peppers, seeded and minced

½ green bell pepper, diced

½ cup raw honey

3 tbsp freshly squeezed lemon juice, from approximately 1 lemon

1 tsp sea salt, plus more

½ cup starter culture (Appendix B)

1. In a large saucepan or pot on the stovetop over medium heat, combine the rhubarb and water. Simmer until the rhubarb softens and begins to fall apart, about 10 to 15 minutes.

2. Transfer the rhubarb to a blender, food processor, or large bowl. Add the remaining ingredients (except the starter culture) and blend until a chunky purée is formed. (If you're working by hand, just toss everything together well.) Taste and adjust seasoning.

3. Stir in the starter culture and transfer the salsa to a quart (liter) glass jar.

4. Leave at room temperature for 1 to 2 days. Store in the fridge for up to 3 to 4 weeks. While you can eat this salsa immediately, it does taste significantly better after a few days—if you have the time to wait.

Other Vegetable Recipes

Why stop at krauts, salsas, and relishes? Keep going! Turn your vegetables into flavorful chutney mixtures and sticks. They make great appetizers or toppings for salads, adding probiotics and crunch.

Carrot Chutney

Sweet carrots and sour cranberries combine with nuts, ginger, and cloves in this delicious chutney. You can make chutneys from many hard fruits and vegetables. Combine with savory spices and you might just come up with a winner.

Yield:	Prep time:	Ferment time:	Ferment type:
1 quart (1 liter)	20 minutes	3 to 5 days	lacto

½ cup raisins

3 cups tightly packed shredded carrots

1 cup fresh or frozen cranberries

½ cup chopped walnuts

1 tsp sea salt

¼ cup starter culture (Appendix B)

pinch of ground cloves

½ tsp dried ginger or 1 inch (2.5cm) fresh ginger, shredded

2 tbsp unrefined sugar

1. In a small bowl, combine the raisins with enough water to cover them. Leave for 15 minutes, then drain, squeezing out some excess water.

2. In a medium bowl, combine the raisins, carrots, cranberries, walnuts, salt, starter culture, cloves, dried or fresh ginger, and sugar. Mash with a potato masher to release the carrot juices.

3. Into a wide-mouth quart (liter) jar or another fermenting container, pack the mixture 1 inch (2.5cm) from the container's rim. Cover tightly with a lid or an airlock.

4. Leave at room temperature for 3 to 5 days. Store in the fridge for up to 1 year.

Carrot Chutney

Pickled Radishes

Pickled Radishes

Delicious atop a green salad, these crunchy, tasty radishes can also be added to egg, meat, or grain salads.

Yield:	Prep time:	Ferment time:	Ferment type:
1 quart (1 liter)	5 minutes	3 to 5 days	lacto

30 radishes, trimmed and cut into quarters

3 garlic cloves, crushed

¼ medium red onion, thinly sliced

1-inch (2.5cm) piece of fresh ginger, cut into ¼-inch (0.5cm) slices or chunks

½ tsp mustard powder

1 dried bay leaf

½ tsp ground coriander

¼ cup starter culture (Appendix B)

1 cup Basic Brine (page 41), plus more

1. In a wide-mouth quart (liter) jar or another fermenting container, combine the radishes, garlic, onion, ginger, mustard powder, bay leaf, coriander, and starter culture.

2. Add the brine, including more as needed to cover the ingredients, but stop 1 inch (2.5cm) from the container's rim.

3. Place a regular-mouth jar lid on top to hold the vegetables below the brine. Cover tightly with a lid or an airlock.

4. Leave at room temperature for 3 to 5 days. Store in the fridge for up to 1 year.

Variation: This recipe is easily adaptable. Keep the radishes, water, salt, and starter culture, but feel free to vary the other ingredients as you like.

Costa Rican Chilero

Chilero is a spicy Costa Rican mixture of carrots, onions, and sweet and spicy peppers. Like with many ferments, the flavor improves with aging. In today's markets, you'll find chilero pickled in vinegar. My friend Marillyn's husband urged her to make a lacto-fermented version. She did—and from the very first jar, it became a family favorite. This is that recipe.

Yield:	Prep time:	Ferment time:	Ferment type:
1 quart (1 liter)	10 minutes	3 days	lacto

3 cups grated carrots

1 medium yellow onion, thinly sliced

1 sweet red pepper, finely chopped

1 to 2 cayenne or jalapeño peppers, finely chopped

2 garlic cloves, minced

1 tbsp sea salt

¼ cup starter culture (Appendix B)

1. In a medium bowl, combine the carrots, onion, peppers, and garlic. Transfer to a wide-mouth quart (liter) jar or another fermenting container. Gently push down the vegetables.

2. In a small bowl, mix the salt and starter culture. Add this mixture to the jar.

3. Add enough water to cover the mixture, leaving 1 inch (2.5cm) from the container's rim. Cover tightly with a lid or an airlock.

4. Leave at room temperature for 3 days. Store in cool storage for up to 1 year.

Spinach Sticks

Lemon and dill add great flavors to fermented spinach stalks. Dark, leafy greens contain oxalic acid, an antinutrient that prevents mineral absorption. Thankfully, fermentation neutralizes oxalic acid in vegetables that contain it.

Yield:	Prep time:	Ferment time:	Ferment type:
1 quart (1 liter)	10 minutes	2 to 3 days	lacto

7 cups spinach stalks cut into 1- to
    4-inch-long (2.5 to 10cm) pieces

4 garlic cloves, crushed

2 lemon quarters

2 tsp dill seeds

2 cups Basic Brine (page 41),
    plus more

1. Into a wide-mouth quart (liter) jar or another fermenting container, tightly pack the spinach stalks, garlic, lemons, and dill seeds.

2. Add the brine, including more as needed to cover the ingredients, but stop 1 inch (2.5cm) from the container's rim.

3. Place a regular-mouth jar lid on top to hold the ingredients below the brine. Cover tightly with a lid or an airlock.

4. Leave at room temperature for 2 to 3 days. Store in the fridge for up to 1 year.

Variation: Try out other stalks, such as chard or kale. If there's another spice you want to add, go for it.

Spinach Sticks

Asparagus Spears

Asparagus Spears

Crunchy, fresh, garlicky, and lemony, these fermented asparagus spears are a healthy snack. Foods containing lactic acid, like all lacto-fermented foods, are helpful to people with weak digestive systems. Lactic acid assists circulation and digestion as well as the pancreas and other digestive organs. The bottom line is it helps your digestive system work better rather than taxing it.

Yield:	Prep time:	Ferment time:	Ferment type:
1 quart (1 liter)	10 minutes	2 to 3 days	lacto

½ tsp peppercorns

¼ tsp celery seeds

½ tsp mustard powder

½ tsp pickling spice

2 garlic cloves, thinly sliced

40 young asparagus stalks, bottom ends trimmed, plus more

¼ lemon

¼ cup starter culture (Appendix B)

2 cups Basic Brine (page 41), plus more

1. In a wide-mouth quart (liter) jar or another fermenting container, combine the peppercorns, celery seeds, mustard powder, pickling spice, and garlic.

2. Break the asparagus stalks in half to fit in the jar, leaving free 1 inch (2.5cm) from the container's rim. Pack the stalks upright—as many as will fit.

3. Push the lemon wedge in between the asparagus spears.

4. Add the starter culture. Add the brine, including more as needed to cover the ingredients, but stop 1 inch (2.5cm) from the container's rim. Cover tightly with a lid or an airlock.

5. Leave at room temperature for 2 to 3 days. Store in the fridge for up to 1 year.

Garlicky Carrot Sticks

Often a staple food for kids, carrot sticks just got better. Ferment them for increased nutrition, a soft yet crunchy texture, and a boost of garlic flavor.

Yield:	Prep time:	Ferment time:	Ferment type:
½ gallon (2 liters)	10 minutes	5 to 7 days	lacto

12 medium carrots, cut into quarter sticks

4 garlic cloves

2 inches (5cm) fresh ginger, cut into ¼-inch (0.5cm) slices

½ cup starter culture (Appendix B) (optional)

4 cups Basic Brine (page 41), plus more

1. In a wide-mouth ½-gallon (2-liter) jar or another fermenting container, combine the carrots, garlic, ginger, and starter culture (if using).

2. Add the brine, including more as needed to cover the ingredients, but stop 1 inch (2.5cm) from the container's rim. Place a regular-mouth jar lid on top to hold the ingredients below the brine. Cover tightly with a lid or an airlock.

3. Leave at room temperature for 5 to 7 days. Store in the fridge for up to 1 year.

Variation: For the child who doesn't like garlic or ginger, omit them and just pickle the carrot sticks plain. Or for a sure child-pleaser, combine 4 cups of shredded carrots, 2 to 3 tablespoons of shredded ginger, ½ tablespoon of sea salt, and ¼ cup of starter culture. Ferment for 3 to 5 days to make ginger carrots. They're delicious!

Dilly Green Beans

Put up some of your summer green bean harvest to also enjoy these salty and dilly green beans in the off-season. Choose a preserving variety of green beans for best results. If the temperature is warm enough, you can ferment the green beans in as early as five days. Best keep an eye on them!

Yield:	Prep time:	Ferment time:	Ferment type:
1 quart (1 liter)	20 minutes	1 to 2 weeks	lacto

4 cups green beans, ends snapped off 1 inch (2.5cm) shorter than the height of a quart (liter) jar

3 garlic cloves, sliced in thirds

1 tbsp dill seeds or 2 to 3 fresh dill heads

2 tsp pickling spice

2 to 3 cups Basic Brine (page 41), plus more

1. Into a wide-mouth quart (liter) jar or another fermenting container, pack the green beans upright. Add the garlic, dill, and pickling spice.

2. Add the brine, including more as needed to cover the ingredients, but stop 1 inch (2.5cm) from the container's rim. Place a regular-mouth jar lid on top to hold the ingredients below the brine. Cover tightly with a lid or an airlock.

3. Leave at room temperature for 1 to 2 weeks. Store in the fridge for up to 1 year.

Garlic & Dill Pickled Okra

I used to think okra was slimy. That all changed the day I met this recipe! These homemade crispy, crunchy okra pickles, introduced to me by my friend Dawn, are every bit as good as sauerkraut or cucumber pickles. Plus, they stabilize blood sugar, fight fatigue, and protect the gut.

Yield:	Prep time:	Ferment time:	Ferment type:
1 pint (½ liter)	30 minutes	3 to 10 days	lacto

12 to 16 fresh okra pods

2 tsp sea salt

1 cup purified water

1 tsp dill seeds

½ tsp mustard seeds

½ tsp whole black peppercorns

2 garlic cloves, thinly sliced

¼ cup yellow onions, sliced or cut into chunks

1. Wash the okra pods and trim the tops (but don't cut them off completely).

2. In a small bowl, combine the salt and water until the salt dissolves.

3. In a 1-pint (½-liter) glass canning jar, combine the dill seeds, mustard seeds, and peppercorns. Pack the okra vertically into the jar. Stuff the garlic slices and onion pieces throughout the okra. Add the brine, but leave room for fermenting weights. Place fermenting weights on top of the okra and press down. Cover with a fermenting lid.

4. Leave at room temperature for 3 to 10 days or until fermented to suit your taste. Once fermented, remove the weights and replace the fermenting lid with a regular lid.

5. Refrigerate to let the okra age a few more days (or weeks) if desired or enjoy when cold. The okra will stay crunchy for several weeks in the fridge.

Pickled Cayenne Peppers

These are crazy spicy and will make you sweat if you eat too many. They also get spicier with age. Use the juice to spice up stews and soup or anything else that can use some heat. For a big pot of chili, 2 tablespoons is just right.

Yield:	Prep time:	Ferment time:	Ferment type:
1 quart (1 liter)	10 minutes	2 to 3 days	lacto

1lb (450g) cayenne peppers

2 garlic cloves, crushed or minced

1 tbsp sea salt

¼ cup starter culture (Appendix B)

1. Wearing gloves, wash and slice the peppers. Place the peppers in a wide-mouth quart (liter) jar or another fermenting container. Lightly press down on them to add more until the jar is well packed. Add the garlic.

2. In a small bowl, combine the salt and starter culture. Add this brine to the jar.

3. Add enough water to cover the mixture, leaving 1 inch (2.5cm) from the container's rim. Cover tightly with a lid or an airlock.

4. Leave at room temperature for 2 to 3 days. Store in a dark pantry or cool storage for up to several months.

Pickled Jalapeño Peppers

These naturally fermented jalapeño peppers—a recipe from my friend Lindsey—are raw and full of enzymes and beneficial, gut-loving bacteria! If you love spicy food but you've never fermented before, this is a perfect place to start.

Yield:	Prep time:	Ferment time:	Ferment type:
1 quart (1 liter)	5 minutes	3 days	lacto

20 jalapeño peppers, sliced ⅛ to ¼ inch (3mm to 0.5cm) thick

4 to 6 garlic cloves, thinly sliced

2 tsp sea salt

2 tbsp starter culture (Appendix B)

1. In a quart (liter) glass canning jar, combine the peppers and garlic. Pack them until they fill the jar to the neck.

2. Add the salt and starter culture. Fill the jar with filtered water. Cover tightly with a lid or an airlock.

3. Leave at room temperature for 3 days. You can ferment up to 6 months for a very strong batch. Check the jar twice a day and burp the lid to let out built-up gases. Store in cold storage for up to several months.

Pickled Turnips & Beets

These turnips and beets are salty, crunchy, and garlicky. Use them to top your salads. When you run out, your family will ask for more. It's best not to shred, grate, or use very tiny pieces of beets. This exposes too much sugar to the fermenting organisms, from which they create alcohol instead of lactic acid.

Yield:	Prep time:	Ferment time:	Ferment type:
1 quart (1 liter)	10 minutes	5 to 7 days	lacto

1¾ cups peeled, quartered, and sliced beets

1¾ cups peeled, quartered, and sliced turnips

3 garlic cloves, sliced in thirds

¼ cup starter culture (Appendix B)

2 cups Basic Brine (page 41), plus more

1. Into a wide-mouth quart (liter) jar or another fermenting container, pack the turnips, beets, and garlic. Add the starter culture.

2. Add the brine, including more as needed to cover the ingredients, but stop 1 inch (2.5cm) from the container's rim. Add a regular-mouth lid to weigh down the ingredients below the brine. Cover tightly with a lid or an airlock.

3. Leave at room temperature for 5 to 7 days. Store in the fridge for up to 1 year.

Variation: You can use various vegetables in this recipe. Imagine a medley of carrots, cauliflower, broccoli, turnips, beets, garlic, and onions. Delicious!

Pickled Garlic

Why rely on other ferments to get your little nibbles of spicy, salty, pickled garlic? Ferment a jar of garlic on its own! I often end up with lots of pickled garlic from other vegetable ferments. As the other vegetables get used up, I pull out cloves or chunks of garlic and add them to salads or salad dressings or as a condiment for cooked dishes. If you're adding pickled garlic (or any lacto-fermented food as a condiment) to hot, cooked food, let the food cool a bit before adding the garlic to preserve the probiotic benefits. This pickled garlic recipe comes in handy when you've got a lot of garlic to preserve. Garlic is an undisputed superfood with medicinal benefits. Fermentation makes it even more powerful. Don't eat a ton though—a little goes a long way. Before eating, test your reaction to it by eating a small portion. Some people get an upset stomach from raw or pickled garlic. If that's you, try smearing it on bread or eating it with something else to see if that helps you react less.

Yield:	Prep time:	Ferment time:	Ferment type:
1 quart (1 liter)	10 minutes	5 to 7 days	lacto

3¾ cups peeled garlic cloves

¼ cup starter culture (Appendix B)

2 cups Basic Brine (page 41), plus more

1. Into a wide-mouth quart (liter) jar or another fermenting container, pack the garlic. Add the starter culture.

2. Add the brine, including more as needed to cover the ingredients, but stop 1 inch (2.5cm) from the container's rim. Add a regular-mouth lid to weigh down the garlic below the brine. Cover tightly with a lid or an airlock.

3. Leave at room temperature for 3 to 5 days. Store in the fridge for up to 1 year.

Variation: Substitute peeled pearl onions for the garlic—now you're making Pickled Pearl Onions.

Fruits

In this chapter, we enter the exciting and delicious world of fruit fermentation. I'll tell you how to adjust the process of fermentation to account for the extra sugar in fruits. We'll go over what supplemental sweeteners you can use in fruit fermentation. We'll cover the best ingredients. And finally, I'll share an exciting set of fruit fermentation recipes to tempt every tummy.

The Challenges of Sugar

Let's discuss the fermentation of fruits, preserving whole fruits, and creating chutneys and traditional jams. This chapter deals with lactic-acid fruit fermentation. (A few alcoholic fruit fermentations are included in Chapter 9.) Lactic-acid fruit fermentation is much like vegetable fermentation in that *lactobacilli*, the friendly bacteria, are the primary workers. (Yeasts are also present, but they're not key players unless the fermentation is alcoholic.) Again, the bacteria produce lactic acid and carbon dioxide as they eat and multiply.

Take note of two significant differences between the lactic-acid fermentation of fruits and vegetables: Fruits might spoil or turn alcoholic. These differences stem from one fact: Most fruits have more sugar than vegetables do. This affects fermentation and storage.

During fermentation, the higher sugar content makes the fruit more susceptible to spoiling organisms. How do we account for this? We ferment for shorter times and we almost always use a starter culture (see Chapter 4 for options) to get competing organisms crowded out from the beginning. You could get around the inclusion of a starter culture by using more salt in your fruit fermentations, but that's not a popular choice. Not many are fans of heavily salted fruit—a notable exception being the spiced preserved lemon recipe later in this chapter. So we're back to using a starter culture and a reasonable amount of salt.

During long-term storage, the higher sugar content leads to two eventualities:

- Nonalcoholic fruit ferments can become alcoholic during long-term storage because of yeasts producing alcohol while consuming remaining sugar. Less active *lactobacilli*, lower acid levels, and ready food (sugar) give the yeasts a chance to step in and start working.

- There's a greater likelihood that fruits will spoil in storage. The higher sugar and lower acid levels of most ferments are attractive to spoiling organisms. The best way to avoid higher alcohol levels and spoiling is to consume your fruit ferments within a few weeks. Again, there are exceptions, like when fermenting high-acid fruits, such as lemons or limes.

Choosing Sweeteners

Some fruit ferments call for additional sweeteners, although you can omit these in many recipes. I prefer to use unrefined sweeteners, such as Sucanat or rapadura, maple syrup, raw honey, or palm sugar. Sucanat and rapadura are unrefined sugars. They're made from whole sugar cane and produced by extracting juice from the sugar cane, then boiling the juice to remove excess water. After that, the resulting sweet syrup is hand-paddled to cool and dry it, leaving behind dry brown granules where all the sugar cane molasses is preserved. Unrefined sugars contain minerals on which fermenting organisms thrive.

Regarding honey, keep in mind that honey's antibacterial properties can interfere with or prevent fermentation unless it's diluted. Straight honey is almost impervious to fermentation, while diluted honey will ferment. I use it in ferments where it's diluted by water (including water from fruits or vegetables).

Stevia is a sweet-tasting herb you can use in fermentation—either in liquid or powder form. But while stevia tastes sweet, it doesn't provide additional sugar (or food) for fermenting organisms. Look for stevia products that don't include many (or any) additional ingredients. I prefer the NuNaturals brand or a powdered green leaf stevia. See Appendix B for sources for stevia.

Recipes in This Chapter

You should use the highest-quality fruits and other ingredients possible, opting for unsprayed to avoid pesticide residues that can interfere with fermentation. You can judge whether a fruit ferment is done by the "All Is Well" guidelines shared in Chapter 4. When you think it's finished fermenting, transfer the fruit to cold storage, which is also outlined in Chapter 4.

This chapter's recipes are organized with the actual fruit ferment recipes first, followed by a small set of recipes that use finished ferments.

Chutney Recipes

Fermented chutneys are wonderful introductory fermented foods for wary eaters. Because they're usually not sour, almost everyone loves them.

Five-Spice Apple Chutney

Apples and nuts spiced with anise, pepper, cinnamon, cloves, and fennel—this chutney is delicious mixed into yogurt or kefir or scooped onto pancakes or waffles. You can even serve it alongside grilled meats.

Yield:	Prep time:	Ferment time:	Ferment type:
½ gallon (2 liters)	25 minutes	2 to 3 days	lacto

½ cup freshly squeezed lemon juice

½ cup starter culture (Appendix B)

1 cup water, plus more

6 cups coarsely chopped apples (any type)

¼ cup unrefined sweetener, such as Sucanat or rapadura

1 cup chopped pecans or walnuts

1 cup raisins

1 tsp sea salt

4 tbsp Chinese five-spice powder

1. In a medium bowl, combine all the ingredients. Into a ½-gallon (2-liter) jar or crock, pack the mixture to 1 inch (2.5cm) from the container's rim. Add more water if necessary to submerge all the ingredients. Cover tightly with a lid or an airlock.

2. Leave at room temperature for 2 to 3 days. Store in the fridge for up to 2 weeks or in the freezer for up to 2 to 3 months.

Variation: This recipe is easily adaptable. Use pears instead of apples or ground cinnamon instead of Chinese five-spice powder. For a great baby food, omit the nuts, chop the apples finer, and ferment for 1 day less.

Cherry, Walnut & Mint Chutney

Dressing cherries up with walnut and mint, this finished chutney offers hints of cordial flavors.

Yield:	Prep time:	Ferment time:	Ferment type:
1 quart (1 liter)	10 minutes	2 to 3 days	lacto

2¾ cups tightly packed coarsely chopped sweet cherries (washed and pitted)

1 cup chopped walnuts

⅛ tsp ground cloves

½ cup unsweetened shredded coconut

1 tbsp chopped fresh mint leaves or 1 tsp dried mint

2 tbsp unrefined sweetener

¼ cup starter culture (Appendix B)

1 tsp sea salt

1. In a medium bowl, combine all the ingredients. Into a ½-gallon (2-liter) jar or crock, pack the mixture to 1 inch (2.5cm) from the container's rim. Cover tightly with a lid or an airlock.

2. Leave at room temperature for 2 to 3 days. Store in the fridge for up to 2 weeks or in the freezer for up to 2 to 3 months.

Variation: If you don't have ground cloves, use ½ teaspoon of whole cloves, but leave them out of the mixture until the end. When all the ingredients have been packed into the jar, press the whole cloves into the mixture. Just before serving, remove them so no one has to eat them.

Cinnamon & Peach Chutney

Combining juicy, sweet peaches with fragrant cinnamon, this chutney is sure to please—especially as a topping for creamy vanilla ice cream.

Yield:	Prep time:	Ferment time:	Ferment type:
1 quart (1 liter)	10 minutes	2 to 3 days	lacto

2¾ cups tightly packed chopped fresh peaches

1 cup chopped walnuts

1 cup raisins

1 to 2 tbsp unrefined sweetener

3 tsp dried cinnamon

grated rind from 2 lemons

juice from 2 lemons

¼ cup starter culture (Appendix B)

1 tsp sea salt

1. In a medium bowl, combine all the ingredients. Into a wide-mouth quart (liter) jar or crock, pack the mixture to 1 inch (2.5cm) from the container's rim. Cover tightly with a lid or an airlock.

2. Leave at room temperature for 2 to 3 days. Store in the fridge for up to 2 weeks or in the freezer for up to 2 to 3 months.

Savory Spiced Rhubarb Chutney

This is delicious paired with bacon and liver or alongside sautéed summer squash. You can use rhubarb stalks in chutneys, relishes, and pies, but don't use or eat the leaves—they're toxic. While the stalks contain low levels of oxalic acid (reduced through fermentation or steaming), the leaves contain much higher, toxic levels that can cause acute poisoning and even death.

Yield:	Prep time:	Ferment time:	Ferment type:
1 quart (1 liter)	10 minutes	2 to 3 days	lacto

1 (10-inch [25cm]) stalk of 1-inch-thick (2.5cm) young rhubarb, diced

¼ cup diced onions (any type)

½ cup raisins

3 tbsp sunflower seeds

2 tbsp unrefined sweetener

⅛ tsp ground nutmeg

¼ tsp ground ginger

¼ cup starter culture (Appendix B)

1 tsp sea salt

¼ tsp whole anise seeds

¼ tsp whole coriander seeds

¼ tsp whole cloves or ¼ tsp ground cloves (optional)

¼ tsp whole allspice or ¼ tsp ground allspice (optional)

1. In a medium bowl, combine the rhubarb, onions, raisins, sunflower seeds, sweetener, nutmeg, ginger, starter culture, and salt.

2. Use a mortar and pestle to grind the anise seeds, coriander seeds, whole cloves (if using), and whole allspice (if using). If you're using ground cloves or ground allspice, add them now. Stir the spices into the other ingredients.

3. Into a wide-mouth quart (liter) jar or crock, pack the mixture to 1 inch (2.5cm) from the container's rim. Add water as needed to make sure the mixture is submerged. Cover tightly with a lid or an airlock.

4. Leave at room temperature for 2 to 3 days. Store in the fridge for up to 2 weeks or in the freezer for up to 2 to 3 months.

Relish & Sauce Recipes

Fruits make delicious sauces—and relishes too! We love to eat these probiotic fruit ferments with yogurt, alongside main dish meats, and on top of desserts, such as cheesecake or pie.

Cranberry, Orange & Apple Relish

My mom makes this relish every year for Thanksgiving and Christmas as well as any other time she feels like it. I recently started fermenting it for more nutrition, plus I like the nice kick and effervescence that fermenting gives it.

Yield:	Prep time:	Ferment time:	Ferment type:
1 quart (1 liter)	10 minutes	2 to 3 days	lacto

2 oranges, peeled and quartered, seeds removed

2 apples (any type), washed and quartered, cores removed

1 cup fresh or frozen cranberries

2 tsp ground cinnamon

¼ cup unrefined sweetener

1 tsp sea salt

¼ cup starter culture (Appendix B)

1. In a food processor, combine the oranges, apples, cranberries, cinnamon, sweetener, salt, and starter culture. Pulse to chop, but don't purée.

2. Into a wide-mouth quart (liter) jar or crock, pack the mixture to 1 inch (2.5cm) from the container's rim. Cover tightly with a lid or an airlock.

3. Leave at room temperature for 2 to 3 days. Store in the fridge for up to 2 weeks or in the freezer for up to 2 to 3 months.

Variation: You can adjust the amount of the fruits—increasing or reducing or even eliminating any of them. Also, other spices, such as nutmeg, allspice, or cardamom, work very well with this relish.

Spiced Applesauce

Yes, you can take a simple applesauce recipe and ferment it for a few days. The resulting bubbles and extra flavor really make it pop!

Yield:	Prep time:	Ferment time:	Ferment type:
3 cups	10 minutes	2 to 3 days	lacto

3 to 4 medium apples (any type), quartered and cores removed

¼ cup unrefined sweetener

1 tsp ground cinnamon

⅛ tsp ground nutmeg

1 tsp sea salt

¼ cup starter culture (Appendix B)

1. In a food processor or blender, pulse the apples to chop them until you get a chunky purée.

2. In a medium bowl, combine the apples, sweetener, cinnamon, nutmeg, salt, and starter culture.

3. Transfer the mixture to a wide-mouth quart (liter) jar or crock, leaving 1 inch (2.5cm) from the container's rim. Cover tightly with a lid or an airlock.

4. Leave at room temperature for 2 to 3 days. Store in the fridge for up to 2 weeks or in the freezer for up to 2 to 3 months.

Variation: Try making a similarly fermented sauce with peaches, pears, or plums.

Plum Sauce

This is fantastic as an ice cream topping or mixed into yogurt. We take advantage of every plum season by making lots of this. In fact, I purchase an abundance of plums when they're in season. I wash, halve, and pit them, then freeze them in 1-gallon (4-liter) resealable bags. When I want to make fresh plum sauce, I bring some out, let them thaw, and then proceed with this recipe. You can do the same with any frozen fruit except strawberries, which are usually too acidic for fermentation.

Yield:	Prep time:	Ferment time:	Ferment type:
1 quart (1 liter)	10 minutes	2 to 3 days	lacto

3½ cups plums, halved and pitted

¼ to ½ cup unrefined sweetener

1 tsp sea salt

¼ cup starter culture (Appendix B)

1. In a food processor, process all the ingredients until smooth. Transfer the mixture to a wide-mouth quart (liter) jar or crock, leaving 1 inch (2.5cm) from the container's rim. Cover tightly with a lid or an airlock.

2. Leave at room temperature for 2 to 3 days. Store in the fridge for up to 2 weeks or in the freezer for up to 2 to 3 months.

Blueberry Sauce

This delectable, cultured, probiotic blueberry sauce developed by my friend Emily is perfect for topping cheesecake.

Yield:	Prep time:	Ferment time:	Ferment type:
2½ cups	20 minutes	2 days	lacto

2 cups fresh blueberries

½ tsp sea salt

2 tbsp starter culture (Appendix B)

2 tbsp evaporated cane juice or Sucanat, rapadura, maple sugar, or coconut sugar

¼ cup coconut syrup or maple syrup

1. In a glass mixing bowl, combine the blueberries, salt, starter culture, and cane juice or sweetener. Mash the berries until they become saucy.

2. Transfer the sauce to a quart (liter) glass canning jar. Cover with an airlock lid. Leave at room temperature for about 48 hours.

3. Once the sauce has cultured, remove the lid and stir in the coconut syrup or maple syrup. Refrigerate to chill. Store in the fridge for up to 2 weeks or in the freezer for up to 2 to 3 months.

Plum Sauce

Cranberry & Ginger Relish

Ginger adds a punch to the cranberries in this festive holiday (or any day) relish. You can often find crystallized ginger in the bulk section of grocery stores that offer a good selection of natural foods. It's dried ginger that's sprinkled with sugar. One of my friends eats it often as a digestive aid (nothing better than ginger for that), but because she doesn't like the extra sugar, she rinses that off before eating it. My kids enjoy it as a gingery, spicy, sort-of-like-candy-but-better-for-you snack. If you can't find crystallized ginger, substitute a few tablespoons of shredded fresh ginger or a few teaspoons of dried ginger powder.

Yield:	Prep time:	Ferment time:	Ferment type:
3 cups	10 minutes	2 to 3 days	lacto

3½ cups fresh or frozen cranberries, rinsed and drained

zest from 1 medium lemon

⅔ cup unrefined sweetener

½ cup coarsely chopped crystallized ginger

¼ tsp ground ginger, plus more

pinch of sea salt

¼ cup starter culture (Appendix B)

1. In a food processor, process all the ingredients until finely chopped. Transfer the mixture to a wide-mouth quart (liter) jar or crock, leaving 1 inch (2.5cm) from the container's rim. Cover tightly with a lid or an airlock.

2. Leave at room temperature for 2 to 3 days. Store in the fridge for up to 2 weeks or in the freezer for up to 2 to 3 months.

Other Fruit Recipes

Stretch your fruit fermenting skills by turning dried fruits into probiotic fruit butters to spread on toast or mix into yogurt, fermenting lemons into salty sour goodness, and even wowing the kids with fermented fruit leather—a healthy step up from grocery store leather, but they won't be able to tell the difference.

Raspberry & Mint Preserves

Fermentation really brings the mint flavor to the forefront in these preserves, complementing the raspberries for a delicious pancake, waffle, toast, or ice cream topping. Or mix them into yogurt. This isn't as thick as modern preserves, but it's still very delicious. You can make these preserves with any other berry except strawberries, which are too acidic to ferment for these preserves.

Yield:	Prep time:	Ferment time:	Ferment type:
1 quart (1 liter)	10 minutes	2 days	lacto

6 cups fresh raspberries

30 fresh mint leaves, chopped finely

6 tbsp unrefined sweetener

1½ tsp sea salt

¼ cup starter culture (Appendix B)

3 tsp Pomona's Universal Pectin (see Appendix B for sources)

3 tsp Pomona's Universal Pectin calcium water (see Appendix B for sources)

1. In a medium bowl, combine all the ingredients. Mash with a potato masher until the berries are crushed but still chunky.

2. Transfer the mixture to a wide-mouth quart (liter) jar or crock, leaving 1 inch (2.5cm) from the container's rim. Cover tightly with a lid or an airlock.

3. Leave at room temperature for 2 days. Skim off any mold daily and re-cover. Store in the fridge for up to 2 weeks or in the freezer for up to 2 to 3 months.

Fig Butter

When you spread this on toast, you'll think you're eating Fig Newtons! This fig recipe and the following mango butter recipe are examples of what you can do to turn dried raw fruits or vegetables into fermented pastes or butters. This works well when you don't have an extra fridge or cellar to store ferments. Instead, dehydrate summer bounty (which you can store more easily) and reconstitute throughout the winter as needed by using this simple fermentation method. "Raw" means a food hasn't been heated or processed at temperatures exceeding 110°F to 115°F (43°C to 46°C) (with some sources offering 118°F [48°C] as an upper limit). When dehydrating your own raw foods, keep the temperature below 110°F to 115°F (43°C to 46°C). If you're shopping for raw dehydrated foods, avoid sulfur (often added to prevent discoloration) and temperatures much over 115°F (46°C).

Yield:	Prep time:	Ferment time:	Ferment type:
1 pint (½ liter)	10 minutes	2 days	lacto

2 cups unsulphured dried figs

1 cup warm water

¾ tsp sea salt

¼ cup raw honey

2 tbsp starter culture (Appendix B)

1. In a medium bowl, combine the figs and water. Soak for 30 minutes or until softened considerably.

2. Transfer the figs and water to a food processor. Process until the mixture becomes smooth.

3. Add the salt, honey, and starter culture. Process until incorporated.

4. Transfer the mixture to a wide-mouth 1-pint (½ liter) or 1-quart (1-liter) jar, leaving 1 inch (2.5cm) from the jar's rim. Cover tightly with a lid or an airlock.

5. Leave at room temperature for 2 days. Skim off any mold daily and re-cover. Store in the fridge for up to 2 weeks or in the freezer for up to 2 to 3 months.

Mango Butter

Savor this creamy, jelly-like fruit butter made from the "peach of the tropics": mangoes. My friend Marillyn makes this from raw, dehydrated mangoes. She dehydrates extra mangoes when they're in season (May through mid-October) and then creates mango butter during the off-season. This butter—as well as the fig butter—is uncooked and fermented, which preserves the natural goodness of the raw fruit and boosts vitamins, enzymes, and probiotics through fermentation.

Yield:	Prep time:	Ferment time:	Ferment type:
2 quarts (2 liters)	10 minutes	2 days	lacto

6 cups unsulphured dried mangoes

¾ tsp sea salt

¼ cup raw honey

¼ cup starter culture (Appendix B)

1. In a medium bowl, place the mangoes and cover with warm water. Soak until completely soft.

2. In a food processor, combine the mangoes (leaving the water behind), salt, honey, and starter culture. Process until smooth.

3. Transfer the mixture to 2 wide-mouth quart (liter) jars or crocks, leaving 1 inch (2.5cm) from the container's rim. Cover tightly with a lid or an airlock.

4. Leave at room temperature for 2 days. Skim off any mold daily and re-cover. Store in the fridge for up to 2 weeks or in the freezer for up to 2 to 3 months.

Spiced Preserved Lemons

Squeeze the salty spiced lemon juice into mint iced tea or over grilled wild salmon. Or finely dice the lemons and toss them with your favorite salad or dressing. A little goes a long way!

Yield:	Prep time:	Ferment time:	Ferment type:
1 quart (1 liter)	10 minutes	1 month	lacto

3 lemons

6 tbsp sea salt, divided

1 dried bay leaf

8 cardamom pods

1½ tsp whole cloves

1 tsp broken cinnamon stick pieces

juice from 3 lemons

1. Quarter the lemons, stopping before you cut through the bottom to keep the wedges together.

2. Sprinkle 1 tablespoon of salt over each lemon and rub into in all the crevices.

3. Into a wide-mouth quart (liter) jar or crock, pack the lemons. Add the bay leaf, cardamom pods, cloves, and cinnamon.

4. In a small bowl, combine the lemon juice and the remaining 3 tablespoons of salt. Add this mixture to the jar. Add more water until the lemons are covered. Leave 1 inch (2.5cm) from the container's rim.

5. Place a regular-mouth lid plus a weight inside the jar to hold the lemons down. Cover tightly with a lid or an airlock.

6. Leave at room temperature for 1 month. Skim off any mold as needed and re-cover. Store in the fridge for up to 2 weeks or in the freezer for up to 2 to 3 months.

Spiced Preserved Lemons

Pear & Ginger Fruit Leather

What kid doesn't love sweet fruit leather? With this easy recipe, you can make yours gently fermented for a deeper flavor and with more nutrition.

Yield:	Prep time:	Ferment time:	Ferment type:
varies	20 minutes	2 to 3 days	lacto

8 to 9 cups fresh pears, quartered, cored, and cut into 2-inch (5cm) pieces

juice from 1 lemon

¼ cup starter culture (Appendix B)

½ tsp sea salt

¼ unrefined sweetener

½ tsp ground ginger

1 tsp ground cinnamon

1. In a blender or food processor, combine all the ingredients. Blend until smooth. You might need to do this in batches depending on the size of your appliance and the amount of fruit you use.

2. Transfer the mixture to a jar or another fermenting container, leaving 1 inch (2.5cm) from the container's rim. Cover with a lid or an airlock.

3. Leave at room temperature for 2 to 3 days. Burp daily if not using an airlock to release pent-up gases.

4. If the mixture is very watery, strain it through two to three layers of 90-thread-count cheesecloth for a few hours until thickened up. (Drink the juice or add it to smoothies.)

5. Place dehydrator tray liners or unbleached parchment paper on dehydrator trays. Spread the fruit mixture on the trays to your desired thickness—not too thick and not too thin.

6. Run the dehydrator at 110°F (43°C) or less until the fruit is smooth and no longer sticky, about 8 to 24 hours. Cut the fruit into strips. Roll up (if desired) or store in sheets in airtight bags or containers. Store in a cool, dry pantry for up to 9 months.

Condiments

Chapter

7

In this chapter, we'll quickly cover the similarities between fermenting condiments and the fruits and vegetables of previous chapters. Because the steps are basically the same, we'll get into the recipes almost straight away. After we cover a bunch of fermented condiments, we'll put them to use later in the chapter with a selection of recipes that use the fermented condiments in delicious dishes.

Fermenting Condiments

Fermenting condiments is very similar to fermenting fruits and vegetables in previous chapters. All are examples of lacto-fermentation, during which beneficial bacteria produce lactic acid as a by-product of consuming the foods. The lactic acid helps preserve the food for a long time—a definite plus to making homemade fermented condiments! Finally, the fermentation boosts vitamins, enzymes, and the number of beneficial organisms.

You don't need much of any lacto-fermented food to benefit. In fact, it's better to eat small quantities of lacto-fermented foods often rather than indulge in large amounts every so often. Just a few tablespoons daily of some fermented food can help keep you regular, support your digestive system, and prevent disease.

To ferment your favorite condiment, you need a starter culture. Let's say you're converting a ketchup recipe to a lacto-fermented recipe. The original recipe is a cooked recipe—meaning you cook the mixture when making the ketchup or you use tomato paste that was cooked at some point. This means the ketchup mixture lacks beneficial organisms for the fermentation. (They were abundant on the raw ingredients, but cooking has destroyed them.) The answer for this? Always, always, always include a starter culture (I give options in Chapter 4) in the mixture when you set it out to ferment. Use ¼ cup per quart (liter).

Condiment Recipes

In this chapter, you'll find condiments that are made from smooth or chunky puréed mixtures as well as condiments (such as from mushrooms or eggs) that are fermented through being covered with brine. Both are accomplished in the same ways you've already seen.

As always, source the highest-quality ingredients possible for your condiments, choosing unsprayed produce so you don't introduce pesticide residues into your fermented mixtures. Ascertain whether your ferment is done according to the "All Is Well" signs shared in Chapter 4. Unless otherwise stated, you should transfer all condiments to cold storage after the room temperature fermentation is complete.

Ketchup

Fragrant from cinnamon, cloves, and allspice as well as tastefully sweetened with honey or maple syrup, this is a fantastic ketchup. Hardly anyone can tell it's fermented because it lacks any bit of sour taste.

Yield:	Prep time:	Ferment time:	Ferment type:
2 cups	5 minutes	2 days	lacto

12oz (340g) no-salt-added tomato paste

6 tbsp water

⅛ cup starter culture (Appendix B)

2 tbsp apple cider vinegar

¼ tsp mustard powder

¼ tsp ground cinnamon

⅛ tsp ground cloves

⅛ tsp ground allspice

⅛ tsp ground cayenne

½ tsp sea salt

¼ to ⅓ cup honey or maple syrup

1. In a medium bowl, whisk together all the ingredients until smooth. Transfer the mixture to a wide-mouth 1-quart (1-liter) or 1-pint (½-liter) jar, leaving 1 inch (2.5cm) from the jar's rim. Cover tightly with a lid or an airlock.

2. Leave at room temperature for 2 days. Store in the fridge for up to 4 weeks.

Creminis

Dice these mushrooms finely for a salty, meaty, and tart addition to wild salmon, chicken, egg, or cold grain salads.

Yield:	Prep time:	Ferment time:	Ferment type:
1 pint (½ liter)	2 minutes	2 to 3 days	lacto

6oz (170g) cremini mushrooms

5 garlic cloves, crushed

2 tbsp pickling spice

1-inch (2.5cm) piece of fresh ginger, cut into thin slices or chunks

2 tbsp starter culture (Appendix B)

1 cup Basic Brine (page 41), plus more

1. In a wide-mouth quart (liter) jar, combine the mushrooms, garlic, pickling spice, ginger, and starter culture.

2. Add the brine, including more as needed to cover the ingredients. Add a regular-mouth lid and a weight to hold down the ingredients. Cover tightly with a lid or an airlock.

3. Leave at room temperature for 2 to 3 days. Transfer to a 1-pint (½-liter) jar. Store in the fridge for up to 4 weeks.

Honey & Dill Mustard

This spicy mustard is fantastic on sandwiches, with grilled meats, and in dressings and sauces. A little goes a long way.

Yield:	Prep time:	Ferment time:	Ferment type:
1 cup	5 minutes	3 days	lacto

½ cup mustard powder

3 tbsp dried dill or 5 tbsp fresh
   chopped dill

5 tbsp honey

1 tsp sea salt

3 tbsp starter culture (Appendix B)

2 tbsp water

1. In a small bowl, combine all the ingredients. Mix well.

2. Transfer the mixture to a wide-mouth 1-pint (½-liter) jar, leaving 1 inch (2.5cm) from the jar's rim. Cover tightly with a lid or an airlock.

3. Leave at room temperature for 3 days. Store in the fridge for up to 4 weeks.

Dijon Mustard

This is perfect for those who prefer a sweeter, less spicy, milder mustard.

Yield:	Prep time:	Ferment time:	Ferment type:
1 pint (½ liter)	10 minutes	3 days	lacto

2 cups dry white wine

1 large onion (any type), chopped into large pieces

3 garlic cloves, minced

1 cup mustard powder

3 tbsp raw honey

1 tbsp extra-virgin olive oil

2 tsp sea salt

3 tbsp starter culture (Appendix B)

1. In a small saucepan on the stovetop over medium heat, combine the wine, onion, and garlic. Bring to a boil, then lower the heat to low. Simmer for 5 to 7 minutes. Transfer the pan to an ice-water bath to cool to room temperature. Remove and discard the garlic and onion.

2. Stir in the mustard powder until smooth. Add the honey, olive oil, and salt.

3. Place the saucepan on the stovetop over medium-low heat. Cook until thickened, about 5 to 10 minutes, stirring constantly. Transfer the saucepan to an ice-water bath to cool to room temperature.

4. Stir in the starter culture and mix well.

5. Transfer the mixture to a wide-mouth 1-pint (½-liter) jar, leaving 1 inch (2.5cm) from the jar's rim. Cover tightly with a lid or an airlock.

6. Leave at room temperature for 3 days. Store in the fridge for up to 4 weeks.

Variation: Use less white wine for a thicker mustard.

Guacamole

This tastes just like fresh guacamole and is absolutely spectacular with homemade tortilla chips and salsa. I also recommend deep-frying wedges of Sourdough Crêpes (page 211) to serve with this.

Yield:	Prep time:	Ferment time:	Ferment type:
2 cups	5 minutes	7 hours	lacto

2 large ripe avocados, peeled and pitted

4 garlic cloves, crushed

juice from ½ lime

½ tsp sea salt

2 tbsp starter culture (Appendix B)

1. In a medium bowl, combine all the ingredients. Mash well.

2. Transfer the mixture to a clean small bowl. Cover with plastic wrap, pressing it to the surface of the guacamole.

3. Leave at room temperature for 8 to 12 hours or overnight. Transfer to the fridge until ready to serve.

4. When ready to serve, skim off the browned top layer or mix it in. Store in the fridge for up to 4 weeks.

Guacamole

Fermented Honey

More fragrant than usual and slightly sour, fermented honey is great spread on toast or bagels for a delicious digestion aid. Honey never spoils, although it can ferment when stored in warm temperatures with enough moisture content. This natural occurrence is sometimes surprising. This recipe will help you recreate what can happen to long-stored honey.

Yield:	Prep time:	Ferment time:	Ferment type:
1 quart (1 liter)	2 minutes	3 months	lacto

3 cups raw honey   ½ cup warm water

1. In a wide-mouth quart (liter) jar, whisk together the honey and water until fully incorporated. Cover tightly with a lid or an airlock.

2. Leave in a warm location (around 80°F [27°C]) for 3 months to 1 year until fragrant and slightly sour. Store in the pantry or cool storage for up to 1 year.

Variation: Mix this into Cream Cheese (page 274) for a topping or fruit dip.

Spinach Dip

This garlicky green dip travels well and makes a great snack after you've been gardening or playing outside all day.

Yield:	Prep time:	Ferment time:	Ferment type:
3 cups	10 minutes	2 to 3 days	lacto

1 cup water

8 cups tightly packed chopped fresh spinach

4 garlic cloves

1¼ tsp sea salt

3 tbsp starter culture (Appendix B)

1. Place the water in a small pot on the stovetop over medium heat. Place a steamer basket in the pot and place the spinach in the basket. Cover and steam until cooked, about 2 minutes. Drain and let cool.

2. In a blender or food processor, combine the spinach, garlic, salt, and starter culture. Process until combined but still a little chunky.

3. Into a wide-mouth 1-pint (½-liter) or 1-quart (1-liter) jar, pack the mixture well. Cover tightly with a lid or an airlock.

4. Leave at room temperature for 2 to 3 days. Store in the fridge for up to 4 weeks.

Spinach Dip

Variation: Make this dip with any dark, leafy green: chard, kale, or beet greens. Fermentation is a great means of preparing dark, leafy greens. If you remember from Chapter 2, the oxalic acid they contain is neutralized through fermentation.

Spicy Cilantro Pesto

This intoxicating pesto—made earthy and pungent by the cilantro—adds flavor to potatoes, pasta, and soups.

Yield:	Prep time:	Ferment time:	Ferment type:
1 cup	5 minutes	12 hours	lacto

2 cups fresh cilantro

2 to 4 garlic cloves

¼ cup raw pumpkin seeds or pine nuts

¼ to 1 tsp hot or mild chili powder

1 tsp sea salt

1 tbsp starter culture (Appendix B)

¼ to ½ cup extra-virgin olive oil, plus more

1. In a food processor or blender, pulse the cilantro until well chopped. Add the garlic, pumpkin seeds, chili powder, salt, and starter culture. Chop well.

2. While running the food processor, slowly add the olive oil via the liquid chute. Keep adding olive oil until the mixture forms a thick paste.

3. Transfer the mixture to a wide-mouth 1-pint (½-liter) jar. Cover with a lid or an airlock.

4. Leave at room temperature for 8 hours. Store in the fridge for up to 4 weeks.

Horseradish

This is typically served with steaks or roasted meats, but you can also mix this hot fermented condiment into dressings or dips for extra mustardy heat. You'll want to prepare this in a well-ventilated area, preferably outside.

Yield:	Prep time:	Ferment time:	Ferment type:
1 cup	15 minutes	5 to 7 days	lacto

1 cup peeled and chopped
    horseradish root

1 tsp sea salt

1 tbsp starter culture (Appendix B)

4 tbsp water, plus more

1. In a food processor, combine all the ingredients. Pulse until chopped, then let run for a few minutes until the mixture is blended and smooth. Add water 1 tablespoon at a time as needed to make a smooth paste.

2. Transfer the mixture to a wide-mouth 1-pint (½-liter) or ½-pint (¼-liter) jar. Cover with a lid or an airlock.

3. Leave at room temperature for 5 to 7 days. Store in the fridge for up to 6 months.

Lemon & Dill Sauce

Creamy and fresh with lemon and dill, this sauce goes well with any grilled fish.

Yield:	Prep time:	Ferment time:	Ferment type:
½ cup	5 minutes	none	lacto

¼ cup mayonnaise

¼ cup Kefir (page 250)

1 tbsp freshly squeezed lemon juice

1 tbsp chopped fresh dill or 1 tsp
    dried dill

pinch of ground black pepper

1. In a small bowl, whisk together all the ingredients.

2. Refrigerate until ready to serve. Store for up to 2 weeks.

Nut Butter

Nutty, earthy almond butter gets a flavor and nutrition boost from fermentation.

Yield:	Prep time:	Ferment time:	Ferment type:
2 cups	10 minutes	7 to 12 hours	lacto

2 cups raw almonds

½ tsp sea salt

toasted expeller-pressed sesame oil

2 tbsp starter culture (Appendix B)

1. In a food processor, combine the almonds and salt. Pulse for 30 seconds to chop. Let the machine run through these stages:
   - The almonds are chopped to a fine meal or flour.
   - A paste forms at the bottom of the bowl.
   - A ball of pasty almonds spins around inside the bowl on top of the blades.
   - The blade shaves away the ball of almond paste into a warm, free-flowing almond butter. (If necessary, stop the machine and scrape down the sides of the bowl during this process.) This can take 5 minutes.

2. If you don't get a paste or butter, add 1 tablespoon of sesame oil at a time until you get almond butter circulating freely.

3. Add the starter culture and pulse to mix until smooth. Transfer the mixture to a wide-mouth 1-pint (½-liter) or ½-pint (¼-liter) jar.

4. Leave at room temperature for 1 to 2 days. Transfer to cool storage.

5. Let the butter warm up to room temperature before serving or spreading. Store in the fridge for up to 4 weeks.

Variations: Use peanuts, hazelnuts, or cashews instead of almonds. Or toast the nuts before using for more flavor.

Hot Chili Sauce

This condiment is very hot and very smoky. You can remove the seeds from the peppers for a milder chili sauce.

Yield:	Prep time:	Ferment time:	Ferment type:
1 pint (½ liter)	15 minutes	3 to 5 days	lacto

16 fresh serrano, jalapeño, sriracha, or other hot peppers (about 1lb [450g]) total), stems removed

2 garlic cloves, crushed

1 tsp sea salt

2 tbsp starter culture (Appendix B)

1. In a food processor, combine the peppers, garlic, salt, and starter culture. Pulse to chop and then run until a paste forms.

2. Transfer the mixture to a wide-mouth 1-pint (½-liter) jar. Cover with a lid or an airlock.

3. Leave at room temperature for 3 to 5 days or until bubbly.

4. Place a fine mesh sieve over a small bowl. Spoon the chili mixture into the sieve. Use the back of a spoon to press the mixture against the sieve to strain the sauce.

5. Transfer the sauce to a bottle. (Use the pulp to add heat to other dishes.) Store in the fridge for up to 4 weeks.

Hot Pepper Sauce

Easy, tangy, spicy, and full of probiotic goodness, this lacto-fermented pepper sauce from my friend Dawn will kick your favorite foods up a notch (or three!).

Yield:	Prep time:	Ferment time:	Ferment type:
2 cups	20 minutes	1 day	lacto

1½ cups jalapeños, sliced (remove the seeds and membranes for a milder sauce)

½ cup sliced red onions

2 garlic cloves, thinly sliced

1½ cups puréed Roma tomatoes (about 4 tomatoes)

½ tsp ground allspice

1 tsp sea salt

2 to 3 tsp raw honey, coconut syrup, stevia, or another preferred sweetener (optional)

1. In a clean and sterilized 1-pint (½-liter) glass canning jar, combine the jalapeños, onions, and garlic.

2. In a small bowl or glass measuring cup, combine the tomato purée, allspice, and salt. Add the mixture to the jar. (For a smooth sauce, blend all these ingredients.) Gently tap the jar to dislodge air bubbles. Pack the vegetables into the liquid. Add fermenting weights to keep them submerged. Secure the jar with your preferred fermenting lid or airlock.

3. Leave at room temperature for 48 hours (less if warm).

4. Add optional sweetener to taste. Store in the fridge for up to 4 weeks.

Clam Dip

This is a delicious addition to sliced vegetables, tortilla chips, or pita chips.

Yield:	Prep time:	Ferment time:	Ferment type:
2 cups	5 minutes	none	lacto

1 cup Cream Cheese (page 274)

¼ cup mayonnaise or Sour Cream (page 260)

2 (6½oz [185g]) cans of minced clams, drained

⅓ cup bell peppers (any color), finely diced

1 minced shallot or 1 tbsp finely diced yellow onions

2 tbsp fresh parsley leaves, minced

½ tsp Worcestershire sauce (look for brands without high-fructose corn syrup, such as French's and Annie's)

⅛ tsp dried cayenne pepper

¼ tsp paprika

⅛ tsp ground black pepper

¼ tsp sea salt (optional)

1. In a small bowl, whisk together the cream cheese and mayonnaise or sour cream until smooth. Stir in the clams, bell peppers, shallot or onions, parsley, Worcestershire sauce, cayenne pepper, paprika, and black pepper. Add the salt (if using).

2. Refrigerate the dip until ready to serve. Store for up to 1 week.

Recipes Using Condiments

You can use your fermented condiments and sauces in other recipes to take them to another level, increasing nutrition from the probiotics and enzymes that will assist with digestion and also with more complex sour, salty, or spicy flavors. You'll also find recipes for brining olives and pickling eggs, which make great additions to these and many other dishes.

Sour Cream & Guacamole Crêpes

Slightly warmed sour cream and guacamole ooze out of warm crêpes and make a delicious complement to an egg and sausage breakfast.

Yield:	Prep time:	Ferment time:	Ferment type:
8 crêpes	5 minutes	none	lacto

8 Sourdough Crêpes (page 210)
1 cup Sour Cream (page 260)

1 cup Guacamole (page 108)

1. In a seasoned cast-iron skillet on the stovetop over medium heat, warm the crêpes one by one.
2. Place 2 tablespoons of guacamole and sour cream on each crêpe. Roll up the crêpes and serve immediately. Store in the fridge for up to 3 days.

Variation: Use jam instead of guacamole for a sweet breakfast crêpe.

Olives

Old-fashioned curing yields olives with appealing sour tones and aromas—given by the lactic and acetic acids produced during the long brine.

Yield:	Prep time:	Ferment time:	Ferment type:
20 pounds (9 kilograms)	1 hour	3 to 6 months	lacto & aceto

2 cups sea salt, plus more

2 gallons (7½ liters) cool water, plus more

4 cups apple cider vinegar, plus more

20lb (9kg) large ripe green olives (Sevillano, Barouni, or Ascolano recommended)

1. In a large bucket or pot, combine the salt and water. Stir until the salt dissolves. Add the apple cider vinegar. Set aside.

2. Sort the olives and discard bruised ones. Make a slit in the olives, but don't cut into the pit. Transfer the olives to a large fermenting vessel, such as a 5-gallon (18-liter) food grade bucket, leaving 1 inch (2.5cm) from the container's rim.

3. Pour the brine over the olives—enough to cover—and save the remaining brine in case you need more later. Place a plate or another flat object on top of the olives to hold them below the brine. Add weights if necessary. Loosely cover with a lid or cloth.

4. Leave at room temperature for about 2 months. The first 4 to 5 days, a lot of gas and bubbles will be produced, possibly frothing over. Add more brine as needed to keep the olives fully submerged. If you run out of brine, make more according to this formula: For every 1 gallon (4 liters) of water, use 1 cup of sea salt and 2 cups of apple cider vinegar.

5. When the bubbling stage is over, cover tightly and store for 2 to 4 more months or until the olives are no longer bitter. Store in a cool, dark place for up to 1 year.

Variation: If you're preserving a smaller variety of olive (such as Manzanillo or Mission), use 1½ cups of sea salt per 1 cup of water for the brine.

Wild Red Salmon Salad

Delicious on toasted English Muffins (page 209), this salad is fresh with dill and the flavors of salmon and feta.

Yield:	Prep time:	Ferment time:	Ferment type:
2 cups	5 minutes	none	lacto

2 (7oz [200g]) cans of wild red salmon, drained

¼ crumbled Feta (page 279)

¼ tsp garlic powder

½ tsp dried dill

⅛ to ¼ tsp sea salt

pinch of ground black pepper

1. In a small bowl, combine all the ingredients. Mix to incorporate, but don't mash—leave the salmon flaky. Adjust the seasonings to taste.

2. Store in the fridge for up to 3 days.

Wild Red Salmon Salad on an English Muffin

Pickled Eggs

These spiced yellow eggs make a delicious addition to a tuna, wild salmon, or chicken salad.

Yield:	Prep time:	Ferment time:	Ferment type:
1 quart (1 liter)	10 minutes	3 to 5 days	lacto

10 large hard-boiled eggs, cooled and peeled

¼ small red onion, thinly sliced

3 garlic cloves, crushed or chopped coarsely

½ tsp ground black pepper

¼ tsp red pepper flakes

½ tsp dill seeds

½ tsp mustard powder

½ tsp ground turmeric

1 dried bay leaf

¼ cup starter culture (Appendix B)

1 cup Basic Brine (page 41), plus more

1. In a wide-mouth quart (liter) jar, combine the eggs, onion, garlic, black pepper, red pepper flakes, dill seeds, mustard powder, turmeric, bay leaf, and starter culture. Add the brine, including more as needed to cover the ingredients, but stop 1 inch (2.5cm) from the jar's rim.

2. Use a regular-mouth lid as a weight to hold down the ingredients. Cover with a lid or an airlock.

3. Leave at room temperature for 2 to 3 days. Store in the fridge for up to 4 weeks.

Fermented Jalapeño Deviled Eggs

These jalapeño deviled eggs from my friend Lindsey are oh so nourishing!

Yield:	Prep time:	Ferment time:	Ferment type:
24 deviled eggs	20 minutes	none	lacto

12 large hard-boiled organic
   or pastured eggs

¼ cup mayonnaise

2 tbsp Dijon Mustard (page 107)

2 to 3 tbsp Pickled Jalapeño
   Peppers (page 81)

1 to 2 tbsp brine from Pickled
   Jalapeño Peppers

1 tbsp fermented garlic from
   Pickled Jalapeño Peppers

½ tsp sea salt

½ tsp ground black pepper

chipotle powder

24 fresh cilantro leaves

1. Cut the eggs in half. Place the egg whites on a platter.

2. In a blender or food processor, combine the egg yolks, mayonnaise, mustard, peppers, pepper brine, fermented garlic, salt, and black pepper. Pulse until the filling is as smooth as desired.

3. Fill the egg whites with the mixture. Or transfer the mixture to a piping bag and pipe the filling into the egg whites. Sprinkle the chipotle powder over the top of each egg. Garnish each egg half with a cilantro leaf.

4. Chill until ready to serve. (You can make these eggs up to 2 days in advance.) Store in the fridge for up to 2 days.

Variation: You can also ferment hard-boiled eggs in juice from another ferment.

Angel Eggs

Smoky paprika and homemade mustard and mayonnaise make these eggs—usually called deviled eggs—a delicious gift from heaven.

Yield:	Prep time:	Ferment time:	Ferment type:
24 eggs	5 minutes	none	lacto

12 large hard-boiled eggs, cooled and peeled

2 tsp Honey & Dill Mustard (page 106) or Dijon Mustard (page 107)

1 tbsp minced red or yellow onions

½ tsp sea salt

⅛ tsp ground black pepper

1 tsp paprika

1. Slice each egg in half lengthwise with a sharp knife. Gently remove the egg yolks and place them in a small bowl. Place the egg whites on a platter.

2. In a small bowl, combine the yolks, mustard, mayonnaise, onions, salt, and pepper. Mash until smooth. Scoop the yolk mixture into the egg whites. Sprinkle each egg with a pinch of paprika. Cover and chill until ready to serve. Store in the fridge for up to 2 days.

Angel Eggs

Nonalcoholic Beverages

In this chapter, we'll explore fermented nonalcoholic beverages, such as fruit and vegetable juices and natural sodas. I'll tell you about the basic principles involved as well as how to bottle natural sodas (if you wish). And, of course, I'll also share a bunch of recipes to get you going.

Brewing Beneficial Beverages

While the next chapter covers alcoholic beverages, in this chapter, we focus on beverages fermented through lactic- and acetic-acid-producing yeasts and bacteria. Sometimes, depending on the organisms involved, other acids and/or alcohol are also produced. It shouldn't be a surprise that a great deal of carbon dioxide is produced—this is what makes natural sodas so deliciously bubbly.

The fermented beverages in this chapter are nutritious and some of them (such as kvass) are even considered superfoods or supertonics. This chapter's beverages offer the nutrition of the fruits, vegetables, roots, and other foods that make them up, but fermentation boosts nutrition by producing beneficial acids, increasing vitamins and enzymes, and proliferating the probiotic organisms.

Each beverage starts with a liquid mixture, to which we add a starter culture. Sometimes, you'll use a liquid starter culture or whey. They contain lactic-acid-producing yeasts and/or bacteria. In other recipes, you'll capture and nurture wild yeasts in a mother culture—often called a "bug." And still other recipes call for very specific mother cultures that contain particular strains of bacteria and yeasts growing together in a mutual colony (such as for kombucha or water kefir, discussed later in this chapter).

Whatever the particular starter, the procedure is usually similar: Combine the starter with the liquid mixture and follow the recipe's recommended time and temperature to create your fermented beverage. The sodas especially will build up carbonation and you'll have the option of bottling those in Grolsch-style bottles. Let's talk a little bit more about bottling now.

Bottling Natural Sodas

As I mentioned in Chapter 4 (and will describe with regard to alcoholic beverages in Chapter 9), you'll want to look for sturdy flip-top bottles of the Grolsch style. See Appendix B for recommendations on where to buy these. A less expensive option is to reuse store-bought kombucha bottles, as they're sturdy enough and work well for storing fermented beverages.

The idea with bottling is to build up carbonation for a pleasing, soda-like result. The fermenting organisms give off carbon dioxide as long as they're still eating. Thus, it's important when you transfer your liquids to bottles that the mixture *still* contains food (sugar) for the organisms. Alternatively, you can add fresh sugar for that purpose. However, sugar can come from surprising sources. For example, you could bottle your sodas with a few raisins at the bottom or add freshly squeezed juice to the mixture.

How long to bottle depends on the strength of the culture inside, how much food is present for the organisms to eat, and the warmth of the environment. In a warmer environment, say between 75°F and 85°F (24°C to 29°C), the organisms will be more active—eating more and producing more gases. In general, building up carbonation in bottled natural sodas takes 3 to 10 days, with warmer temperatures requiring fewer days and vice versa.

You can test for carbonation levels by opening a bottle. If you don't hear the pleasing sound of released gases, it isn't ready yet. Give the batch more time, checking daily. When a bottle is ready, refrigerate or chill the batch to hold the carbonation and sweetness level. The fridge also gives your sodas a refreshing chill. It's always a good idea to open your natural sodas outside, over a sink, or even with an upside-down bowl held over the top (just in case).

Sealed carbonated beverages can get very bubbly and possibly blow up! Because of their sugar levels, fruit sodas are especially susceptible. When checking your fermented beverage for doneness, do it outside or over a sink. If they're carbonated to your liking, refrigerate or transfer to cold storage immediately to prevent any more carbonation from building up. Chilling also slows down the work of the organisms. They eat much less sugar and, therefore, you preserve residual sweetness by chilling beverages sooner rather than later.

A bottle opened for testing isn't lost. Close it back up and leave at room temperature to replace the carbonation let out (provided there's even a small amount of sugar for the organisms to consume). Or drink or chill it right away—but it will be more flat.

If you don't have bottles or room to store bottles in your fridge, you can leave fermented beverages out at room temperature in jars. However, be sure to open the jars daily to release gases and prevent explosions. Expect your beverages to get less sweet the more time goes by. Beverages left sealed at room temperature (even if periodically opened to release gases) don't usually go bad, but they do get more sour. Let's get started with nonalcoholic fermented beverages!

Making Water Kefir

Juice Recipes

There's juicing—and then there's juicing! You can blend fruits and vegetables in a high-powered blender, leaving a thick, pulpy mixture. On the other hand, a juicing appliance extracts the juices from raw foods, separating them from the pulp. The juices are smooth and very pleasing to drink. When you drink juice (without fiber), the food nutrients skip digestion and go right into the bloodstream for quick utilization.

Veggie Tomato Juice

Clear, fresh, smooth tomato juice gets a boost from other vegetables, lemon, and honey.

Yield:	Prep time:	Ferment time:	Ferment type:
4¼ cups	5 minutes	12 hours	lacto

8 medium Roma tomatoes, quartered	1 garlic clove
1 medium carrot, ends trimmed	1 small cucumber, ends trimmed
1 medium celery stalk, ends trimmed	1 medium lemon, peeled and quartered
¼ bell pepper (any color), seeds removed	1 tbsp raw honey
⅛ medium onion (any type), ends trimmed and skin removed	½ tbsp sea salt
	¼ cup starter culture (Appendix B)

1. In a juicer, combine the tomatoes, carrot, celery, bell pepper, onion, garlic, cucumber, and lemon. You can run the pulp through the juicer again to extract more juice. Discard the pulp. Transfer the juice to a ½-gallon (2-liter) jar.

2. Whisk in the honey, salt, and starter culture. Leave 1 inch (2.5cm) from the jar's rim. Cover with a lid or an airlock.

3. Leave at room temperature overnight or for 12 hours. Chill for 2 to 3 hours or until cold. Shake before serving. Store in the fridge for up to 2 weeks, but it's best when consumed within 3 days.

Snappy Tomato Juice

This is a sharp—but not spicy—tomato juice for the person who wants something a bit more intriguing.

Yield:	Prep time:	Ferment time:	Ferment type:
2 cups	5 minutes	12 hours	lacto

6 medium Roma tomatoes, quartered

⅛ medium onion (any type), ends trimmed and skin removed

¼ bell pepper (any color), seeds removed

½ serrano pepper, seeds removed

1 garlic clove

½ tbsp sea salt

3 tbsp starter culture (Appendix B)

1. In a juicer, combine the tomatoes, onion, peppers, and garlic. You can run the pulp through the juicer again to extract more juice. Discard the pulp. Transfer the juice to a wide-mouth quart (liter) jar.

2. Whisk in the salt and starter culture. Leave 1 inch (2.5cm) from the jar's rim. Cover with a lid or an airlock.

3. Leave at room temperature overnight or for 12 hours. Chill for 2 to 3 hours or until cold. Shake before serving. Store in the fridge for up to 2 weeks, but it's best when consumed within 3 days.

Green Veggie Juice

Beautifully green and with mild vegetable flavors complemented by apple, lemon, and cilantro, this juice is sure to please.

Yield:	Prep time:	Ferment time:	Ferment type:
4½ cups	5 minutes	12 hours	lacto

3 medium cucumbers, ends trimmed

1 medium carrot, ends trimmed

3 medium celery stalks, ends trimmed

1 medium lemon, peeled and quartered

½ medium sweet apple, such as Fuji

8 cilantro stalks, with leaves

½ tbsp sea salt

¼ cup starter culture (Appendix B)

1. In a juicer, combine the cucumbers, carrot, celery, lemon, apple, and cilantro. You can run the pulp through the juicer again to extract more juice. Discard the pulp. Transfer the juice to a ½-gallon (2-liter) jar.

2. Whisk in the salt and starter culture. Leave 1 inch (2.5cm) from the jar's rim. Cover with a lid or an airlock.

3. Leave at room temperature overnight or for 12 hours. Chill for 2 to 3 hours or until cold. Shake before serving. Store in the fridge for up to 2 weeks, but it's best when consumed within 3 days.

Variation: You can leave out the carrot for a brilliantly green juice.

Kvass Recipes

Kvass is a fermented beverage from Eastern Europe. Although usually made with rye bread, the recipes here feature beets and carrots—and we know what nutritional powerhouses those vegetables are!

Beet Kvass

Beet kvass, a traditional Ukrainian beverage, is an excellent blood tonic, promotes regularity, aids digestion, alkalizes the blood, cleanses the liver, and is a good treatment for kidney stones and other ailments. Earthy, rich, sweet, and salty—a few ounces will provide a great start to your day.

Yield:	Prep time:	Ferment time:	Ferment type:
1 quart (1 liter)	5 minutes	2 days	lacto

3 medium beets (about 3 to 4 inches [7.5 to 10cm] in diameter), peeled and chopped into ¾- to 1-inch-wide (2 to 2.5cm) pieces

1½ tbsp plus 1 scant tbsp sea salt, divided

¼ cup starter culture (Appendix B)

1. In a ½-gallon (2-liter) jar or another fermenting container, combine the beets, 1½ tablespoons of salt, and starter culture. Add water to fill, leaving 1 inch (2.5cm) from the container's rim. Cover tightly with a lid or an airlock. Leave at room temperature for 2 days. It might have a few foamy-type bubbles at the top, but this isn't a bubbly fermented beverage.

2. Transfer all but about 10% (doesn't have to be exact) of the liquid to a wide-mouth quart (liter) jar. Cover and transfer to the fridge. This is the first batch. It will keep for many weeks.

3. To make a second batch, add the remaining 1 scant tablespoon of salt to the ½-gallon (2-liter) container with the beets. Add water to fill, leaving 1 inch (2.5cm) from the container's rim. Cover tightly with a lid or an airlock. Leave at room temperature for 2 days.

4. Transfer the liquid to a wide-mouth quart (liter) jar. Cover and transfer to the fridge. This is the second batch. It will keep for many weeks. Discard or compost the beet pieces.

Variation: The second batch will be weaker than the first and it might be possible to get a third (even weaker) batch. To do so, don't transfer all the kvass in step 4 and then repeat steps 3 and 4 to make the third batch. For future batches with fresh beets, feel free to use finished kvass instead of the starter culture in step 1.

Beet & Carrot Kvass

This is a sweeter, carroty cousin to regular beet kvass.

Yield:	Prep time:	Ferment time:	Ferment type:
1 quart (1 liter)	5 minutes	2 days	lacto

1 large carrot, ends trimmed and coarsely chopped into ½-inch (1.25cm) pieces

1 medium beet (about 3 to 4 inches [7.5 to 10cm] in diameter), peeled

and chopped into ¾- to 1-inch-wide (2 to 2.5cm) pieces

1½ tbsp plus 1 scant tbsp sea salt, divided

¼ cup starter culture (Appendix B)

1. In a ½-gallon (2-liter) jar or another fermenting container, combine the carrots, beets, 1½ tablespoons of salt, and starter culture. Add water to fill, leaving 1 inch (2.5cm) from the container's rim. Cover tightly with a lid or an airlock. Leave at room temperature for 2 days.

2. Transfer all but about 10% (doesn't have to be exact) of the liquid to a wide-mouth quart (liter) jar. Cover and transfer to the fridge. This is the first batch. It will keep for many weeks.

3. To make a second batch, add the remaining 1 scant tablespoon of salt to the ½-gallon (2-liter) container with the carrots and beets. Add water to fill, leaving 1 inch (2.5cm) from the container's rim. Cover tightly with a lid or an airlock. Leave at room temperature for 2 days.

4. Transfer all the liquid to a wide-mouth quart (liter) jar. Cover and transfer to the fridge. This is the second batch. It will keep for many weeks. Discard or compost the carrot and beet pieces.

Variation: The second batch will be weaker than the first and it might be possible to get a third (even weaker) batch. To do so, don't pour off all the kvass in step 4 and then repeat steps 3 and 4 to make the third batch. For future batches with fresh carrots and beets, feel free to use finished kvass instead of the starter culture in step 1.

Beet Kvass

Soda Recipes

Fermented sodas begin with yeast. While you can buy yeast, you can also catch your own wild yeast—to save money and for the greatest health benefits. One of the easiest and most reliable ways to catch wild yeast is through a "ginger bug" (created in the following recipe). Once caught, maintain it indefinitely by feeding it more ginger and sugar (about 1 tablespoon each) every other day. When the jar gets full, pour off the liquid to a new jar (leaving the spent ginger and sugar behind). Use this ginger bug as a base for ginger soda or you can create new flavors by adding fruit juices, herbs, or barks.

Ginger Soda

Gingery and mildly sweet, this bubbly, chilled drink is great on a hot day.

Yield:	Prep time:	Ferment time:	Ferment type:
1 gallon (4 liters)	30 minutes	10 days	lacto

one 5- to 6-inch (12.5 to 15.25cm) piece of fresh ginger, scrubbed but not peeled

organic evaporated cane juice (lightly refined sugar)

⅓ to ½ cup freshly squeezed lemon juice

1. Fill a wide-mouth quart (liter) jar two-thirds full with water.

2. Grate 1 tablespoon of fresh ginger into the jar. Add 1 tablespoon of cane juice. Stir well to dissolve the sugar and incorporate as much air as possible. Cover with a cloth napkin or paper towel. Secure with a rubber band.

3. Leave the jar in a warm location (between 75°F and 85°F [24°C to 29°C]). Insulate the jar by wrapping it in a towel if the room temperature is cool.

4. Every 24 hours, add 1 tablespoon each of grated ginger and cane juice. Stir well, then taste. It should be slightly sweet and mildly gingery. Adjust the grated ginger and juice accordingly.

5. Every day for 3 to 7 days, check for little bubbles at the outside top edge of the liquid. If you see bubbles, give the mixture a stir and listen for a fizzing sound from bubbles breaking. When this happens, stop adding ginger and cane juice. This is the starter—also called a "ginger bug."

6. Fill a 1-gallon (4-liter) jar two-thirds full of water. Grate ⅓ packed cup of ginger and add to the jar. Add 1½ cups of cane juice, 1 cup of starter, and ⅓ cup of lemon juice. Add more water (if needed) to fill the jar to its shoulder (where the jar starts narrowing in diameter). Stir well to incorporate lots of air and mostly dissolve the sugar, then taste. It should be slightly sweet and gingery. This is the syrup/soda base—also called the "wort."

7. Cover with a cloth napkin or paper towel. Secure with a rubber band. Leave the jar in a warm location (between 75°F and 85°F [24°C to 29°C]). Insulate the jar by wrapping it in a towel if the room temperature is cool.

8. For 3 days, stir the mixture every 12 hours. Taste at each stirring. Add some cane juice if it loses all sweetness. It should stay mildly sweet throughout the 3 days. When you see bubbles forming at the top of the mixture or if it releases carbonation when you stir the mixture, you can proceed. If you don't see any bubbles by the end of day 3, add 1 more cup of starter and wait another 1 to 2 days (stirring and adjusting the sugar every 12 hours).

9. Adjust the sweetness by adding sugar as needed to make a mildly sweet mixture. You want it to be perfectly delicious and even a little on the sweet side because it will get less sweet during the bottling stage.

10. Transfer the mixture through a strainer to a container with a pour spout. Fill five 25-ounce (¾ liter) Grolsch-style bottles (or another size) to 2 inches (5cm) from each bottle's rim. Cap the bottles.

11. Leave at room temperature (or slightly warmer) for 3 to 5 days to build up carbonation, during which time the soda will also get less sweet. When carbonated to your liking (see earlier in this chapter for tips on checking this), transfer to the fridge for chilling until ready to serve. Store in the fridge indefinitely, but it's sweetest when consumed within 3 days.

Ginger & Rhubarb Soda

For this tangy soda, the tartness of rhubarb is mellowed and sweetened by ginger and sugar.

Yield:	Prep time:	Ferment time:	Ferment type:
1 gallon (4 liters)	30 minutes	10 days	lacto

4 cups rhubarb stalks cut into
½-inch (1.25cm) pieces

½ gallon (2 liters) water, plus more

1½ cups evaporated cane juice
(lightly refined sugar)

1 cup starter (ginger bug) from
Ginger Soda (page 132),
plus more

1. In a 3-quart (3-liter) pot on the stovetop over medium heat, place the rhubarb and cover with water. Simmer until the rhubarb begins to get mushy, about 10 minutes. Strain the rhubarb using a fine mesh strainer and discard. Let the liquid cool to room temperature.

2. In another 3-quart (3-liter) pot on the stovetop over medium-low heat, combine the cane juice and water. Stir until the sugar dissolves. Remove the pot from the heat and let the liquid cool to room temperature.

3. In a 1-gallon (4-liter) jar, combine the rhubarb juice, simple syrup, and ginger bug. Mix well, then taste. If the rhubarb and ginger flavors are too strong for your liking, add 1 cup of water at a time until you like it. It should be very sweet with a pleasing rhubarb and ginger flavor. Cover with a lid or an airlock.

4. Leave the jar in a warm location (between 75°F and 85°F [24°C to 29°C]). Insulate the jar by wrapping it in a towel if the room temperature is cool.

5. For 3 days, stir the mixture every 12 hours. Taste at each stirring. Add some cane juice if it loses all sweetness. It should stay mildly sweet throughout the 3 days. When you see bubbles forming at the top of the mixture or if it releases carbonation when you stir the mixture, you can proceed. If you don't see any bubbles by the end of day 3, add 1 more cup of starter and wait another 1 to 2 days (stirring and adjusting the cane juice every 12 hours).

6. Refrigerate and drink without building up additional carbonation or proceed with step 8 for bottling to build up carbonation.

7. Adjust the sweetness by adding cane juice as needed to make a mildly sweet mixture. You want it to be perfectly delicious and even a little on the sweet side because it will get less sweet during the bottling stage. Transfer the mixture through a strainer to a container with a pour spout. Fill 6 Grolsch-style bottles to 2 inches (5cm) from each bottle's rim. Cap the bottles.

8. Leave at room temperature (or slightly warmer) for 3 to 5 days to build up carbonation, during which time the soda will also get less sweet. When carbonated to your liking (see earlier in this chapter for tips on checking this), transfer to the fridge for chilling until ready to serve. Store in the fridge indefinitely, but it's sweetest when consumed within 3 days.

Cultured Cream Soda

Dress up any natural soda with some cream and honey—and voilà, you've got yourself a deliciously refreshing drink!

Yield:	Prep time:	Ferment time:	Ferment type:
1 glass	5 minutes	none	lacto

crushed ice

Basic Water Kefir (page 140)
  or another natural soda

¼ cup cream (not heavy)

stevia drops (optional)

1. Fill a 16-ounce (450g) glass one-half full with crushed ice.

2. Add the water kefir or natural soda to about three-fourths full. Add the cream.

3. Stir the ingredients just before drinking. Sweeten with stevia drops (if using).

Store in the fridge indefinitely, but it's sweetest when consumed within 3 days.

Pomegranate Soda

I make this for my family in the winter when pomegranates are at the market. The hardest part is getting all the seeds out, but it's worth it. Sediment might accumulate at the bottom of this or many other ferments. This is normal: You can stir it back in or pour your beverage off the top, leaving the sediment behind.

Yield:	Prep time:	Ferment time:	Ferment type:
¾ gallon (3 liters)	20 minutes	1 day	lacto

seeds from 4 large pomegranates

¾ cup starter culture (Appendix B) or Basic Water Kefir (page 140)

½ gallon (2 liters) water, plus more

stevia drops

1. In a large bowl, mash the seeds with a potato masher until slightly chopped. (You can also pulse them in a food processor.)

2. In a 1-gallon (4-liter) jar, combine the seeds, starter culture or water kefir, and water. Add more water or water kefir to fill the jar, leaving 1 inch (2.5cm) from the jar's rim. Cover with a lid or an airlock.

3. Leave at room temperature for 1 day. Strain out the seeds. Chill in the fridge.

4. Serve with 5 drops of stevia per glass. Store in the fridge indefinitely, but it's sweetest when consumed within 3 days.

Variation: Use Basic Water Kefir (page 140) instead of water for a more bubbly pomegranate soda.

Water Kefir Recipes

Water kefir is a mildly bubbly and sweet soda-like fermented beverage. Its mother culture, originating in Mexico, is a colony of yeast and lactic-acid-producing bacteria called "water kefir grains"—much like the dairy kefir grains you'll see in Chapter 12, except dairy-free. Submerge water kefir grains in sweetened water, where they consume the sugar and, in return, give all the great probiotic benefits of other ferments. This culture produces alcohol—usually less than 1%—and shorter fermentation times will keep the alcohol production lowest. Its basic taste is neutral and well suited to taking on fruit or other flavors in additional fermentations.

Many people consume water kefir as a natural soda, while others drink it because it's dairy-free. Water kefir grains don't multiply as readily as dairy kefir grains, but the probiotic and immune-supporting benefits are similar. Water kefir grains don't get used up and you can transfer them from batch to batch indefinitely. They look somewhat like translucent pebbles (while dairy kefir grains look like clumps of cauliflower). Water kefir grains typically take on the color of their sweetener. The darker the sweetener, the browner the grains, with grains grown on refined sugars being close to transparent and colorless.

You'll probably use dehydrated water kefir grains unless you can get fresh grains from a friend. You must rehydrate them for use in fermentation: Combine ½ cup of water and ¼ cup of unrefined sweetener in a small pot. Heat over medium-low heat to dissolve the sweetener. Remove the pot from the heat. Add 2½ cups of cold water. Place the sweet water in a quart (liter) jar. Add 2 teaspoons of dehydrated water kefir grains. Cover with a cloth napkin or paper towel. Secure with a rubber band. Let this mixture sit for 3 to 4 days or until the grains are plump. The mixture will be slightly bubbly. You might see occasional bubbles rising to the surface. Don't let the mixture sit for more than 5 days, and in warmer temperatures, the process might complete more quickly. Now the grains are ready for use in recipes.

Making water kefir always includes a first fermentation, with further fermentations optional. As you'll see in the upcoming Basic Water Kefir recipe, follow this ratio for the first fermentation: ¼ cup of water kefir grains per ¾ gallon (3 liters) of sweetened water. (The sweet water is ¾ cup of sugar dissolved in ¾ gallon [3 liters] of water.) None of this is set in stone. You can use more or less sugar or more or less sweetener with good results. More sweetener will extend the fermentation time, while more grains will shorten the fermentation time. A 1-gallon (4-liter) jar is a handy fermenting vessel and a simple cloth or paper napkin secured with a rubber band makes a great cover.

I prefer to place the grains free-floating in the sweet water. As they eat the sugar and release carbon dioxide, they might float up and down in the jar and make really pleasing popping noises. You'll know it's finished when much of the sweetness is reduced and the beverage is mildly bubbly.

In general, water kefir shouldn't be fermented for more than about 3 days (and some people ferment in as little as 1 day to yield a fairly sweet beverage). Otherwise, the grains start decaying from the prolonged lack of food. You'll need to strain the grains out of the liquid with a simple mesh strainer, although you can skip this by putting your water kefir grains in a muslin bag during the fermentation. (See Appendix B for sources for muslin bags.) Tie the bag and submerge it in the jar of sweet water. When the first fermentation is done, just pull out the bag and transfer it to a fresh batch. However, if your grains are thriving and multiplying, they can quickly fill the bag, get stifled, and stop performing. In that case, I recommend leaving them free-flowing.

You can ferment the water kefir a second time for a few days more by mixing the liquid (sans grains) with dried or fresh fruits or fruit juice. You'll see examples of this with the recipes. You can also do the second fermentation in soda bottles to build up carbonation at the same time or you can add a third fermentation devoted to bottling (discussed earlier in this chapter). So many options!

When bottled, water kefir shouldn't be left out indefinitely. It will continue to build up pressure as long as the organisms have something to eat. But it tends to lose some natural carbonation once refrigerated. It's best to plan on serving your water kefir within a few days of bottling and refrigerate it just before serving.

When water kefir grains aren't in use, store them submerged in sugar water–1½ teaspoons of sugar dissolved in ½ cup of water–in a small covered jar in the fridge for 1 week at a time. If not used in that time, use fresh sugar water.

Water kefir is a very easy ferment, but it can have bigger pitfalls than other ferments. Water kefir grains have a high need for mineral supplementation. If the grains don't get enough minerals, they fail to thrive, start shrinking in size, and produce smelly and overall poor water kefir. You can supply their need for minerals in three ways:

- Use mineral-rich water, such as hard well water.

- Use the least refined sweeteners, such as Sucanat or rapadura. These retain the sugar cane's naturally present minerals.

- Supplement the grains with mineral drops. Minerals drops are nearly always beneficial and I highly recommend using them even if your water and sugar are the best they can be. I call for them in the recipes at the rate of about ⅛ teaspoon per batch. See Appendix B for where to purchase them.

You can try leaving out the mineral drops. Alternatives include using ½ teaspoon of baking soda or ½ rinsed and pastured (not conventional) eggshell per batch. Just add the baking soda or the eggshells free-floating in the first fermentation so they're present when the grains are in the mixture. The eggshells will need to be strained out, though, and if they're mixed up with the grains, this can be time-consuming. Ultimately, it will be up to your experimentation to find the right combination of minerals to keep your grains happy.

Too long a ferment isn't good for the longevity of the water kefir grains—the mother culture of this ferment. When fermented too long, you might end up with syrupy, vinegary, or otherwise strong-smelling water kefir. The grains might suffer and show it by shrinking in volume. Typically, because water kefir grains are slow to multiply and grow, don't be alarmed if they stay the same size—unless you also notice "off" smells or textures in the ferment. If you run into trouble, don't toss the grains. All's not necessarily lost. If you can improve anything (water, sweetener, minerals, or timing), take steps to do so immediately. Then ferment the grains repeatedly in smaller, shorter duration batches. A little TLC might help them bounce back to full strength.

Now let's get into some water kefir recipes. First, you'll see the general procedure for making Basic Water Kefir, which is how all first fermentations should proceed. Following that, I'll give you two recipes for a second fermentation.

Basic Water Kefir

Mildly bubbly, this nondairy kefir makes a family-friendly natural soda you can drink plain or use in the next recipes, flavoring it up or turning it into cream soda.

Yield:	Prep time:	Ferment time:	Ferment type:
¾ gallon (3 liters)	20 minutes	2 to 4 days	lacto

¾ cup unrefined sugar

¾ gallon (3 liters) water, divided, plus more

¼ cup water kefir grains (active and hydrated; see Appendix B for sources)

¼ tsp mineral drops, divided

1. In a 3-quart (3-liter) pot on the stovetop over medium heat, combine the sugar and 1 cup of water. Stir until the sugar dissolves. Remove the pot from the heat and add ½ gallon (2 liters) of cool or cold water to cool down the mixture. Let cool to room temperature.

2. Transfer the sugar water to a 1-gallon (4-liter) jar. Add the remaining 11 cups of water to fill the jar to three-fourths full. (This should be cold water.)

3. Stir in the water kefir grains and ⅛ teaspoon of mineral drops. Cover with a cloth napkin or paper towel. Secure with a rubber band. Leave at room temperature for 1 to 2 days.

4. Transfer the liquid through a strainer to a fresh 1-gallon (4-liter) jar. Transfer the kefir grains to another batch of water kefir or store in the fridge as described earlier in this chapter.

5. To the finished water kefir, add the remaining ⅛ teaspoon of mineral drops. Proceed with one of the following variations.

Vanilla Cream Soda: Add 3 tablespoons of pure vanilla extract. Refrigerate until ready to drink. Store indefinitely, although the sweetness reduces over time.

Other Flavors: Add 2 to 3 tablespoons of desired extract flavors, such as almond, orange, or lemon. Add 20 to 30 stevia drops per 1 gallon (4 liters) if not sweet enough. Store indefinitely, although the sweetness reduces over time.

Bottling: Add 1 teaspoon of any unrefined sweetener to each bottle and fill to the top with vanilla cream soda (or another flavor). Leave at room temperature for 2 to 3 days to build up carbonation. Follow the bottling instructions discussed earlier in this chapter. Store in the fridge or at cool room temperature until ready to drink. Store indefinitely, although the sweetness reduces over time.

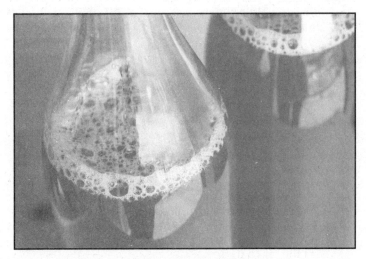

Bottled Water Kefir

Strawberry Water Kefir

Strawberry Water Kefir

What better way to use juicy, sweet, in-season strawberries than to make a beneficial and tasty carbonated natural beverage?

Yield:	Prep time:	Ferment time:	Ferment type:
¾ gallon (3 liters)	5 minutes	1 to 2 days	lacto

1 batch of Basic Water Kefir (page 140)

2 cups coarsely chopped fresh strawberries

1. In a 1-gallon (4-liter) jar, combine the water kefir and strawberries. Cover tightly with a lid. Don't use an airlock if you want to build up carbonation. Use plastic wrap underneath the lid if it's not airtight.

2. Leave at room temperature for no more than 24 hours or less if room temperature is very warm.

3. Strain the strawberries. Tightly cover the strawberry water kefir in the 1-gallon (4-liter) jar or transfer to Grolsch bottles or smaller canning jars with tight lids.

4. Leave at room temperature for 1 to 2 days to build up carbonation or as you desire. Transfer to the fridge before serving. Store indefinitely, although the sweetness reduces over time.

Variations: Use any fresh fruit or combination to flavor the water kefir, leaving the fruit in the water kefir for up to 24 hours. You can leave dried fruits in the water kefir to ferment for several days. To make Blueberry & Pomegranate Water Kefir, use ¾ to 1 cup of blueberry and pomegranate juice instead of fresh strawberries. To make Grape Water Kefir, use 2 cups of grape juice instead of fresh strawberries.

Lemon & Ginger Water Kefir

I'm a sucker for anything with lemon and ginger—and this water kefir certainly delivers a punch.

Yield:	Prep time:	Ferment time:	Ferment type:
¾ gallon (3 liters)	5 minutes	1 to 3 days	lacto

1 batch of Basic Water Kefir (page 140)

4 tbsp peeled and grated fresh ginger

¼ cup freshly squeezed lemon juice

1 tsp pure vanilla extract

1. In a 1-gallon (4-liter) jar, combine all the ingredients. Cover tightly with a lid. Don't use an airlock if you want to build up carbonation. Use plastic wrap underneath the lid if it's not airtight.

2. Leave at room temperature for 1 to 2 days or less if the room temperature is very warm.

3. Strain the ginger. Tightly cover the water kefir in the 1-gallon (4-liter) jar or transfer to Grolsch bottles or smaller canning jars.

4. Leave at room temperature for 12 to 24 hours to build up carbonation. Transfer to the fridge before serving. Store indefinitely, although the sweetness reduces over time.

Kombucha Recipes

From Russia comes kombucha, an old and beneficial fermented beverage. It's also delicious! It's sweet, sour, and naturally carbonated by fermenting gases. Fizzy and dark, acidic and sweet, kombucha originated in the Ural Mountains. Reported benefits of consuming kombucha include lowering blood pressure, cleansing, boosting your immune system, and fighting cancer and other degenerative diseases. Just a few ounces of kombucha a day can help with any of these issues.

The mother culture is called a "SCOBY." SCOBY is an acronym for what this is: a Symbiotic Colony of Bacteria and Yeast. The organisms exist in a tough, layered, mushroom-like disc shape. A SCOBY is very versatile. Even a piece of it will grow over time to fit the exact dimensions of the fermenting container. As it consumes the sugar in brewed tea, the SCOBY grows a fresh whitish layer on top. Over time, it can grow to be many inches (centimeters) thick. I keep mine about 1 to 2 inches (2.5 to 5cm) thick, peeling off the older layers to share with friends or feed to livestock (because it's also good for them!). When not in use, store the SCOBY in a glass jar in a cool, dark location covered with finished kombucha. It can keep for many months this way.

As the bacteria and yeast consume the sugar, they produce vitamin B and three kinds of acids: lactic, acetic (vinegar), and glucoronic. You're familiar with the first two acids, but I've not mentioned the third acid before.

Our liver produces glucoronic acid in small quantities. It binds toxins and helps flush them out of our bodies. Kombucha contains significant amounts of glucoronic acid, making it a powerful detoxifier. In my opinion, one should drink as much water as one does kombucha because its detoxification powers also make it dehydrating.

You'll get more glucoronic acid if you choose granulated sugar instead of unrefined sweeteners for brewing your kombucha. Also, glucoronic acid is highest at about the eighth day of fermentation. However, temperature is a factor: Cooler temperatures slow down the fermentation, while warmer temperatures speed it up. A quick test with a pH strip is the only way to know for sure. At a pH of 2.6, the beverage is the healthiest. Interestingly, the process of fermentation reduces caffeine and fluoride in tea. Because kombucha can contain a small amount of alcohol, pregnant or nursing mothers should exercise caution when consuming it.

Don't have finished kombucha handy to get your first batch going? You can substitute apple cider vinegar. Because the SCOBY produces vinegar in addition to other beneficial acids, a little raw vinegar also provides a good starter liquid.

Green Tea Kombucha

I choose green tea for my basic kombucha—rather than the usual black tea—because it makes a lighter and sweeter yet slightly earthy drink.

Yield:	Prep time:	Ferment time:	Ferment type:
¾ gallon (3 liters)	20 minutes	5 to 10 days	lacto & aceto

SCOBY (kombucha starter)
  (see Appendix B for sources)

1½ cups finished kombucha
  (homemade or store-bought
  with active cultures)

6 green tea bags

1 cup sweetener (any kind)

3½ quarts (3½ liters) water, divided,
  plus more

1. In a 1-gallon (4-liter) jar, combine the SCOBY and finished kombucha. Cover with a cloth napkin or paper towel. Secure with a rubber band. Set aside.

2. In a 3-quart (3-liter) pot on the stovetop over medium heat, combine the tea bags, sweetener, and 3 cups of water. Bring to a boil, then remove the pot from the heat. Cover and let steep for 15 minutes.

3. Squeeze the liquid from the tea bags and then discard them. Add 2 quarts (2 liters) of cool water to the pot.

4. Transfer the cooled-down tea to the 1-gallon (4-liter) jar. Add the remaining 3 cups of water (plus more as needed) to fill to the shoulder of the jar (where the jar starts narrowing in diameter).

5. Cover with a cloth napkin or paper towel. Secure with a rubber band. Leave at room temperature for 5 to 10 days or until bubbly and slightly sweet and sour.

6. Transfer the finished kombucha mixture to another 1-gallon (4-liter) container, leaving the SCOBY and 1½ cups of kombucha behind. (Use a wooden spoon to hold the SCOBY back.) Repeat steps 2 through 5 to make more batches.

7. Transfer the finished kombucha to bottles or tightly lidded jars. Leave at room temperature for 1 to 2 days to build up carbonation, then chill until needed. Store indefinitely, but it gets more sour and vinegary over time.

Variation: For a darker, richer kombucha (the most traditional variety), use black tea instead of green tea.

Spiced Green Tea Kombucha

Chai spices—cardamom, black pepper, cloves, anise, cinnamon, and vanilla (depending on brand of tea bag)—make this kombucha fragrant and delicious.

Yield:	Prep time:	Ferment time:	Ferment type:
¾ gallon (3 liters)	20 minutes	5 to 10 days	lacto & aceto

SCOBY (kombucha starter)
(see Appendix B for sources)

1½ cups finished kombucha
(homemade or store-bought
with active cultures)

4 green tea bags

2 chai tea bags

1 cup sweetener (any kind)

3½ quarts (3½ liters) water,
divided, plus more

1. In a 1-gallon (4-liter) jar, combine the SCOBY and finished kombucha. Cover loosely. Set aside.

2. In a 3-quart (3-liter) pot on the stovetop over medium heat, combine the tea bags, sweetener, and 3 cups of water. Bring to a boil, then remove the pot from the heat. Cover and let steep for 15 minutes.

3. Squeeze the liquid from the tea bags and then discard them. Add 2 quarts (2 liters) of cool water to the pot.

4. Transfer the cooled-down tea to a 1-gallon (4-liter) jar. Add the remaining 3 cups of water (plus more as needed) to fill to the shoulder of the jar (where the jar starts narrowing in diameter). Cover with a cloth napkin or paper towel. Secure with a rubber band.

5. Leave at room temperature for 5 to 10 days or until bubbly and tastes slightly sweet and sour. Transfer the finished kombucha to another 1-gallon (4-liter) container, leaving the SCOBY and 1½ cups of kombucha behind. (Use a wooden spoon to hold the SCOBY back.) Repeat steps 2 through 5 to make more batches.

6. Transfer the finished kombucha to bottles or tightly lidded jars. Leave at room temperature for 1 to 2 days to build up carbonation, then chill until needed. Store indefinitely, but it gets more sour and vinegary over time.

Variation: For a darker spiced kombucha, use black tea instead of green tea.

Honey Kombucha

Wildflower honey as a sweetener creates a mildly floral and delicious kombucha.

Yield:	Prep time:	Ferment time:	Ferment type:
¾ gallon (3 liters)	20 minutes	5 to 10 days	lacto & aceto

SCOBY (kombucha starter)
(see Appendix B for sources)

1½ cups finished kombucha
(homemade or store-bought
with active cultures)

6 green tea bags

3½ quarts (3½ liters) water,
divided, plus more

1 cup raw honey (wildflower
recommended)

1. In a 1-gallon (4-liter) jar, combine the SCOBY and finished kombucha. Cover loosely. Set aside.

2. In a 3-quart (3-liter) pot on the stovetop over medium heat, combine the green tea bags and 3 cups of water. Bring to a boil, then remove the pot from the heat. Cover and let steep for 15 minutes.

3. Squeeze the liquid from the tea bags and then discard them. Add the honey and 2 quarts (2 liters) of cool water to the pot. Stir until the honey dissolves.

4. Transfer the cooled-down tea to the 1-gallon (4-liter) jar. Add the remaining 3 cups of water (plus more as needed) to fill to the shoulder of the jar (where the jar starts narrowing in diameter).

5. Cover with a cloth napkin or paper towel. Secure with a rubber band. Leave at room temperature for 5 to 10 days or until bubbly and tastes slightly sweet and sour.

6. Transfer the finished kombucha to another 1-gallon (4-liter) container, leaving the SCOBY and 1½ cups of kombucha behind. (Use a wooden spoon to hold the SCOBY back.) Repeat steps 2 through 5 to make more batches.

7. Transfer the finished kombucha to bottles or tightly lidded jars. Leave at room temperature for 1 to 2 days to build up carbonation, then chill until needed. Store indefinitely, but it gets more sour and vinegary over time.

Variation: Combine black or green tea with chai for a spiced honey kombucha.

Ginger & Grapefruit Kombucha

On hot days, nothing satisfies thirst like a cold, bubbly beverage. This kombucha from my friend Kresha just so happens to fit the bill perfectly. It's light, citrusy, and refreshing. And, of course, nourishing and probiotic—because it's kombucha.

Yield:	Prep time:	Ferment time:	Ferment type:
1 quart (1 liter)	10 minutes	1 to 2 days	lacto

3 cups Green Tea Kombucha
(page 145)

1-inch (2.5cm) piece of fresh ginger,
cut into matchsticks

½ to 1 cup freshly squeezed
Ruby Red grapefruit juice
(from 2 grapefruits)

1. In a 1-quart (1-liter) glass canning jar or Grolsch-style flip-top bottle, combine the kombucha, ginger, and grapefruit juice, leaving 1 inch (2.5cm) from the container's rim. Cover tightly with a lid.

2. Leave at room temperature (68°F to 72°F [20°C to 22°C]) for 1 to 2 days.

3. Transfer to the fridge until well chilled. When ready to drink, open carefully because kombucha sometimes bubbles fiercely and sometimes not! Serve cold. Store indefinitely, but it gets more sour and vinegary over time.

Kanji

Other Nonalcoholic Recipes

Once you've mastered your sodas, kefir, and kombucha, why not try these other refreshing fermented, nonalcoholic beverages? Perhaps the children won't love the *kanji* (it's spicy), but you're sure to find something to please the young and old. I especially recommend the sparkling apple cider!

Kanji

Hot and spicy from a chili pepper and mustard seeds, this fermented beverage (similar to kvass) from Northern India is my husband's and my favorite supertonic.

Yield:	Prep time:	Ferment time:	Ferment type:
1 quart (1 liter)	5 minutes	2 days	lacto

1 large carrot, ends trimmed and coarsely chopped into ½-inch (1.25cm) pieces

1 medium beet (about 3 to 4 inches [7.5 to 10cm] in diameter), peeled and chopped into ¾- to 1-inch-wide (2 to 2.5cm) pieces

1 green chili pepper, split in half lengthwise, with seeds

pinch of red pepper flakes

1 tbsp mustard seeds

1½ tbsp plus 1 scant tbsp sea salt, divided

¼ cup starter culture (Appendix B)

1. In a ½-gallon (2-liter) jar or another fermenting container, combine the carrot, beet, chili pepper, red pepper flakes, mustard seeds, 1½ tablespoons of salt, and starter culture. Add water to fill, leaving 1 inch (2.5cm) from the container's rim. Cover tightly with a lid or an airlock. Leave at room temperature for 2 days.

2. Transfer all but about 10% (doesn't have to be exact) of liquid to a wide-mouth quart (liter) jar. Cover and transfer to the fridge. This is the first batch. It will keep for 2 to 3 weeks.

3. To make a second batch, add the remaining 1 scant tablespoon of salt to the ½-gallon (2-liter) container with the vegetables. Add water to fill, leaving 1 inch (2.5cm) from the container's rim. Cover tightly with a lid or an airlock. Leave at room temperature for 2 days.

4. Transfer all the liquid to a wide-mouth quart (liter) jar. Cover and transfer to the fridge. This is the second batch. It will keep for 2 to 3 weeks. Discard or compost the solid ingredients.

Variation: The second batch will be weaker than the first and it might be possible to get a third (even weaker) batch. To do so, don't pour off all the kanji in step 4 and then repeat steps 3 and 4 to make the third batch. For future batches, feel free to use finished kanji instead of the starter culture in step 1.

Coconut Water

Sweet and refreshing water from coconut gets a boost through fermentation— you'll love it!

Yield:	Prep time:	Ferment time:	Ferment type:
2 to 3 cups	10 minutes	1 day	lacto

1 medium to large young green drinking coconut	1 tbsp water kefir grains (active and hydrated; see Appendix B for sources)

1. Near or over a sink, use a sharp knife to cut a triangular-shaped deep hole through the coconut flesh (much like cutting eyes or a nose on a pumpkin). Pull out the triangular piece you just cut. Carefully transfer the coconut water to a wide-mouth quart (liter) jar.

2. Add the water kefir grains. Cover with a lid or an airlock. Leave at room temperature for 24 hours.

3. Remove the kefir grains and transfer them to a new batch of coconut water or store in the fridge in a small lidded jar in sugar water (1½ teaspoons of sugar dissolved in ½ cup of water) for up to 1 week. If you won't use them again within 1 week, replace the sugar water with fresh sugar water weekly. With good care and a consistent food source, they should last indefinitely.

4. Refrigerate the coconut water until ready to serve. Store in the fridge for up to 2 weeks.

Variation: You can use rinsed dairy kefir grains instead of water kefir grains. See Chapter 12 for more information about dairy kefir grains or Appendix B for where to purchase them. If you use dairy kefir grains to ferment a nondairy beverage, you can't usually ferment dairy with them again, but you'll be able to make at least several more batches of coconut water with them.

Lemonade

Delightfully refreshing with real lemon goodness, this probiotic lemonade is a favorite with kids—and adults!

Yield:	Prep time:	Ferment time:	Ferment type:
1 gallon (4 liters)	10 minutes	2 to 3 days	lacto

3 quarts (3 liters) cool water, divided

¾ cup evaporated cane juice (lightly refined sweetener)

juice from 14 lemons (about 3½ cups)

1 cup starter culture (Appendix B)

stevia drops (optional)

1. In a 3-quart (3-liter) pot on the stovetop over medium heat, combine ½ quart (½ liter) of water and the sugar. Stir until the sugar dissolves. Remove the pot from the heat. Add the remaining 2½ quarts (2½ liters) of water.

2. Transfer the sugar water to a 1-gallon (4-liter) jar. Let cool to room temperature. Add the lemon juice and starter culture. Add more water to fill, leaving 1 inch (2.5cm) from the jar's rim. Cover with a lid or an airlock.

3. Leave at room temperature for 2 to 3 days or until the sweetness is reduced to where you like it.

4. Chill before serving with 5 drops of stevia (if using) per glass if you desire more sweetness. Store indefinitely, but the sweetness reduces over time.

Variations: To make limeade, use lime juice instead of lemon juice. To make orangeade, use orange juice instead of lemon juice. Or use a combination of lemons, limes, and oranges to equal 3 cups.

Sparkling Apple Cider

The skin of unwashed organic apples is teeming with microscopic organisms—tiny yeasts and bacteria that feed off the natural sugars in apple cider and turn it into a bubbly, sparkling, sweet-and-tart glass of fall flavor! No need to add sugar or spices to this recipe created by my friend Lindsey.

Yield:	Prep time:	Ferment time:	Ferment type:
varies	1 hour	2 days	lacto

locally grown sweet apples (such as
    Fuji) or whatever's in season

1. Use a juicer or cider press (if available) to juice (or press) the apples—skin, stems, peels, and all! If you're using a cider press, you don't even have to worry about stray leaves or sticks because they'll be filtered out. As long as you're sure your apples are organic and have never been sprayed with anything, you don't even need to wash them first. If you're using a juicer, remove the leaves and sticks before juicing, but don't worry about the skins or stems. Whether using a juicer or cider press, there won't be any leaves, seeds, or stems in the finished cider.

2. Transfer the cider to flip-top Grolsch-style bottles or quart (liter) jars. Cap or cover the bottles or jars. Leave on a countertop for 2 to 4 days. (You can go longer, but the cider will lose most of its sweetness and become slightly alcoholic the longer it ferments.)

3. As the yeasts and bacteria get to work eating the apples' sugar, they'll begin to release carbon dioxide, especially by the end of the second day. Make sure to check and burp your jars at least once a day!

4. Once the apple cider tastes like you want and has the fizz (sparkle!) you like, transfer it to the fridge. Store in the fridge for up to 2 weeks, but it's best when consumed within 3 days.

Honey-Sweetened Ginger Beer

This tasty beverage from my daughter Haniya is a probiotic, GAPS-friendly (Gut and Psychology Syndrome), nonalcoholic, natural soda. And it's a ferment sweetened with honey! Learn how this is possible so you can make this bubbly, pizzazz-y, traditionally fermented drink!

Yield:	Prep time:	Ferment time:	Ferment type:
1 gallon (4 liters)	30 minutes	21 hours	lacto

2 to 3 medium-sized fresh pieces of ginger (if your grocery store has old, dry roots, try a health food store instead)

2 tbsp plus ¾ cup raw honey, divided, plus more

⅓ cup freshly squeezed lemon juice

1. Make the starter ("ginger bug") by filling a quart (liter) jar two-thirds full with filtered water. Wash (but don't peel) and grate the ginger. Add 1 tablespoon of grated ginger to the jar. Add 1 tablespoon of honey. Stir well to dissolve the honey and to incorporate lots of air. This ferment is aerobic and needs air. Cover with a cheesecloth and rubber band.

2. Leave in a warm place to ferment (between 75°F and 85°F (24°C to 29°C). Cover or insulate the jar with towels if the temperature is cooler. You can also keep the starter on a seedling warming mat.

3. Every 12 hours (morning and night), stir and taste your starter. Does it need another feeding? Is it too sweet? Is it too strong? You want to keep the mixture mildly gingery and slightly sweet. Depending on how it tastes, either hold off on feeding it or feed it about 1 tablespoon of grated ginger, 1 tablespoon of honey, and 2 tablespoons of water (to keep the honey diluted). You might need to feed it every 24 hours or every couple days. It takes anywhere from 3 to 7 days to get a strong ginger bug. The length of time depends on temperature, stirring, and honey content. It's ready when you see a layer of bubbles on the top of the starter and it fizzes when you stir. This is the carbonation releasing. If you ever notice that bubbles were forming but have since stopped, simply dilute the starter with more water.

4. In a 1-gallon (4-liter) jar, combine 1 cup of ginger bug, ⅓ cup of well-packed grated ginger (plus more if desired), lemon juice, and the remaining ¾ cup of honey. Fill to the shoulder with water (where the jar starts narrowing in diameter). This is now called the "wort" (soda before fermentation). Stir the wort well to incorporate lots of air and to dissolve the honey, then taste. It should be sweet and gingery but not too strong.

5. Cover with cheesecloth and a rubber band. Leave in a warm location, cover with towels, or keep on a seedling warming mat if the temperature is cooler.

6. Stir every 12 hours (morning and night) for 3 to 7 days, tasting as you go. Add more honey if it loses all sweetness but not too much because you want only a slightly sweet ginger beer. The wort is ready for bottling when there's a layer of bubbles on top and it fizzes when you stir. If you're not seeing any bubbles and your room temperature has been warm, add another cup of starter. Stir well. Give it another day or two for bubbles and fizz to form. Taste the wort and add any additional flavors, such as dried fruit, preserves, or overripe fruit.

7. Bottle the ginger beer by using a funnel with a strainer to fill flip-top Grolsch bottles or 1-pint (½-liter) glass canning jars 1½ to 2 inches (3.75 to 5cm) from the container's rim. This will ensure no bottles break as the carbonation builds up. Cap or cover the bottles or jars. Set aside in the same warm location where you fermented the bug and wort. Leave for 3 to 7 days depending on the temperature.

8. Open and test for doneness on about day 3. If it fizzes, it's done! If not, cap and leave for another 24 hours, then check again. Keep checking every day until the ginger beer is carbonated to your preference. The longer it sits, the less sweet it becomes.

9. When done, refrigerate the bottles. Once chilled, enjoy! Store in the fridge indefinitely, but it's sweetest when consumed within 3 days.

Alcoholic Beverages

Chapter

9

In this chapter, I'll cover a brief history of beer-making—how it got started and how it's changed in today's world—and then I'll explain how alcoholic fermentation differs from lactic- and acetic-acid fermentation. To get your own beverages brewing, I'll take you through the basic process of extract brewing, including what tools and equipment you need. You'll soon be ready to start one of the home-brew recipes I've included to introduce you to this traditional skill.

Brewing Alcoholic Beverages

I learned how to make beer from Gerard Van Assche, a beer-maker and co-president of the Umpqua Valley Brewer's Guild. No doubt influenced by Gerard's appreciation for tradition, my approach to alcohol fermentation is different from many others. Conventional beer-making can be complicated in terms of steps, procedures, and ingredients, and as such, the simplicist in me rebels. What I'll share with you now is a bare-bones, simple approach to getting started and excelling in traditional brewing.

The biggest difference between my approach and conventional methods is that most brewing texts, websites, and recipes yield highly alcoholic and minimally nutritious beverages. That's not entirely a bad thing. Home brewing usually produces superior beers no matter what approach you take. However, in this book, you'll explore brews that are lower in alcohol (and therefore less taxing on brain cells and liver) and more nutritious (because of using other herbs besides hops).

As used in modern beers to balance the sweetness, "hops" refers to the flower of the hops plant (which has many varieties). Although used occasionally in history, they've been used exclusively since around 1520 CE for reasons political and monetary. While hops do balance the sweetness and lend flavor, they offer other undesirable effects: They make the drinker drowsy and suppress sexual vitality.

For these reasons—and to impart various medicinal and beneficial properties into our brews—the recipes in this chapter will return to the tradition of using herbs.

Beers are either lagers or ales. Lagers are fermented at cold temperatures for long periods of time, with yeasts that work at the bottom of the fermenting container. Ales are fermented at warmer temperatures for shorter periods of time and the yeasts ferment at the top of the carboy (a 5-gallon [18-liter] fermenting container). The recipes in this book are ales.

Beer in History

Women were the first brewers, making and perfecting brews for their households. The first beer was likely a surprise (just like the first cheese, sourdough bread, and sauerkraut). I think this surprise was the result of a set of discoveries. First, people discovered that when grains are moist and warm, they germinate (or sprout) and get sweet. Although they didn't know it then, what happens is the bound-up complex carbohydrates get converted into simple sugars or malts to feed the new sprout. At this point, the sprouted grains taste and smell sweet.

The second discovery was this (as beer historians speculate): Perhaps someone left a bowl of cooked barley porridge or dried sprouted barley in the rain on a mildly warm day. The abundant wild yeasts had a field day consuming those sugars in a perfectly wet environment, producing a bubbly concoction of carbonated alcohol. Now enters our unassuming housewife, who tastes the liquid and then shares the taste and sensation with others in the household, who are all equally pleased.

This could very well have been the world's first beer, which households continued to produce for themselves for thousands of years. When towns sprang up, water supplies became contaminated, making the mildly alcoholic and contamination-resistant home beers one of the few safe liquids to consume. At about the same time, small-town breweries took over the task of beer-making and were appreciated for conveniently providing brews for all who lived in the area. Today, household brewers and local breweries have been mostly supplanted by mega-breweries.

What have we lost by this shift from home brews to mega-breweries? Certainly three things but possibly more: We've lost the flavor diversity that herbs give to traditional brews; the nutritional and medicinal benefits that come from using herbs, grasses, and roots; and the nutrition of consuming wild yeasts (suspended in the alcoholic liquid) and their B vitamin by-products, which are destroyed or removed through modern beer pasteurization and filtering.

Alcoholic Fermentation vs. Other Types

Let's cover the differences between alcoholic and lactic-acid (or acetic-acid) fermentation. First, in alcoholic fermentation, the yeasts produce alcohol (ethanol) rather than lactic acid or acetic acid. There's not much more to say about that. Second, rather than being either aerobic (like acetic-acid fermentation) or anaerobic (like lactic-acid fermentation), alcoholic fermentation involves both.

The first stage is aerobic. Because no alcohol is produced during this stage, we can't call it a fermenting stage. However, it's so important that fermentation wouldn't occur without it. Here's how it works: When yeasts are added to the liquid being fermented, you must incorporate a great deal of oxygen by shaking up the mixture. Then over a four- to eight-hour period, called the "respiration stage," the yeasts grab energy and other things they'll need for reproduction and fermentation. During the respiration stage, the yeasts reproduce, produce carbon dioxide, and change the flavor of the brew—but no alcohol is produced.

Then the brew moves into the anaerobic second stage: fermentation. The yeasts continue to reproduce until the mixture is full and then they convert the sugars in the sweet liquid into carbon dioxide, flavor compounds, and alcohol. This stage lasts three to seven days, at which time the yeasts create a sediment called "glycogen" (an energy source that yeasts can consume during dormancy). The yeasts and the sediment fall to the bottom of the fermenting container. From here on out, fermentation slows tremendously.

The third difference is a particular of preparation. I venture to suppose that each brewer has their own take on how sterile an environment is provided for the yeasts. Rather than using salt or acidity (or the other protection methods mentioned in Chapter 3) to protect the growing yeast population, many beer brewers employ two methods of killing off any competing organisms: heating the mixture to be fermented and sterilizing equipment. These steps give the yeast starter culture the high ground from the beginning.

While high heat and sterilization seem to be the norm, they're not always the rule. For example, when traditional elderflower champagne is made, the flowers are combined with water and sugar only. No yeast is added and the mixture isn't heated. Elderflowers are abundant in the yeasts needed to create the champagne. Heat would kill them and adding another culture simply isn't necessary. There are more intricate complexities of alcohol brewing, but these basics are all you really need to get started. If you'd like more information, see Appendix B.

The Process of Brewing Alcohol

Although we covered two stages of alcoholic fermentation previously, now I'm going to go into more detail about the steps. This account will be much more practical and is, in fact, the process you'll follow for all the alcohol fermentation recipes in this book. This is a great, simple approach to making beer. If any questions arise in the recipes, come back to this section to refresh yourself with the process. These instructions assume you'll be making a 5-gallon (18-liter) batch and any tools used are described in the next section. Use good water (see Chapter 4 for more discussion on this) and make sure all equipment, tools, and utensils are sterilized (also discussed in Chapter 4).

The Tea

This is also called the "wort." Start by putting fresh or dried herbs and/or specialty grains in a filter sock (also called a "hop sack"). Tie it up and add it to a 2½-gallon (10-liter) or bigger pot with 1 gallon (4 liters) of water. The herbs and specialty grains are for flavor and the amount is flexible. One recipe (the Nettle & Lemon Beer recipe later in this chapter) calls for 5 cups of herbs and 3 cups of specialty grains. If you use only herbs, your beer will end up grassy, so using grains is recommended to improve the overall flavor.

Slowly bring the mixture to a boil and simmer gently for 40 minutes to a few hours depending on how much flavor you desire. You don't usually cover this mixture. Lower the heat. Transfer the filter sock to a strainer and pour about 1 quart (1 liter) of fresh water at a time through the filter sock to the pot, gently rinsing the herbs and grains. Don't squeeze the filter sock—this can impart harsh flavors into the beer.

The Boil

Now we add sugar to the tea. The sugar might be light or dark malted barley extract, maple syrup, honey, brown sugar, molasses, unrefined sugar, or other choices. Because granulated sugar lends a cidery taste to the beer, it's not normally recommended. The darker the sugar, the darker the brew. The more sugar, the more alcohol in the end product. Two cups of malted barley extract yield an alcohol level in finished ales of about 1%.

Grains and Herbs in a Filter Sock

Rinsing the Grains and Herbs in a Filter Sock

In this chapter, we focus on extract brewing, where the recipes call for sugar syrups already collected from sprouted and dried grains. This makes for simpler beginning brewing. At some point, though, you might want to get into all-grain brewing, which involves extracting your own sugar from malted grains. This adds about three hours of time to a recipe and is a rewarding process for many home brewers.

Stir the sugar into the mixture until it's completely dissolved. Keep the heat low (to prevent scorching the sugar) while bringing the entire mixture to a boil. Remove from the heat. This final boil kills any organisms that might be present in the sugar, making sure the yeasts (which will be added later) have no competition.

The Chill

Add cool or cold water to the mixture to bring the total volume up to 2 gallons (8 liters). Cover the pot to keep the mixture sterile. Place the pot in an icy water bath, the fridge, or the freezer to cool it down as quickly as possible. The temperature you're after depends on a number of factors. First, you're going to mix this with 3 more gallons (12 liters) of water, which will affect the finished temperature. Second, you're going to add yeast to the 5-gallon (18-liter) mixture and you want that to be an ideal temperature for the variety of yeast you're using.

The simplest strategy is to cool the 2-gallon (8-liter) mixture down quite a bit before mixing it with 3 gallons (12 liters) of water in a 5-gallon (18-liter) carboy. Use a thermometer to check the total mixture's temperature. If it is too warm for the yeast, cool it down more. If it is too cool for the yeast, warm it up by letting it come to room temperature or by using a warm water bath.

The Aeration

Rotate and shake the carboy to get it all shaken up well. You need to get lots of froth on top—a sign that it's good and aerated. The yeasts need this oxygen to fuel up on energy and other good stuff for the fermentation.

The Pitch

This is when you add (or "pitch") the yeast into the carboy. Use yeast saved from a previous brew or a new packet of yeast. See the upcoming section "Brewing Tools & Ingredients" for information on yeasts. Repeat the process of rolling and shaking the carboy to get the yeasts mixed in well. Add a blow-off tube (also discussed in "Brewing Tools & Ingredients") to the carboy.

The Primary Ferment

Out of sunlight (perhaps covered with a cloth or an old T-shirt), give the mixture five to seven days for the yeasts to do most of their work. As mentioned before, the first four to eight hours aren't fermentation but rather the time when the yeasts grab energy from oxygen. The next two to three days are when the yeasts are most active and a blow-off tube is best to funnel off the foam that's produced. When the yeasts' activity slows down, you can switch to a regular airlock. Don't shake the mixture up when switching tops. We want the yeasts and sediment to settle fairly completely to the bottom of the carboy by the end of the fermentation. When the sediment has fallen, you can proceed with bottling. If you used honey for your primary sweetener (meaning it's the only sweetener you used), the fermentation can take months.

The Bottling

Use a siphon hose to transfer the beer to a bottling bucket. (Learn more about these tools later in this chapter.) This stage is called "racking." Be careful not to disturb the sediment/yeasts at the bottom of the carboy.

Add more sugar to the beer and mix in gently. Don't overagitate. Again, use any sweetener you prefer in the amount of ¾ cup, but avoid granulated sugar because of the cidery taste it lends. Sweetening here provides the yeasts with additional food so they'll produce carbon dioxide in the bottles—that's your carbonation.

Instead of adding sugar during the bottling stage, you can save back 1 pint (½ liter) of the sweet tea mixture (in a sanitized jar) and use it instead of additional sugar. This is called "Krausening." Put the bottling bucket in a raised position, such as on a countertop, with the spigot facing you. Use a bottling hose or wand inserted into the spigot to fill the bottles. With the hose or wand inserted fully into the bottles, fill the bottles to the top. When you remove the hose or wand, the beer will be at the perfect level, leaving a 1- to 1½-inch (2.5 to 3.75cm) space for the carbonation. If you're using Grolsch-style bottles, secure the lids. If you're using bottles with removable caps, use a bottle capper to crimp down the lids.

The Bottle Conditioning

A secondary fermentation occurs after you bottle the beer. Leave your bottles at room temperature or even in cooler storage for five to seven days or longer.

You can drink the beer after five to seven days or let it age more. If you used honey for your primary sweetener, you should let it age for about 1 year. In very warm locations, because bottles might explode, it's best to keep them at a reasonable room temperature or cooler storage. And that's the process of brewing your own beer! Let's now talk about the tools and ingredients you need.

Brewing Tools & Ingredients

Unlike other, more flexible forms of fermentation, making your own home brews means you need some gadgets. There's some leeway, though, so don't be too scared. First, we'll talk about the tools and then we'll cover the ingredients.

Tools & Equipment

What I'll include here is a general list of the most basic home brewer's tools and equipment. Take this list with you to your local beer-making supply store and get their advice too. I won't include basic kitchen utensils, such as wooden stirring spoons and measuring cups.

Big Sink

You can get by with a small sink (that's all I have currently), but a big sink helps with being able to rinse, wash, sterilize, and water-bathe the larger containers you'll use in home brewing.

Bottle Brush

You should make a habit of rinsing containers and bottles right after use to prevent the buildup of dried-out solids that are hard to clean. Still, sometimes you'll need a little extra help with cleaning. A beer-supply store will have a long-handled bottle brush. You can even bend the brush into various positions for hard-to-reach places.

Sanitizing Solution

Some people use a bleach solution, but others say this contributes a metallic flavor to the brew. My friend Gerard recommends the commercial solution Star-San (see Appendix A for sources), which causes no "off" flavor. You might also consider using vinegar, although it might contribute a flavor. Don't use raw vinegar because you don't want to introduce competing acetic-acid-producing organisms. I prefer to pour boiling water over all my tools for a simple sterilization.

2½-Gallon (10-Liter) Pot

When choosing a 2½-gallon (10-liter) pot, choose stainless steel if you can to minimize reactions. You need this to simmer your tea.

Thermometer

It's helpful to know the temperature of your fermenting mixture so you can provide the right environment for the yeast culture. A basic, long-stemmed thermometer that ranges from 40°F to 200°F (4°C to 93°C) works well.

Filter Sock

Also called a "hop sack," a filter sock is like a big tea bag. You can get it at a beer-supply store or paint store. You'll need it to create the "tea" with herbs and specialty grains. After use, rinse it well in cool water and save it for the next time. Unless it gets contaminated somehow, it doesn't need to be sterilized before each use. Being boiled in the tea takes care of sterilizing it. You don't absolutely need this if you want to use a fine strainer though.

Large Strainer

Use a food-grade plastic or stainless steel large strainer. You'll need this when it comes time to rinse the herbs and grains in the filter sock.

5-Gallon (18-Liter) Carboy With Airlock

The carboy is a giant 5-gallon (18-liter) container. You can get it in glass for about $35 or get a less expensive food-grade plastic variety (used for bottled water). The airlock is the special apparatus (discussed in Chapter 4) that puts a water barrier between the liquid and the outside air, but it lets the gases produced by the yeasts escape. The airlock should fit into a rubber cork, which sits inside the carboy's top opening. Beer-supply stores usually have these ready to go for you or you can search the Internet for do-it-yourself instructions.

Blow-Off Tube

For the first two to three days of primary fermentation, the yeasts will be most active, producing a lot of gas and foam, which can plug an airlock, spilling beer foam everywhere. Unless your carboy has a lot of extra space, you'll need to use a blow-off tube during this time rather than an airlock. The blow-off tube is a 1¼-inch-diameter (3cm) piece of flexible, transparent tubing. You can find one at a beer-supply shop. Insert one end of the tube into the carboy opening. Use a long piece of plastic wrap as "tape" around the tube and the carboy opening to hold them together (as well as prevent air from going into the carboy). Place the other end of the tube in a container of water, which prevents air from going through the tube into the carboy but lets the yeasts' gases get out.

Funnel

You need a food-handler's funnel with a long tapered neck to pour your sweet "tea" into the carboy. This is the best way to do it without making a big mess!

Siphoning Tube

Use a narrow, transparent, flexible tube to siphon off the beer after the primary fermentation. You don't want to tip or otherwise move the carboy to pour the beer out or you'll disturb the sediment at the bottom and get it into your beer. Siphoning is the way to avoid this. Beer-supply shops sell various solutions—some easier to use than others. You need a tube that's long enough to reach from near the bottom of the inside of the carboy all the way to your bottling bucket.

5-Gallon (18-Liter) Bottling Bucket

Use a 5-gallon (18-liter) bottling bucket to mix your beer (after the primary fermentation) with additional sweetener before it goes into the bottles. This is basically a 5-gallon (18-liter) bucket with a spigot at the bottom, letting you easily fill your bottles. Quite often, beer-supply stores make these by drilling a hole near the bottom and then inserting a washer and the spigot. If the washer is too small, beer leaks out. In this case, buy a bigger washer from a hardware store. You can skip using a bottling bucket entirely if you're planning to place your sweetener directly into the bottles before filling them.

Bottling Wand

A bottling wand will help you fill the bottles very neatly and without spilling. You can use a siphoning tube, but the bottling wand gives you more control. You connect the plain end to the spigot on the bottling bucket. Insert the spring end into a beer bottle. Depress the spring and turn on the spigot so the beer will flow. Fill the bottle with beer to the top and release the pressure on the bottle wand shut-off spring. Remove the wand from the bottle. The displaced wand leaves the right amount of beer in the bottle for good carbonation.

Bottles

You have two choices: Use Grolsch or Grolsch-style bottles with permanent ceramic caps and rubber or plastic seals or reuse today's commercial beer bottles.

There are advantages and disadvantages to both. The Grolsch bottles are more expensive but can last a very long time. Reused conventional bottles are easy to come by—ask your friends to save you some or visit a store to buy some back for the cost of the state bottle recycling deposit. Bottles can be as little as 5 cents! The seals on Grolsch-style bottles wear out over time but can be replaced. Reused beer bottles need new caps. They're inexpensive in my area—144 for $3.99—but still a continuing expense. If you're using new caps, you'll need a capper (discussed in the next section). Finally, the Grolsch bottles can be larger than conventional beer bottles. If sharing beer with others, you might find it easier to part with the less expensive and smaller conventional bottles—and a bonus is they fit perfectly in recycled cardboard beer carriers.

Over time, both types of bottles can develop cracks or weak spots from the stress of built-up pressure. Discontinue use if this happens. Bottles are best cared for by rinsing immediately after use. Wash in hot soapy water or the dishwasher. Store in a dust-free, clean cupboard or otherwise clean area until ready to fill again. You can place a clean towel over the top to prevent dust from settling on them. If you use the hot cycle of the dishwasher and they stay very clean through storage, you might not need to resterilize before filling.

How many bottles do you need? If you're using repurposed, conventional 12-ounce (340-gram) bottles, you'll need 50 for a full 5-gallon (18-liter) batch of beer. Grolsch and Grolsch-style bottles vary in size, with newer bottles being smaller. Some are 16 ounces (450 grams), some are 25 ounces (710 grams), and some are even larger. Five gallons (18 liters) is 640 ounces (18 kilograms). Divide that by the capacity (in ounces) of your bottles and you'll know how many bottles you need for a 5-gallon (18-liter) batch.

Bottle Capper

You'll need a bottle capper if you're adding new caps to conventional bottles. From the various styles, the most useful and pleasing seems to be single-handled and adjustable. The two-handled styles are harder to use. Having an adjustable capper is helpful if you have an assortment of bottle sizes. A decent adjustable capper is about $32 in my area.

Those are the basic tools. Stopping in at your local brew shop is the best way to get set up. The people are usually very friendly and frugal-minded and are probably also willing to share money-saving shortcuts. Now let's talk about the ingredients.

Brewing Ingredients

Basically, you need four ingredients when brewing beer: water, sugar, yeast, and herbs. The herbs are optional because you can make beer from just the first three (although it will lack much flavor). Herbs actually include *anything* you might use for flavor or medicinal effect: actual herbs, hops, grasses, grains, vegetables, fruits, or anything else you can dream up.

What about wine? Wine starts with fruit and its juice provides three of the basic beer-brewing components: water, sugar, and herbs. All *you* need to add is yeast. And, of course, the right anaerobic, clean environment.

Let's talk about what you should keep in mind when sourcing yeast and herbs.

Yeasts

Some companies keep traditional and modern strains of yeast going and offer them for sale to home brewers. Each strain has its own characteristics, imparts unique flavors, and prefers optimum fermenting temperatures. You'll see these qualities when shopping. (See Appendix B for a recommended online supplier or visit your local brewing shop.)

Some yeasts come ready to dump into the carboy (called "smack packs"), while others require a wake-up phase. Refer to the yeast's package instructions for how to do this. The recipes in this book are written for smack packs, but you can use yeast that requires waking up if you follow the wake-up instructions first.

A packet of yeast is about $8 and provides enough culture to ferment a 5-gallon (18-liter) batch of home brew. You need never buy another packet after the first if you save the first batch's yeast and sediment in the fridge for the next batch. (Make sure to use a sterilized jar.)

Which yeast do you need? For light beers, a yeast that works almost universally with all flavors is American Ale yeast. It's good with herbs, fruit, spices, and hops. On the other hand, Scottish Ale yeast is good for dark brews (and it also works well for light brews).

Before companies got into propagating yeasts for brewers' convenience, families kept their own varieties of yeasts alive in creative ways. For example, in Norway, people used a birch log or juniper branch. They placed one of these inside the fermenting barrel during the primary fermentation. The yeasts settled at the bottom as well as coated the log or branch. After the beer was drawn off, they placed the log or branch somewhere to dry out. Then they inoculated the next batch of brew with these yeasts, along with fresh branches or logs to capture yeasts for the next time.

In this book's recipes, I call for particular strains of yeast. Choose another yeast if you'd like, but adjust the fermentation time and temperature according to what's recommended for your yeast.

Herbs

The sky's the limit with what you can use to flavor beers. Not only typical herbs fit this category but also grasses, fruits, vegetables, grains, and anything else you might use. You'll see what I mean when you peruse the recipes, but let me give you some examples now.

You can use fresh or dried plants, such as mint, marjoram, borage, red clover, spruce, pine, nettles, yarrow, lavender, or rosemary. Choose the ones you want based on their medicinal properties or just because you like a certain flavor. If you're using fresh, use three times as many as dried. You saw when I discussed making the "tea" that a good amount of dried herbs to place in the filter sock is about 5 cups dried with 3 cups of specialty grains. But really, whatever amount you'd like is fine—the more herbs, the stronger the flavor and effect.

You can add specialty grains, which brewers usually get from a brew shop. We're talking barley or other grains in a million (okay, not quite) different styles. You've got roasted or toasted, special varieties, and lots of variants. They each impart particular flavors and you'll get information from the brew shop staff or catalog. Because the specialty grains are usually roasted or otherwise heated, they don't offer any viable enzymes into the process. Additionally, they're not usually a source of sugar for the yeasts.

You can use fruits, vegetables, or roots, such as carrots, beets, or dandelion roots. Everything should be well boiled when making the tea to prevent introducing competing organisms for the yeasts. This also goes for herbs and specialty grains.

Now that we've covered the history, the particulars of alcohol fermentation, the overall methods, and information on tools and ingredients, you're ready to start brewing. Let's get going!

Czech Porter

A darker cousin of the Czech Pilsner, this rich and malty beer has hints of roasted coffee and chocolate as well as floral hops notes. Don't forget: You can save the yeast and sediment in a clean, sterilized jar in the fridge. Then use it for your next batch of dark beer—even months later.

Yield:	Prep time:	Ferment time:	Ferment type:
5 gallons (18 liters)	3 hours	14 days	alcohol

2 cups Special Belgian Coffee Roast grains

2 cups Chocolate Patent Malt grains

5 gallons (18 liters) water, divided

1oz (30g) Czech Saaz hops

3¼ cups dark malt syrup extract, divided

1 package of Czech Pilsner yeast

1. Place the grains in a filter sock. Tie the sock. In a 2½-gallon (10-liter) pot, submerge the sock in 1 gallon (4 liters) of water.

2. Place the pot on the stovetop over medium heat. Slowly bring to a boil, then simmer uncovered for 40 minutes to a few hours. During the last 20 minutes of simmering, open the filter sock and add the hops.

3. Still over a gentle simmer, transfer the filter sock to a strainer over the pot. Rinse with 1 quart (1 liter) of hot water. Don't squeeze the sock. Discard the grains and hops. Rinse the filter sock and place it somewhere to dry out.

4. Add 2 cups of malt syrup to the pot and stir well. Slowly bring to a boil while stirring. Remove the pot from the heat.

5. Add 3 quarts (3 liters) of water to the pot. Transfer the pot to an ice water bath to cool the mixture as quickly as possible. Keep the pot covered.

6. Add the remaining 3 gallons (12 liters) of water to a carboy. Use a funnel to add the grain and hops mixture. This mixture should be around 70°F (21°C). If too warm, use the ice water bath to cool it down.

7. Shake the carboy to introduce a lot of air. Add the yeast. Shake the carboy again to introduce more air. Place an airlock or a blow-off tube on top of the carboy. Leave at room temperature for 5 to 7 days or until the yeast activity slows and the yeasts and sediment settle at the bottom.

8. Siphon the beer into a bottling bucket, trying not to disturb the sediment. Add the remaining 1¼ cups of malt syrup. Stir well without overagitating.

9. Raise the bottling bucket to a higher location, such as a countertop. Insert a bottling wand into the bucket spigot. Fill and cap the bottles.

10. Let the bottles sit at room temperature for 5 to 7 days and then keep them in a cooler location until you're ready to drink. Chill before serving if desired. Store indefinitely in cool storage.

Scottish Ale

This is another darker cousin of traditional ales but with the magic of heather flowers and Nordic Lyndon flowers.

Yield:	Prep time:	Ferment time:	Ferment type:
5 gallons (18 liters)	3 hours	14 days	alcohol

2 cups Honey Malt grains

2 cups Crystal 120L grains

2 cups Belgian Biscuit grains

5 gallons (18 liters) water, divided

3¼ cups dark malt syrup extract, divided

2oz (60g) dried heather flowers

4oz (110g) dried Lyndon flowers

2 black tea bags

1 package of Scottish Ale yeast

1. Place the grains in a filter sock. Tie the sock. In a 2½-gallon (10-liter) pot, submerge the sock in 1 gallon (4 liters) of water.

2. Place the pot on the stovetop over medium heat. Slowly bring to a boil, then simmer uncovered for 40 minutes to a few hours.

3. Still over a gentle simmer, transfer the filter sock to a strainer over the pot. Rinse with 1 quart (1 liter) of hot water. Don't squeeze the sock. Discard the grains. Rinse the filter sock and place it somewhere to dry out.

4. Add 2 cups of malt syrup to the pot and stir well. Slowly bring the mixture to a boil while stirring.

5. In a small pot on the stovetop over medium heat, combine the flowers, black tea bags, and 1 quart (1 liter) of water. Bring to a simmer, then cover and let steep for 20 minutes. Use a strainer to strain the flowers and tea bags. Discard. Transfer the tea to a bigger pot. Remove the big pot from the heat.

6. Add 2 quarts (2 liters) of water to the big pot. Transfer the pot to an ice water bath to cool the mixture as quickly as possible. Keep the pot covered.

7. Add the remaining 3 gallons (12 liters) of water to a carboy. Use a funnel to add the grain and tea mixtures. This mixture should be around 70°F (21°C). If too warm, use the ice water bath to cool it down.

8. Shake the carboy to introduce a lot of air. Add the yeast. Shake the carboy again to introduce more air. Place an airlock or a blow-off tube on top of the carboy. Leave at room temperature for 5 to 7 days or until the yeast activity slows and the yeasts and sediment settle at the bottom.

9. Siphon the beer into a bottling bucket, trying not to disturb the sediment. Add the remaining 1¼ cups of malt syrup. Stir well without overagitating.

10. Raise the bottling bucket to a higher location, such as a countertop. Insert a bottling wand into the bucket spigot. Fill and cap the bottles.

11. Let the bottles sit at room temperature for 5 to 7 days and then keep them in a cooler location until you're ready to drink. Chill before serving if desired. Store indefinitely in cool storage.

Ginger Ale

This is a peppery, sweet concoction that aids digestion and leaves you feeling satisfied but wanting a little more. Don't have a juicer? Boil 2 pounds (1 kilogram) of shredded ginger in 1 quart (1 liter) of water for 30 minutes, then strain out the pulp. Reduce the amount of water added in step 6 by 1 quart (1 liter).

Yield:	Prep time:	Ferment time:	Ferment type:
5 gallons (18 liters)	3 hours	14 days	alcohol

4 cups Aromatica grains

2 cups Crystal 120L grains

2 cups Special Roast grains

5 gallons (18 liters) water, divided

juice from 2lb (1kg) freshly peeled ginger

juice from 2 lemons

3¼ cups light malt syrup extract, divided

1 package of American Ale yeast

1. Place the grains in a filter sock. Tie the sock. In a 2½-gallon (10-liter) pot, submerge the sock in 1 gallon (4 liters) of water.

2. Place the pot on the stovetop over medium heat. Slowly bring to a boil, then simmer uncovered for 40 minutes.

3. Still over a gentle simmer, transfer the filter sock to a strainer over the pot. Rinse with 1 quart (1 liter) of hot water. Don't squeeze the sock. Discard the grains. Rinse the filter sock and place it somewhere to dry out.

4. Add the ginger juice and lemon juice. Bring to a simmer.

5. Add 2 cups of malt syrup and stir well. Slowly bring to a boil while stirring.

6. Add 3 quarts (3 liters) of water to the pot. Transfer the pot to an ice water bath to cool the mixture as quickly as possible. Keep the pot covered.

7. Add the remaining 3 gallons (12 liters) of water to a carboy. Use a funnel to add the grain and juice mixture. This mixture should be around 70°F (21°C). If too warm, use the ice water bath to cool it down.

8. Shake the carboy to introduce a lot of air. Add the yeast. Shake the carboy again to introduce more air. Place an airlock or a blow-off tube on top of the carboy. Leave at room temperature for 5 to 7 days or until the yeast activity slows and the yeasts and sediment settle at the bottom.

9. Siphon the beer into a bottling bucket, trying not to disturb the sediment. Add the remaining 1¼ cups of malt syrup. Stir well without overagitating.

10. Raise the bottling bucket to a higher location, such as a countertop. Insert a bottling wand into the bucket spigot. Fill and cap the bottles.

11. Let the bottles sit at room temperature for 5 to 7 days and then keep them in a cooler location until you're ready to drink. Chill before serving if desired. Store indefinitely in cool storage.

Rosemary Ale

This creamy and floral ale warms your heart and settles your stomach. You can substitute dried rosemary for fresh. Use three times less—or 1⅓ quarts (1⅓ liters).

Yield:	Prep time:	Ferment time:	Ferment type:
5 gallons (18 liters)	3 hours	14 days	alcohol

4 cups Aromatica grains

2 cups Crystal 80L grains

5 gallons (18 liters) water, divided

4 quarts (4 liters) fresh rosemary cut into 2-inch (5cm) pieces

3¼ cups light malt syrup extract, divided

1 package of American Ale yeast

1. Place the grains in a filter sock. Tie the sock. In a 2½-gallon (10-liter) pot, submerge the sock in 1 gallon (4 liters) of water.

2. Place the pot on the stovetop over medium heat. Slowly bring to a boil, then simmer uncovered for 40 minutes.

3. Still over a gentle simmer, transfer the filter sock to a strainer over the pot. Rinse with 1 quart (1 liter) of hot water. Don't squeeze the sock. Discard the grains. Rinse the filter sock.

4. Fill the filter sock with the rosemary. Tie the sock and submerge it in the pot. Simmer for 15 minutes.

5. Still over a gentle simmer, transfer the filter sock to a strainer over the pot. Rinse with 1 quart (1 liter) of hot water. Don't squeeze the sock. Discard the herbs. Rinse the filter sock and place it somewhere to dry.

6. Add 2 cups of malt syrup and stir well. Slowly bring the mixture to a boil while stirring.

7. Add 2 quarts (2 liters) of water. Transfer the pot to an ice water bath to cool the mixture as quickly as possible. Keep the pot covered.

8. Add the remaining 3 gallons (12 liters) of water to a carboy. Use a funnel to add the grain and rosemary mixture. This mixture should be around 70°F (21°C). If too warm, use the ice water bath to cool it down.

9. Shake the carboy to introduce a lot of air. Add the yeast. Shake the carboy again to introduce more air. Place an airlock or a blow-off tube on top of the carboy. Leave at room temperature for 5 to 7 days or until the yeast activity slows and the yeasts and sediment settle at the bottom.

10. Siphon the beer into a bottling bucket, trying not to disturb the sediment. Add the remaining 1¼ cups of malt syrup. Stir well without overagitating.

11. Raise the bottling bucket to a higher location, such as a countertop. Insert a bottling wand into the bucket spigot. Fill and cap the bottles.

11. Let the bottles sit at room temperature for 5 to 7 days and then keep them in a cooler location until you're ready to drink. Chill before serving if desired. Store indefinitely in cool storage.

Chocolate & Lavender Ale

Two powerful aphrodisiacs—chocolate and lavender—combine in one beverage that's simultaneously stimulating and calming . You can substitute fresh lavender for dried. Use 6 ounces (170 grams) of fresh lavender petals.

Yield:	Prep time:	Ferment time:	Ferment type:
5 gallons (18 liters)	3 hours	14 days	alcohol

2 cups Honey Malt grains

2 cups Crystal 120L grains

2 cups Belgian Biscuit grains

5 gallons (18 liters) water, divided

2oz (60g) lavender flower powder

4oz (110g) cocoa powder

3¼ cups light malt syrup extract

1 package of American Ale yeast

1. Place the grains in a filter sock. Tie the sock. In a 2½-gallon (10-liter) pot, submerge the sock in 1 gallon (4 liters) of water.

2. Place the pot on the stovetop over medium heat. Slowly bring to a boil, then simmer uncovered for 40 minutes.

3. Still over a gentle simmer, transfer the filter sock to a strainer over the pot. Rinse with 1 quart (1 liter) of hot water. Don't squeeze the sock. Discard the grains. Rinse the filter sock and place it somewhere to dry out.

4. Add the lavender and cocoa powder. Bring to a simmer.

5. Add 2 cups of malt syrup and stir well. Slowly bring the mixture to a boil while stirring.

6. Add 3 quarts (3 liters) of water. Transfer the pot to an ice water bath to cool the mixture as quickly as possible. Keep the pot covered.

7. Add the remaining 3 gallons (12 liters) of water to a carboy. Use a funnel to add the grain, lavender, and cocoa mixture. This mixture should be around 70°F (21°C). If too warm, use the ice water bath to cool it down.

8. Shake the carboy to introduce a lot of oxygen. Add the yeast. Shake the carboy again to introduce more air. Place an airlock or a blow-off tube on top of the carboy. Leave at room temperature for 5 to 7 days or until the yeast activity slows and the yeasts and sediment settle at the bottom.

9. Siphon the beer into a bottling bucket, trying not to disturb the sediment. Add the remaining 1¼ cups of malt syrup. Stir well without overagitating.

10. Raise the bottling bucket to a higher location, such as a countertop. Insert a bottling wand into the bucket spigot. Fill and cap the bottles.

11. Let the bottles sit at room temperature for 5 to 7 days and then keep them in a cooler location until you're ready to drink. Chill before serving if desired. Store indefinitely in cool storage.

Nettle & Lemon Beer

This is the spice trade in a bottle. Its smooth yet fuzzy bubbles tickle your tonsils and strengthen your resolve.

Yield:	Prep time:	Ferment time:	Ferment type:
5 gallons (18 liters)	3 hours	14 days	alcohol

1 cup Aromatica grains

1 cup Special Briess grains

1 cup Crystal 120L grains

2 cups dried nettle leaves

1 cup dried lemon verbena

1 cup dried lemon balm

1 cup dried lemongrass

5 gallons (18 liters) water, divided

3¼ cups light malt syrup extract, divided

1 package of American Ale yeast

1. In a filter sock, combine the grains, nettle leaves, lemon verbena, lemon balm, and lemongrass. Tie the sock. In a 2½-gallon (10-liter) pot, submerge the sock in 1 gallon (4 liters) of water.

2. Place the pot on the stovetop over medium heat. Slowly bring to a boil, then simmer uncovered for 40 minutes.

3. Still over a gentle simmer, transfer the filter sock to a strainer over the pot. Rinse with 1 quart (1 liter) of hot water. Don't squeeze the sock. Discard the grains and herbs. Rinse the filter sock and place it somewhere to dry out.

4. Add 2 cups of malt syrup and stir well. Slowly bring the mixture to a boil while stirring.

5. Add 3 quarts (3 liters) of water. Transfer the pot to an ice water bath to cool the mixture as quickly as possible. Keep the pot covered.

6. Add the remaining 3 gallons (12 liters) of water to a carboy. Use a funnel to add the grain, nettle, and lemon mixture. This mixture should be around 70°F (21°C). If too warm, use the ice water bath to cool it down.

7. Shake the carboy to introduce a lot of air. Add the yeast. Shake the carboy again to introduce more air. Place an airlock or a blow-off tube on top of the carboy. Leave at room temperature for 5 to 7 days or until the yeast activity slows and the yeasts and sediment settle at the bottom.

8. Siphon the beer into a bottling bucket, taking care not to disturb the sediment. Add the remaining 1¼ cups of malt syrup. Stir well without overagitating the mixture.

9. Raise the bottling bucket to a higher location, such as a countertop. Insert a bottling wand into the bucket spigot. Fill and cap the bottles.

10. Let the bottles sit at room temperature for 5 to 7 days and then keep them in a cooler location until you're ready to drink. Chill before serving if desired. They'll keep indefinitely in cool storage.

Beans

Ever have trouble digesting beans? Well, this chapter shares the ins and outs of fermenting beans, including why it's a beneficial method of preparing beans for digestion. We'll also explore some tasty bean recipes to get your digestion moving.

Fermenting of Beans

I feel like a broken record telling you how we're fermenting the same as usual. But that's not completely true for this chapter on fermenting beans.

Here's the first reason why: Beans contain extremely complex sugars (called "oligo-saccharides") that can cause a lot of digestive discomfort. Fermentation breaks down those sugars into simpler components that don't stress out our digestive systems—just like soaking and cooking beans for long periods of time does. But with fermentation, you've got those other benefits I've mentioned time and time again: increased vitamins and enzymes as well as probiotics.

The second reason fermentation of beans is special concerns the soybean. In its unfermented form, soy isn't so good for us to eat. It contains high levels of phytic acid, which prevents mineral absorption in the digestive system. Components in soy interfere with protein digestion. Hormone-mimicking phytoestrogens disrupt gland function and might be linked to infertility and breast cancer. And there are more strikes against it, but I think I've said enough. The good news is that when soy is fermented (as in the making of natto, tempeh, miso, or long-fermented soy sauce), these issues go away, making it fine to eat in moderation. (Traditionally, healthy Asian cultures ate about 2 teaspoons per day of fermented soy foods—and not as a meat replacer but as a condiment to enhance a meal.)

So in this chapter, I offer two bean pastes: Middle Eastern hummus (my family's traditional recipe) and a Mexican variety you can make from any leftover beans. And in the rest of the chapter, we focus on fermenting soy, turning it into natto, tempeh, and miso. Interestingly, we'll use very specific mold and bacteria starter cultures (see Appendix B for places to buy them) to produce the signature fermented soy dishes of the world. And this chapter also includes a bonus recipe for delicious burrito roll-ups.

Hummus

Hummus Recipes

Hummus

Roasted sesame and chickpeas combine for this garlic and lemon-infused signature Middle Eastern bean paste. This hummus is my Arabic family's traditional recipe. My grandmother—for whom I was named—taught my mother to make it. And she taught me. I've heard from others that it's heavy on the tahini. Even though I disagree, you might feel the same and that's okay. Make it your own by reducing the tahini. You could try adding cumin for extra smokiness. Even use cayenne pepper. Hummus is very adaptable.

Yield:	Prep time:	Ferment time:	Ferment type:
2 cups	5 minutes	7 to 12 hours	lacto

2 cups cooked garbanzo beans (chickpeas), rinsed if canned

3 rounded tbsp roasted sesame tahini

juice from 1 lemon

3 garlic cloves

½ tsp sea salt

¼ cup water

¼ cup starter culture (Appendix B)

paprika, fresh parsley, or extra-virgin olive oil

1. In a blender or food processor, combine the beans, tahini, lemon juice, garlic, salt, water, and starter culture. Blend until smooth.

2. Transfer the mixture to a wide-mouth quart (liter) jar. Cover tightly with a lid or an airlock.

3. Leave at room temperature for 7 to 12 hours or up to 1 day. Store in the fridge for up to 2 weeks or in the freezer for up to 2 to 3 months. When serving, garnish with paprika, parsley, and/or extra-virgin olive oil.

Roasted Red Pepper Hummus

In this recipe from my friend Katie Mae, the peppers make it slightly sweet, while the fermentation adds tanginess.

Yield:	Prep time:	Ferment time:	Ferment type:
3 cups	5 minutes	7 to 12 hours	lacto

2 cups soaked and cooked garbanzo beans

2 roasted red bell peppers

⅓ cup tahini

¼ cup extra-virgin olive oil, plus more

¼ cup starter culture (Appendix B)

2 tbsp freshly squeezed lemon juice

1 tsp sea salt

½ tsp paprika, plus more

1. In a blender or food processor, combine all the ingredients. Blend on high until a thick and creamy paste forms. If too thick, add 1 tablespoon of water at a time until it reaches the desired consistency.

2. Transfer the mixture to a wide-mouth quart (liter) jar. Cover tightly with a lid or an airlock.

3. Leave at room temperature overnight. Store in the fridge for up to 2 weeks or in the freezer for up to 2 to 3 months.

Other Bean Recipes

If you can ferment hummus made from beans, why not ferment other beans too? From fermented bean dip to traditional fermented soybean dishes, such as natty or tempeh, here are a selection of recipes to try.

Bean Paste

This condiment is fantastic with breakfast burritos, chips and salsa, tacos, and salads. It really shines as part of Latin American or Mexican meals. Fermenting bean paste can really get bubbly, especially in warm temperatures. I urge you to burp your jar daily to release pent-up gases—and do this over the sink or a towel in case it tries to escape the jar.

Yield:	Prep time:	Ferment time:	Ferment type:
1 quart (1 liter)	5 minutes	1 to 3 days	lacto

1 medium onion, preferably red, ends trimmed and skin removed

3 to 6 garlic cloves

3 or more cups cooked black, pinto, or red beans, drained and rinsed if canned

½ tbsp sea salt

¼ cup starter culture (Appendix B)

1. In a blender or food processor, combine the onions and garlic. Blend until well chopped.

2. Add the beans, salt, and starter culture. Blend until smooth.

3. Transfer the mixture to a wide-mouth quart (liter) jar. Cover tightly with a lid or an airlock.

4. Leave at room temperature for 1 to 3 days. If using a lid, burp your jar once a day to release pent-up gases. Store in the fridge for up to 2 weeks or in the freezer for up to 2 to 3 months.

Mexican Burrito Roll-Ups

Bursting with flavors from various homemade ferments (salsa, sour cream, beans, guacamole, and cheese or anything else you'd like), these roll-ups beat out regular burritos any day.

Yield:	Prep time:	Ferment time:	Ferment type:
8 burritos	5 minutes	none	lacto

8 Sourdough Crêpes (page 210) or flour tortillas

1 cup Bean Paste (page 187), room temperature

1 cup Mild Salsa (page 67) or Spicy Salsa (page 68), room temperature

1 cup Guacamole (page 108), room temperature

1 cup Sour Cream (page 260), room temperature

1 cup shredded cheddar or Colby-Jack cheese

1. In a dry, seasoned cast-iron skillet on the stovetop over medium heat, warm the crêpes one by one.

2. Spread 2 tablespoons of bean paste on each crêpe. Top each with up to 2 tablespoons each of desired other fillings: salsa, guacamole, sour cream, and/or shredded cheese. Roll up the crêpes and serve immediately.

Tempeh

Tempeh is an Indonesian fermented soybean cake—high in protein with a nutty, firm texture and rich, earthy flavor. If you can't get hulled soybeans, you can use regular soybeans and remove the hulls yourself. Soak the beans for 18 hours, then squeeze the beans to split them and make the hulls come off. Because of the soaking, cooking will only take about 30 minutes. You can eat this tempeh raw, steamed, simmered, sautéed, or fried—in a soup, stew, or stir-fry.

Yield:	Prep time:	Ferment time:	Ferment type:
6 cups	5 minutes	1 to 3 days	mold

2 cups hulled soybeans

6 cups water

2 tbsp white vinegar

¾ tsp tempeh starter (see Appendix B for sources)

1. In a medium saucepan on the stovetop over medium-high heat, combine the soybeans and water. Bring to a boil and cook until swelled and softened but still a little firm, about 30 minutes to 1 hour. Drain the beans, discarding the water. Pat the beans dry with a clean towel. Place the beans in a medium bowl and let them cool to room temperature.

2. Add the vinegar and mix well. Add the tempeh starter and mix well again. Spread the bean mixture out in two quart (liter) resealable bags in flat layers about 1 to 1½ inches (2.5 to 3.75cm) thick. Poke holes in the top layer of the bags at ½-inch (1.25cm) intervals for ventilation.

3. Place the containers in a dehydrator at 88°F (31°C) (or between 85°F and 91°F [29°C to 33°C]). Check after 12 hours. Because the fermentation will cause the beans to generate their own heat, you might need to reduce or eliminate the external heat source. Use a thermometer to check the actual temperature.

4. After 24 hours or so, a white culture (an active, growing mushroom culture) will start to cover the surface of the beans. After that, it will grow through the beans and they'll smell nutty. Stop the fermentation when the culture has spread fully throughout beans, about 24 to 48 hours.

5. Cut the tempeh into strips and store tightly wrapped (preferably individually or a few wrapped together) for up to 2 weeks or in the freezer for up to 1 year.

Natto

Stringy and slippery with a strong smell but with a taste worth acquiring for its health benefits, *natto* has been eaten by the Japanese for more than 1,000 years—typically over rice. Natto is a traditional part of a Japanese breakfast, packed with nutrition. During the fermentation, the beneficial bacteria (*bacillus subtilis*) not only improve the digestibility of soybeans, but they also create vitamin K2—essential for radiant skin, a healthy heart, and strong bones. Vitamin K2 isn't found in any other plant food.

Yield:	Prep time:	Ferment time:	Ferment type:
6 cups	5 minutes	1 to 3 days	bacterial

1lb (450g) organic, non-GMO soybeans (about 2 cups)

0.05 gram natto spores (see Appendix B for sources)

2 tsp water, boiled for 5 to 10 minutes to sterilize

1. Wash the soybeans thoroughly. Place in a large pot and cover with triple the amount of water. Soak for 9 to 12 hours or overnight if more convenient.

2. In a colander, drain and rinse the beans. Transfer the beans back to the pot and cover them with water. Place the pot on the stovetop over medium-high heat. Bring to a boil, then cover and simmer for 12 hours or overnight, replenishing the water as needed to keep the beans covered.

3. From here on out, you must sterilize all utensils and bowls that touch the beans or natto spores. To sterilize them, simmer them in boiling water for 2 minutes or pour boiling water over them.

4. Drain the cooked beans and place them in a sterilized 12-cup square or rectangular glass container (preferably one that has an airtight glass lid). The beans should be about 1½ inches (3.75cm) deep. Use additional containers if the beans are too deep. Cover with a sterilized cheesecloth while the beans cool to a warm room temperature. Don't touch them to check.

5. Measure the natto spores with the special spoon that comes with them. Fill the spoon halfway with culture. In a small bowl or cup, combine the spores and sterilized water. Stir well. Pour the spores mixture over the beans. Stir together carefully using a sterilized stainless steel or plastic spoon (not wood).

6. Spread the beans back out if necessary. If any beans spill out, discard them rather than return them to the container.

7. Place a glass lid (or plastic wrap) on the container. If you're using a lid and it's not airtight, place a layer of plastic wrap under the lid.

8. Preheat the oven or a dehydrator to 100°F (40°C).

9. Place the container in the oven or dehydrator. Let the soybean mixture ferment for 22 to 24 hours, keeping the temperature steady at 100°F (40°C). Near the end of the fermentation period, remove the container, open it, and gently stir the soybeans. When done, they should be stringy and slimy, and they might have whitish crystals forming on top. If the natto smells like ammonia, it has overfermented and should be discarded.

10. Place the container in the fridge overnight. Serve for breakfast or keep for later. Store for up to 4 to 6 weeks, during which time the flavor increases, they get stringier, and more white crystals form.

Mugi Miso

Made from fermenting barley, this widely popular chunky miso is mellow, sweet, and flavorful—wonderful in soups and stews. Use mugi miso as a paste to marinate meat, fish, or vegetables. Add to stews or cooked dishes—but add at the end of the cooking time (and be sure not to boil it) for the best flavor. You can also dilute it with water for a delicious soup or gravy base.

Yield:	Prep time:	Ferment time:	Ferment type:
6 cups	5 minutes	6 to 10 months	mold

3¾ cups soybeans

17.6oz (500g) barley koji (see Appendix B for sources)

1 cup plus 2 tsp sea salt, divided, plus more

1. Place the soybeans in a large pot and cover with triple the amount of water. Soak the soybeans overnight. Drain the water, then cover the beans with triple the amount of fresh water.

2. Place the pot on the stovetop over medium-high heat. Bring to a boil, then simmer covered until the soybeans are tender, about 3 to 4 hours.

3. Drain the soybeans, saving 1⅔ cups cooking water. Let the soybeans and reserved cooking water cool in separate containers to room temperature.

4. Add the koji, cooled cooking water, and 1 cup of salt to the pot. Mix well.

5. In a clean, cylindrical ½-gallon (2-liter) crock, sprinkle 1 teaspoon of salt on the bottom and sides. Rub the salt all over, leaving it inside. Place the bean mixture in the crock and pack down well. Sprinkle the remaining 1 teaspoon of salt over the top. Place parchment paper or natural wax paper over the bean mixture. Top that with a lid or plate and a 1-pound (450-gram) weight to maintain the pressure. Cover with a cloth. Secure with a rubber band or tie.

6. Leave in a cool location to ferment for 6 to 18 months. (If the location is warmer, the fermentation might proceed more quickly.) After about 1 month, open up the container to see if liquid has risen to the top. This is tamari (fermented soy sauce). Stir the mixture, bringing the bottom miso up to the top. If there's no tamari, add more weight. Stir again after the second and third months. If you ever find white mold on top, skim it away and discard. This is normal at the surface where air touches the ferment. During the fermentation, the color will change from light to darker, eventually turning a reddish-brown color. It will smell earthy and sweet.

7. You can begin eating the miso after 6 months. Take out what you need and leave the rest in the crock to continue aging. It's best after 1 year. Store in cold storage indefinitely.

Grains

In this chapter, we move on to explore the fermentation of grains. You're likely already familiar with sourdough bread, which is actually fermented dough. Sourdough preparation is a nutritious and easy way to eat fermented grains. This chapter will give you all you need to know about how to care for and use a sourdough starter, along with lots and lots of recipes—most of which use sourdough and a few that don't.

Sourdough Is Fermented Dough

Fermenting grains is most frequently known as the art of sourdough. The word "sourdough" itself reveals the process: The dough is soured. Remember that the organisms in fermentation produce acids, alcohol, and vinegar, and the presence of some or all of those in fermented foods explains why they're called sour. Additionally, because the grains are usually ground up and mixed with water into a dough, I imagine that over time, the words "soured" and "dough" became the one word: sourdough.

We'll talk later about how souring or fermenting grains makes them more digestible. On the practical side of things, souring dough rises: The fermenting organisms give off gases as they eat the simple sugars in flour. The gases lift the dough into fluffy pancakes or round loaves, among other things.

You already read in Chapter 1 how the Egyptians might have been the first to discover soured and leavened bread, possibly by accident. Historians speculate that someone left a lump of dough in a warm place for a while, and when coming upon it again, they found it had puffed up beautifully. (We now know that fermenting organisms did this work.) Then it was baked and the resulting loaf had a pleasant sour tang and was probably easier to digest. Then someone especially observant realized they could save a bit of previously soured dough and add it to the next batch as a starter to get the process "started" again.

This is how people baked bread for centuries. Cultures developed, shared, and nurtured their own particular sourdough starters. Sourdough starters are active colonies of beneficial yeasts and bacteria particular to a region, living in a batter of flour and water. People kept their starters alive through regular feedings of more flour and water. They added portions of the starter to various doughs to achieve leavening, souring, and improvement in digestibility.

Historians say that sourdough starters kept the Western settlers of the United States alive. Settlers and prospectors—whether alone or in a wagon train—carried sourdough pots from east to west. Each evening or as they had need, they'd feed the starter with flour and water and then take out whatever amount was needed to make cakes, pancakes, biscuits, or loaves. Interestingly, old-time experienced prospectors in the United States and Canada are called sourdoughs! I wonder if this had to do with a telltale sourdough bucket or a sour disposition?

What can you make from soured dough or sourdough? You can make almost any dough-based food from soured dough. I've made bread, dinner rolls, hamburger buns, biscuits, muffins, sweet cakes and quick breads, brownies, pot pies, donuts, pasta, cinnamon rolls, English muffins, pancakes, crêpes, gingerbread, waffles, and probably more. Yes—all from sourdough. Look for a lot of those recipes later in this chapter.

What's So Great About Sourdough?

The organisms at work in a sourdough starter and therefore in a soured dough are wild yeasts and bacteria (*lactobacilli*). A starter can last for hundreds of years—really, as long as a person is able to take care of it with regular feedings and by providing a suitable environment. The organisms work together to add B vitamins to grains, break down gluten for better digestion, and neutralize phytic acid and enzyme inhibitors. The organisms are pretty versatile in that they can work in a range of temperatures. Finally, the beneficial acids produced by the wild organisms protect the bread from going stale as easily as unsoured bread.

Phytic acid is an antinutrient that binds to minerals in your gut, preventing mineral absorption and leading to mineral deficiencies. *Enzyme inhibitors* suppress the proper functioning of your digestive enzymes, leading to poor digestion and digestive discomfort.

By contrast, most modern leavened breads are made using a laboratory-produced, selected strain of yeast called "baker's yeast" or "active dry yeast." This yeast must be purchased again and again because it gets used up in the recipes. It has to work quickly or it loses its oomph. Baker's yeast is pretty picky about its environment, requiring just the right temperature and not too much acidity to work well. This yeast isn't capable of predigesting gluten or neutralizing antinutrients. And lastly, breads made with commercial yeast stale easily.

Sourdough's Wild Yeasts & Bacteria

While many fermentations use one type of organism, sourdough relies on the work of yeasts and bacteria. A good sourdough starter is a living colony of these organisms in a good balance: more yeasts than bacteria. This balance in favor of the yeasts is essential to get a good rise because it's the yeasts that really raise a bread through their production of carbon dioxide.

Yeasts and bacteria feed on simple sugars in flour. Flour has simple sugars and complex sugars readily available. The organisms eat the simplest sugars while they release enzymes to break up the more complex ones. Now you know that the predigestion they achieve is really for themselves (to make more food), but we also benefit from it.

As a whole, all the various organisms in the starter do the same things we've discussed before: eat and proliferate as well as give off gas (carbon dioxide), lactic acid, alcohol, and vinegar. What do all these by-products do? Carbon dioxide makes a sourdough starter bubbly and puffs up a rising bread dough. The lactic acid acts as a natural antibiotic in the starter, preventing it from getting overtaken by spoiling organisms. The lactic acid, alcohol, and vinegar give the bread a sour smell and flavor. The vinegar keeps the bread fresh longer.

The organisms have different jobs, preferences, and roles. Some of the yeasts in the starter require oxygen, which is why you'll see instructions on how to incorporate lots of air into a starter. The bacteria do the job of neutralizing phytic acid and enzyme inhibitors—a job the yeasts can't do. Because the yeasts are much better at producing carbon dioxide, if a starter lacks a healthy yeast population, it won't raise bread very well. And finally, the bacteria do a good job cleaning up: They consume any expired yeasts, which keeps a starter fresh and vibrant.

Because the process of sourdough produces lactic acid, vinegar, and alcohol, consider these as examples of fermentations discussed in Chapter 3. However, because mainly lactic acid is produced and this process is what makes sourdough bread so healthy, I personally consider sourdough foods lacto-fermented.

It's All About the Sourdough Starter

You can't make sourdough foods without a starter—and that needs care and maintenance. Because whole books have been written on the subject of keeping sourdough starters, please read up on the subject more. See Appendix B for my recommendations. But here are the essentials to get you started.

Sourdough Starter

Getting a Starter Going

You can get a wet or dried sourdough starter from friends, neighbors, or even local or online shops. (See Appendix B for sources.) Or refer to the first recipe in this chapter for how to make your own sourdough starter from scratch.

Caring for Your Sourdough Starter

Once you have an active starter, you need to care for and feed it regularly. Leave the starter at room temperature, loosely covered in a ceramic or glass bowl or in a crock. Don't tightly cover the container because the starter needs airflow. In the summer, I cover my bowl with a napkin topped by a plate. Air can still get in and out, but fruit flies can't. In the winter, I use only the plate. Avoid using any metal containers or utensils, which can react with the acids in the starter. However, you can use stainless steel utensils to feed and stir the starter twice daily.

Feed your starter equal parts whole grain flour (preferably whole wheat, spelt, or rye) and water twice daily. To 1 or 2 cups of starter, you can feed ¼ or ½ cup of flour with a corresponding amount of water (stirred in at the same time) or go up as high as three times its volume. How much you feed depends on how much starter you need. If you need a quantity larger than triple the volume, build it up through successive feedings. My friend Erin feeds a little more flour than water to keep a thicker starter, which helps make perfect pancakes and other sourdough foods.

Some people feed starters only once daily, but I think this makes for a more sour starter in which *lactobacilli* dominate. This isn't nearly as effective in raising bread.

If you live in a very warm climate, your starter's organisms might go through their food more quickly, which you can tell by watching the stages (discussed in the next section). If you find that the starter completes its stages quickly, consider adding a third daily feeding.

Alternately, you can store a sourdough starter in the fridge for up to 1 week at a time after just being fed. Use an airtight container. Take it out to feed it or use it weekly and then pop it back in the fridge to lay dormant until the next time. There's no need to keep a large volume—just 1 cup will do.

Stages of a Sourdough Starter

An established sourdough starter exhibits normal and regular stages. After a feeding, the organisms produce gases, creating some bubble action. This culminates in a dome shape from the built-up carbon dioxide in the starter. The organisms are also producing acids and alcohol, and as the dome recedes, those liquids start pooling on top. This layer of liquid is called "hooch," which is yellowish. If you scooped into the starter, you'd find it gloppy and gel-like. Depending on the room temperature, this whole process can take from 1 hour to up to 12 hours. Warmer temperatures speed up the process and cooler temperatures slow it down.

When a starter is stored in the fridge, the hooch slowly turns from yellow to a blackish liquid. This is normal and not harmful. However, the hooch is the sourest part of the starter because it's a mixture of all the acids produced by the organisms. You might wish to pour it off (whether it's yellow or black).

Using a Sourdough Starter

With regular feedings, you'll need to use your sourdough starter in recipes to keep up with the volume or you can discard some of it as you go. This might sound wasteful, but a sourdough starter can grow exponentially if its volume isn't reduced. Discarding small amounts is less wasteful than feeding massive amounts of flour to what can quickly become a very hungry and very needy large starter! If you can't keep up with it no matter what amount of starter you're maintaining, refer to the previous section on storing a small amount of starter in the fridge.

How to use it? The most important thing to remember is this: Always reserve some of your starter. *Never use it all.* Let's say you have 2 cups of sourdough starter and you need 1½ cups for a recipe. Take out the 1½ cups for the recipe, leaving the rest in the crock to feed and keep going.

Do you find wet dough after the souring stage is over? During the summer months, when room temperature is warmer, the organisms in the starter work more quickly and produce liquids sooner, making a wetter dough. To account for this, use more flour when making up the dough or sour for a shorter length of time.

For best results in recipes, use the sourdough starter when it's at its peak. You'll know this because it's domed and bubbly. This is when it has the highest number of living organisms. Some recipes don't require a sourdough starter to be at its active stage. Breads that require a good rise will always need your starter to be at its best. In the recipes, you'll see this: "(active and bubbly)."

Grain Notes

Because of the greater nutrition of and higher number of naturally present organisms on whole grains, I recommend using whole grain flours in sourdough recipes. Fresh is best—whether or not you grind your own. Recipes specify if a certain type of flour is required. As with all foods, choose pesticide-free to ensure a more successful fermentation.

All the sourdough recipes in this book are tested around fresh-ground, gluten-containing flours, such as whole wheat, whole wheat pastry, spelt, and einkorn. If you're not using fresh-ground flour, you might find you need less flour to achieve the right consistency. This is expected because flour settles over time. If you live in a very dry climate, you might also use less flour. Gluten-free sourdough is outside the range of this cookbook. Please see Appendix B for resources on gluten-free sourdough baking.

Whole Grain Flour

Whole Wheat Flour

Whole wheat flour comes from grinding the hard white or hard red wheat berry. This flour is used for bread. It has a high gluten content—and gluten provides the strong, stretchy structure for bread when it rises. If the gluten weren't present, the bread wouldn't stay up. Hard red is nuttier and denser, while hard white is sweeter and lighter. In the recipes, I say "whole wheat flour" when I want you to use either hard red or hard white. They're interchangeable. However, with experience, you might learn to prefer one over the other.

Whole Wheat Pastry Flour

Whole wheat pastry flour is ground from soft wheat berries. With little gluten, it doesn't make good bread because it can't provide a strong structure to trap and hold the gases produced by the organisms. However, this flour makes an excellent whole grain alternative to white flour in pastry-like baked goods, such as cakes, muffins, and cookies.

Whole Spelt or Einkorn Flour

Spelt and einkorn are ancient varieties of wheat, often tolerated better by people who are sensitive to wheat. The gluten in spelt and einkorn is more fragile than the gluten in wheat. Although more fragile, these flours create a lighter texture in baked goods—whether breads or pastries. Personally, they're my favorite flours. In the recipes, I specify when spelt or einkorn flour is preferred.

Other Flours

Feel free to use, research, and experiment with other gluten-containing flours, such as rye or kamut (an ancient Egyptian variety of wheat with a nutty flavor). If you're going to use white flour, please choose organic unbleached.

Other Soured Grain Dishes

Cultures around the world lend us fermented grain dishes besides what we know as sourdough. From India, we get flatbreads called *dosas*, which are made from fermented grains or legumes. The Ethiopian staple flatbread *injera* is made from fermented teff, the smallest grain in the world. The Scots make *calders*—fermented oat porridge. A large pot of oatmeal is cooked up, then transferred to a kitchen cupboard drawer. For the rest of the week, family members would take slices of the cooled, congealed, and souring oat porridge along with them to the fields.

This chapter mainly focuses on what we today call sourdough, but I include some other fermented grain recipes that don't require maintaining or keeping a sourdough starter. Additionally, grains are a key ingredient in many fermented beverages. Those recipes are included in Chapter 9.

To Cook or Not to Cook?

As you know, I've cautioned you not to cook fermented foods to preserve vitamins, enzymes, and probiotics. Fermenting grains (with the exception of traditional alcoholic beverages) is an exception to this rule. Quite frankly, you'd be hard-pressed to find a fermented grain recipe that isn't cooked.

Rather than bemoan the loss of vitamins, enzymes, and probiotics, let's look at the positive: The act of fermentation neutralizes antinutrients, ensuring better mineral absorption. This in itself is a great improvement over eating quick breads or modern yeast breads.

Now let's get into some sourdough recipes, beginning with instructions to make your own sourdough starter. Once the sourdough recipes conclude, I'll share some other fermented grain recipes with you.

Sourdough Starter

Fresh-ground whole grain flours are a rich source of wild organisms. The wild organisms are ripe for the cultivating, which is what we do when we nurture a little flour and water into a colony of wild organisms called a sourdough starter. If you can't get fresh-ground flour, choose a whole grain flour, such as wheat, rye, spelt, or einkorn, from a store that gets good turnover, ensuring the flour is relatively fresh. Don't use white flour—whether bleached or unbleached—because it's not likely to carry any wild organisms. Sometimes, a sourdough starter doesn't double or triple in size. If your batter is on the thin side, this is normal. On the other hand, if your starter is getting quite big, you can give it a little more room by moving it to a 1-quart (1-liter) jar.

Yield:	Prep time:	Ferment time:	Ferment type:
2 cups	Varies	5 days	lacto

whole grain flour   water

1. In a wide-mouth 1-pint (½-liter) jar, combine ⅜ cup of flour and ¼ cup of water. Stir vigorously, scraping down the sides. Cover loosely with a cloth napkin or paper towel. Secure with a rubber band.

2. Leave at room temperature for 12 hours. If you see a few bubbles, add ⅜ cup of flour and ¼ cup of water to the jar. Stir vigorously, scraping down the sides. Cover loosely and leave for 12 hours. If you don't see bubbles at this stage, just stir again. Scrape the sides, cover, and leave for 12 hours more.

3. If you see bubbles, discard half the starter, add ⅜ cup of flour and ¼ cup of water to the jar. Stir vigorously, scraping down the sides. Cover loosely and leave for 12 hours. If you don't see bubbles at this stage, dump out the mixture and start again with step 1.

4. Discard half the starter, then add ⅜ cup of flour and ¼ cup of water to the jar. Stir vigorously, scraping down the sides. Cover loosely and leave for 12 hours.

5. Continue with this routine until the starter consistently shows bubbles, doubles or triples in size between feedings, and is at least 1 week old. Then it's ready to use.

Recipe Notes: In a jar or ceramic bowl covered with a cloth napkin or towel, keep at room temperature and feed twice daily, taking out amounts as needed to make recipes. Or store ½ to 2 cups of starter in a lidded 1-pint (½-liter) jar in the fridge for up to a week at time, taking it out at least weekly to feed and use in recipes.

Sourdough Starter

Breakfast Recipes

"Breakfast is the most important meal of the day," we're told. Unless you're following a special diet that has you fasting, make your breakfast breads more nutritious and wow-worthy with fluffy pancakes, crunchy waffles, toasted English Muffins, or any of the following recipes.

Waffles

These crispy and fluffy waffles can't be beat when topped with fresh fruit and yogurt or butter and maple syrup. You can also enjoy waffles when camping— look for cast-iron waffle irons with long handles that are safe to extend over fire.

Yield:	Prep time:	Ferment time:	Ferment type:
6 to 7 waffles	5 minutes	none	lacto

¼ cup melted salted butter, plus more

2 large eggs

½ tsp sea salt

1 tsp pure vanilla extract

2 tbsp honey or maple syrup, plus more

2 cups Sourdough Starter (page 204), fed within the last 12 hours

1 tsp baking soda

1. Preheat a waffle iron.

2. In a medium bowl, whisk together the butter, eggs, salt, vanilla extract, and honey or maple syrup. Add the sourdough starter and whisk well.

3. Sprinkle the baking soda over the waffle batter. Whisk well.

4. Follow the manufacturer's instructions for cooking the waffles.

5. Transfer the waffles to plates. Serve with butter and maple syrup. Store in an airtight plastic bag of container in the fridge for up to 1 day (separated by parchment paper) or in the freezer for up to 1 month. These reheat beautifully in a toaster.

Variation: Add 1 tablespoon of cocoa powder or cinnamon during step 2 to heighten the flavor.

Fluffy Skillet Pancakes

Crispy and surprisingly light, these sourdough pancakes are the fluffiest around! For the best-ever pancakes, use a cast-iron skillet and no flipping! This recipe makes good use of baking soda's reaction with the acids in the starter—to puff up the batter. It also sweetens the potentially sour flavor of sourdough foods.

Yield:	Prep time:	Ferment time:	Ferment type:
4 pancakes	5 minutes	none	lacto

4 tbsp melted salted butter, plus more

1 large egg

½ tsp sea salt

1 tsp pure vanilla extract

2 tbsp honey or maple syrup, plus more

2 cups Sourdough Starter (page 204), fed within the last 12 hours

1 tsp baking soda

1. Heat two cast-iron 8- or 10-inch (20 or 25cm) skillets or one griddle on the stovetop over medium-low heat. Grease with a small amount of butter.

2. In a medium bowl, whisk together the 4 tablespoons of butter, egg, salt, vanilla extract, and honey or maple syrup. Add the sourdough starter and whisk well. Transfer half the mixture to another medium bowl.

3. Sprinkle ½ teaspoon of baking soda on the batter in one of the bowls. Whisk quickly and well. Quickly pour the batter to fill the skillets to 1 inch (2.5cm) thick or to make 1-inch-thick (2.5cm) pancakes on the griddle. Cook until bubbly in the center and firmed up all over, about 4 to 5 minutes.

4. Make sure the top oven rack isn't in the top position. Turn on the oven broiler. Transfer the skillets or the griddle to the oven and cook until the top is browned and the pancakes are cooked through, about 3 minutes. Transfer the pancakes to plates or a cooling rack. Repeat with the second bowl of batter.

5. Serve the pancakes with butter and maple syrup. Store in the fridge for up to 1 day (separated by parchment paper) or in the freezer for up to 1 month. These reheat beautifully in a toaster.

Variation: Press blueberries or other add-ins into the pancakes after step 3.

Biscuits

These are fluffy, buttery, and flaky beyond belief—and my family adores them.

Yield:	Prep time:	Ferment time:	Ferment type:
12 biscuits	12 minutes	5 to 8 hours	lacto

6 tbsp cold salted butter, cut into ¼-inch (0.5cm) cubes

2½ cups whole wheat pastry flour or 2¾ cups whole spelt flour, plus more

½ cup Sourdough Starter (page 204), fed within the last 12 hours

¾ cup whole milk, plus more

½ tsp sea salt

1½ tsp baking powder

½ tsp baking soda

1. In a medium bowl, combine the butter and flour. Use a pastry cutter or a knife and fork to cut into the flour until the butter is the size of peas.

2. Add the sourdough starter and milk. Don't overmix, but combine into a dough that just holds together, adding more milk as needed.

3. Cover with a tea towel or plastic wrap and leave at room temperature for 5 to 8 hours. If the temperature is very warm, sour the dough in a cooler location or fridge.

4. Preheat the oven to 425°F (220°C). Uncover the dough. Sprinkle the salt, baking powder, and baking soda over the top. Fold over about 15 times to incorporate the dry ingredients, but avoid overhandling the dough.

5. Flour a cutting surface and place the dough on it. Use a rolling pin to gently roll out the dough to a 1-inch-thick (2.5cm) rectangle. Use a pizza cutter or knife to cut the rectangle into 12 to 15 squares. Place the squares on an ungreased baking tray.

6. Place the tray in the oven and bake until golden brown, about 8 to 10 minutes. Remove the tray from the oven and transfer the biscuits to a cooling rack. Store in an airtight plastic bag or container at room temperature for up to 2 to 3 days or in the freezer for up to 2 months.

Variation: Make thicker or thinner biscuits if you'd like. Just roll the dough to a different thickness and then cut. Your yield will differ.

English Muffins

These are hearty yet light and chewy just like an English muffin should be. You'll probably find yourself making these all the time. Although the recipe calls for making them on a griddle, you can also use cast-iron skillets. I suggest a cover to turn the skillet into a "mini" oven to let the muffins fully bake inside.

Yield:	Prep time:	Ferment time:	Ferment type:
12 muffins	12 minutes	8 to 12 hours	lacto

½ cup Sourdough Starter (page 204), fed within the last 12 hours

1 cup whole milk

2 cups whole wheat or whole grain flour, plus more

1 tsp sea salt

1 tsp baking soda

honey (optional)

1. In a medium bowl, combine the sourdough starter and milk. Add the flour and mix well. Add more flour as needed to make a thick and somewhat sticky dough. Cover with a tea towel or plastic wrap. Leave at room temperature for 8 to 12 hours.

2. Preheat an 8- or 10-inch (20 or 25cm) cast-iron skillet on the stovetop over medium-low heat. Remove the cover from the dough. Sprinkle the sea salt and baking soda over the dough. Drizzle the honey (if using) over the top. Mix thoroughly using a wooden spoon.

3. Transfer the dough to a clean countertop and knead for 2 to 3 minutes—just long enough to achieve a smooth dough. Divide the dough into 8 portions and place them on waxed paper. Roughly shape each portion into a ball and place as many as you can in the skillet. Flatten each ball to about ½-inch (1.25cm) thick. Cook until browned on the bottom, about 3 minutes. Adjust the heat to prevent them from browning too quickly.

4. Flip the muffins and cook on the other side for 3 to 5 minutes. Cover to hold in moisture and to cook the muffins on the inside. Transfer the muffins to a cooling rack. Repeat steps 6 through 8 until all the muffins are cooked. Slice when cool. Store in an airtight plastic bag or container at room temperature for up to 2 to 3 days or in the freezer for up to 2 months.

Sourdough Crêpes

Chewy and soft, these are the perfect addition to any meal. Roll them up with your favorite toppings. Might I suggest sour cream and guacamole? Leftover crêpes warm up just like fresh when laid on a warm skillet.

Yield:	Prep time:	Ferment time:	Ferment type:
16 to 18 crêpes	10 minutes	none	lacto

2 cups Sourdough Starter (page 204), fed within the last 12 hours

6 large eggs

6 tbsp salted butter

¼ tsp sea salt

½ cup whole milk, plus more

1. Heat an 8-inch (20cm) cast-iron skillet on the stovetop over medium heat.

2. In a medium bowl, whisk together the sourdough starter, eggs, butter, and salt. Add the milk and whisk well. Add more milk if needed to get a thin batter.

3. Pour ¼ cup of the batter into the center of the skillet. Quickly pick up the skillet and tip it outward in a circle to spread the batter over the bottom of the pan. Cook until the edges peel up from the pan and small bubbles dot the crêpe, about 1 minute.

4. Flip the crêpe with a spatula and cook on the other side for 10 to 20 seconds. Transfer the crêpe to a plate lined with a paper towel. Repeat steps 3 and 4 with the remaining batter to cook all the crêpes.

5. Store in a resealable plastic bag in the fridge for up to 2 days or in the freezer for up to 2 months.

Variation: Make crêpe cakes by layering the finished crêpes with sweet or savory toppings, such as nut butter with jam, frosting with sliced fruit, or sautéed vegetables and cheese. Cut into wedges and serve. Crêpes also make the most delicious homemade tortilla chips—deep-fry wedges of the sourdough crêpes in coconut oil or lard.

Dessert Recipes

Using sourdough for your desserts gives a deeper flavor to cut the absolute sweetness. Plus, those who might get an upset stomach from grains or sweet foods might feel better after eating soured desserts because of how the starter reduces carbs and makes the grains more nutritious and digestible. In the following recipes, you'll also see we like to use unrefined sweeteners that give the desserts more flavor while preventing them from tasting super sweet.

Impossible Brownies

Rich and gooey with a pleasant tang, these brownies are a treat your family will beg for again and again. Sometimes, when I make these, the batter separates in the oven and makes a two-layer brownie. One layer is like a sweet chocolate quick bread and the other a dense and smooth chocolate brownie. Other times, the mixture stays uniform. Both results are pleasing.

Yield:	Prep time:	Ferment time:	Ferment type:
varies	5 minutes	none	lacto

¼ cup salted butter, lightly melted, plus more

4 large eggs

4oz (110g) baking chocolate, melted

½ cup Sourdough Starter (page 204), fed within the last 12 hours

1 cup unrefined sugar

½ tsp pure vanilla extract

1. Preheat the oven to 350°F (180°C). Butter an 8- or 9-inch (20 to 23cm) square or round baking pan.

2. In a medium bowl, whisk together the butter, eggs, chocolate, sourdough starter, sugar, and vanilla extract until very smooth. Pour the batter into the prepared pan.

3. Place the pan in the oven and bake until a toothpick inserted in the center comes out clean, about 25 to 30 minutes. Transfer the pan to a cooling rack to cool for 10 to 15 minutes. Cut into 9 squares.

5. Serve plain or with whipped cream or ice cream. Store in an airtight container in the fridge for up to 4 days or in the freezer for up to 5 days.

Chocolate Sourdough Cake

Light and fluffy and pleasantly tangy, this cake is a crowd-pleaser, even with people who say they hate sourdough. It must be the chocolate. Cake deflated? It's likely the batter was too thin. Next time, use more flour. A thicker cake batter will hold its height better.

Yield:	Prep time:	Ferment time:	Ferment type:
varies	10 minutes	8 to 12 hours	lacto

½ cup Sourdough Starter (page 204), fed within the last 12 hours

⅞ cup whole spelt flour or whole wheat pastry flour

½ cup whole milk

½ cup barely melted coconut oil or butter, plus more

¾ cup unrefined sugar

1 tsp pure vanilla extract

1 large egg

⅜ cup cocoa powder (preferably not Dutch process)

½ tsp sea salt

¾ tsp baking soda

½ tsp finely ground coffee or coffee substitute powder

powdered sugar or Chocolate Cream Cheese Frosting (page 286)

1. In a medium bowl, combine the sourdough starter, flour, and milk. Cover with a tea towel or plastic wrap. Leave at room temperature for 8 to 12 hours or up to 24 hours if that's more convenient for you.

2. Preheat the oven to 350°F (180°C). Rub a little coconut oil or butter all over the inside of an 8- or 9-inch (20 to 23cm) square or round cake pan.

3. In a separate medium bowl, combine the ½ cup coconut oil or butter, sugar, vanilla extract, egg, and cocoa powder. Beat until smooth.

4. Add the soured flour mixture, salt, baking soda, and coffee powder to the wet ingredients. Beat until smooth. Pour the mixture into the prepared cake pan.

5. Place the pan in the oven and bake until a toothpick inserted in the center comes out clean, about 25 to 35 minutes.

6. Remove the pan from the oven and set on a cooling rack. When cool, transfer the cake to a plate. Dust with the powdered sugar or frost with chocolate cream cheese frosting.

Chocolate Sourdough Cake

Sourdough Cobbler

My friend Erin loves sharing tasty sourdough recipes with friends—and this recipe is just that. I also enjoy recipes you can tweak to meet the needs of many. What fruit do you have in your freezer? Are you reducing your sugar intake? Are you dairy-free? Grain-free? This recipe is as flexible as you choose to make it. See Recipe Notes for soaked, gluten-free, and/or dairy-free versions.

Yield:	Prep time:	Ferment time:	Ferment type:
1 cobbler	1 hour	6 to 8 hours	lacto

¼ cup Sourdough Starter (page 204)*

⅔ cup raw whole milk**

1 cup whole grain flour of choice***

½ cup coconut oil or butter, cut into ½-inch (1.25cm) chunks

4 cups berries or other fruits of choice (about 1lb [450g]), frozen or fresh

¼ cup plus ⅓ cup dry sweetener, divided

1 tsp ground cinnamon or preferred spice (optional)

½ tsp baking soda

½ tbsp baking powder

⅛ tsp sea salt

1. In a small bowl, combine the sourdough starter and milk. Stir in the flour until incorporated. Cover with a tea towel and plate. Set aside for at least 6 hours.

2. Place an oven rack in the middle position. Spread the chunks of coconut oil or butter in a 2-quart (2-liter) casserole dish, a 9-inch (23cm) round dish, or an 8-inch (20cm) square baking dish. Place the dish in the oven. Preheat the oven to 350°F (180°C).

3. In a small bowl, combine the fruit, ¼ cup of dry sweetener, and cinnamon. Set aside.

4. Add the baking soda, baking powder, salt, and the remaining ⅓ cup of dry sweetener to the dough. Use clean hands or a mixer to thoroughly combine.

5. Remove the dish from the oven. Place tablespoon-sized drops of prepared batter on top of the oil. Cover all the oil with batter, but don't stir.

6. Spoon the fruit mixture on top of the batter. Cover the batter, but don't stir.

7. Place the dish in the oven and bake for 40 minutes. Cover with parchment paper and bake until the cobbler is browned and no longer gooey in the middle, about 10 minutes more. Continue baking and checking every few minutes until a toothpick inserted in the center comes out clean.

8. Remove the dish from the oven. Enjoy hot or warmed. Store covered in the fridge for up to 5 days.

Recipe Notes:

* No sourdough starter? Make it a soaked flour recipe, eliminating the starter and using 1 cup of flour and ⅔ cup of milk or nondairy milk spiked with 2 tablespoons of lemon juice, whey, yogurt, dairy kefir, or buttermilk. (See Basic Whey recipe on page 39.)

** In place of raw whole milk, you can use homemade nut or seed milk, coconut milk, or fermented dairy.

*** Gluten-free? I encourage you to give this a try. You might want to add a couple teaspoons or so of ground flaxseeds or chia seeds to help the batter hold together.

Bread Recipes

Fresh bread with butter ... mmmm! Now make that bread sourdough and you have more flavor and more nutrition in every bite! Even those who say sourdough bread is too sour should find a less sour bread among this selection of recipes—and I recommend the No-Knead Sourdough Bread to try first.

No-Knead Sourdough Bread

Chewy inside and perfectly crusty outside—and with a fresh-baked aroma to die for—this artisan bread is one on which your family will soon be hooked! Keep the oven air moist for great bread: Place a big metal bowl over small-enough loaves for the first 15 minutes of baking. Or place a pan of just-boiled water on the bottom of the oven. This creates steam to circulate around larger loaves or logs. Try baking your loaves in a lidded casserole dish or in a Dutch oven with a lid. Remove the lid after the first 15 minutes of baking.

Yield:	Prep time:	Ferment time:	Ferment type:
varies	5 minutes	varies	lacto

6 cups water

3 tbsp sea salt

3 cups Sourdough Starter (page 204) (active and bubbly)

13 cups whole wheat flour or whole grain flour, plus more

1. In a 2-gallon (8-liter) bucket or crock, combine all the ingredients. Stir well and cover loosely with a lid. Leave at room temperature for 6 to 8 hours.

2. Transfer the dough to the fridge. Chill for a few hours before using.

3. Preheat the oven to 400°F (200°C). Place the top rack in the center of the oven. Place a baking stone or baking sheet in the oven to heat.

4. Spread a piece of parchment paper on a clean work surface and flour it lightly. Remove the dough from the fridge. Sprinkle some flour over the dough. Scoop out a ball of dough without deflating it. The size depends on how big you want your loaf to be—it will roughly double in size during baking.

5. Place the ball on the parchment paper. Without patting it down, shape the dough into a log or round ball.

6. Return the remaining dough to the fridge for future loaves. It will keep for about 5 days and get more sour over time.

7. If the dough is pretty stiff, let rise at room temperature for about 20 minutes before moving on to step 9. If it's more batter-like and wants to spread out, you can proceed. Use a serrated knife to make one or a few cuts into the top of the loaf—either in X shapes or diagonal parallel cuts.

8. Open the oven and quickly slide the parchment paper (with the dough on it) onto the preheated baking stone or sheet. Bake until the loaf sounds hollow when tapped and is lightly browned. For smaller loaves, such as will fit in a normal-sized toaster oven, this could be 20 minutes. Larger loaves will take 40 to 60 minutes.

9. Remove the bread from the oven and let cool for 15 to 30 minutes before slicing and serving. Repeat these steps as needed to bake loaves from the remaining dough.

10. Store in a sealed plastic bag at room temperature for 1 to 2 days or in the freezer for up to 2 months. If you preslice your bread before freezing, you're more likely to be able to fit it in gallon-size (liter-sized) freezer bag(s), plus you can easily toast as many slices you need to quickly thaw them instead of having to thaw the entire load.

Recipe Note: Slice off one end about ¾-inch (2cm) thick. Rotate the loaf a bit less than 90 degrees and make a similar slice, slightly less than perpendicular to the first slice. Then go back to where you made the first slice and cut another slice of your desired thickness. Repeat, alternating slicing in the two locations. You can slice the entire loaf at once, but it will stay fresh longer if you only slice what you need.

Basic Whole Wheat or Spelt Bread

Fluffy and chewy—and mildly fragrant from the olive oil—this hearty yet light bread will quickly become a family favorite for sandwiches and toast. If the total amount of flour used is 3 to 4 cups and you make two loaves of bread, the loaves might turn out small and wimpy. Instead, make just one loaf from this recipe and use a large bread pan.

Yield:	Prep time:	Ferment time:	Ferment type:
2 loaves	20 minutes	11 hours	lacto

3 cups Sourdough Starter (page 204) (active and bubbly)

1 cup water

1 rounded tbsp sea salt

¼ cup plus 4 tbsp extra-virgin olive oil, divided, plus more

4 to 6 cups whole wheat flour or spelt flour, plus more

1. In a large bowl, combine the sourdough starter, water, salt, and ¼ cup of olive oil. Mix well.

2. Beginning with 2 cups of flour and adding more in increments of ¼ to ½ cup, add 5 to 6 cups of flour total. Mix with a wooden spoon until the dough is shaggy (not yet uniform and smooth). Use your hands to turn the dough when it gets too stiff to stir. Add flour only until the dough cleans the sides of the bowl. It might still be sticky and that's okay.

3. Cover with a plate or towel. Let rest for 15 minutes to absorb excess water.

4. Sprinkle a little flour on a clean work surface and place the dough on the flour. Knead for 4 to 5 minutes. Add more flour to the countertop only if it's making a sticky mess. It's okay if some dough sticks to your hands or the countertop.

5. Cover the dough with a clean tea towel and let rest for 5 minutes. Knead again for 4 to 5 minutes.

6. Rub the original large bowl with 2 tablespoons of olive oil. Place the dough in the bowl, rotating it to grease all the sides with oil. Cover with a clean, dampened tea towel. Place the bowl in a warm place. Let the dough rise until doubled in size or spilling out of the bowl, about 3 to 8 hours depending on room temperature.

7. Punch down the dough and divide it into two parts. Rub the remaining 2 tablespoon of olive oil equally on the inside of two medium bread pans . Shape each piece of dough into a loaf and place each in a bread pan. Rub more oil on top of each loaf to keep them from drying out. Use a serrated knife to cut diagonal slices in the top of each loaf. Let the loaves rise for 1 to 3 hours or until they've filled the pans.

8. Preheat the oven to 400°F (200°C).

9. Place the pans in the oven and bake until nicely browned, about 45 to 60 minutes. Transfer the pans to a cooling rack. Brush the loaves with more olive oil if desired. Let rest for 30 minutes before slicing and serving.

10. Store in a sealed plastic bag at room temperature for 1 to 2 days or in the freezer for up to 2 months. If you preslice your bread before freezing, you're more likely to be able to fit it in gallon-sizes (liter-sized) freezer bag(s), plus you can easily toast as many slices you need to quickly thaw them instead of having to thaw the entire load.

Recipe Note: Using a bread knife or serrated knife, slice the bread into ½-inch to ¾-inch (1.25 to 2cm) slices. You can slice the entire loaf at once, but it will stay fresh longer if you only slice what you need.

Spelt Sandwich Bread

Olive & Feta Swirl Bread

Olives, feta, and a fragrant thyme-based Middle Eastern spice blend called "za'atar" make this tantalizing swirl bread. With the addition of toppings, this bread can easily be too big for a bread pan. That's why it's important to use a little less than half the dough from the basic bread recipe.

Yield:	Prep time:	Ferment time:	Ferment type:
1 loaf	10 minutes	11 hours	lacto

5 tbsp extra-virgin olive oil, divided

half the uncooked dough from
   Basic Whole Wheat or Spelt
   Bread (page 219)

¼ cup crumbled feta cheese

¼ cup sliced black olives

2 tbsp za'atar seasoning blend
   or 2 tsp dried thyme

pinch of sea salt

1. Grease a clean countertop with 1 tablespoon of olive oil. Use a rolling pin to roll out the dough to a ½-inch-thick (1.25cm) rectangle, with its width being a little less than the length of a bread pan.

2. Use a pastry brush to brush the dough with 2 tablespoons of olive oil. Sprinkle the feta, olives, za'atar or thyme, and salt over the top.

3. With clean hands, roll up the dough from one short end to the other. If the loaf is longer than the bread pan, press in the ends to shorten it up.

4. Grease a medium or large bread pan with 1 tablespoon of olive oil. Place the dough on the pan and rub the remaining 1 tablespoon of olive oil over the top. Use a serrated knife to cut diagonal slices in the top of the loaf. Let rise for 1 to 3 hours or until the loaf has filled the pan.

5. Preheat the oven to 400°F (200°C). Place the pan in the oven and bake until nicely browned, about 45 to 60 minutes.

6. Transfer the pan to a cooling rack. Brush the loaf with more olive oil if desired. Let rest for 30 minutes before slicing and serving.

7. Store in a sealed plastic bag at room temperature for 3 to 4 days or in the freezer for up to 2 months. If you preslice your bread before freezing, you're more likely to be able to fit it in gallon-sizes (liter-sized) freezer bag(s), plus you can easily toast as many slices you need to quickly thaw them instead of having to thaw the entire load.

Recipe Note: Using a bread knife or serrated knife, slice the bread into ½- to ¾-inch (1.25 to 2cm) slices. You can slice the entire loaf at once, but it will stay fresh longer if you only slice what you need.

Variation: For a cinnamon and raisin swirl loaf, omit the toppings listed and sprinkle raisins (plumped in water for about 10 minutes), cinnamon, sweetener of choice (like unrefined sugars Sucanat or rapadura, honey, maple syrup, or coconut syrup), and butter over the dough.

Olive & Feta Swirl Bread

Grain-Free Paleo Sourdough Bread

Grain-free sourdough bread recipes might be hard to find, but this one from my friend Megan is a versatile gem you can make into loaves or rolls and eaten as sandwiches or toast. It tastes just like tender, soft, fresh, whole wheat bread!

Yield:	Prep time:	Ferment time:	Ferment type:
1 loaf / 8 to 10 rolls	3 hours	12 hours	lacto

2 cups raw nuts and/or seeds of choice, soaked for 2 hours in warm filtered water, then drained and rinsed*

½ cup purified water

⅛ cup sauerkraut liquid

coconut oil or butter

¾ cup cassava flour

¾ cup chia seeds meal**

2 large organic or pastured eggs

¼ cup tallow or butter, melted and cooled, or avocado oil

2 tbsp raw honey

½ tsp sea salt

½ tsp sifted baking soda

1. In a high-powered blender, combine the nuts or seeds, soaking water, and purified water. Purée until smooth, about 50 seconds. Add the sauerkraut liquid and purée again until just combined, about 10 seconds.

2. Transfer the mixture to a ceramic bowl and cover loosely with a towel or plate. Place in a warm location (ideally 95°F to 105°F [35°C to 38°C]) for 12 hours or overnight. A dehydrator or an oven with the light on works best, but a countertop also works if your home temperature is 70°F (21°C) or higher. Fermentation will still occur, but it will take about 24 hours.

3. Preheat the oven to 325°F (165°C). Grease a sandwich bread loaf pan with coconut oil or butter.

4. In a small bowl, sift together the cassava flour, chia seeds meal, baking soda, and salt.

5. In a stand mixer or food processor, combine the eggs, fat of choice, and honey. Mix on medium speed until completely blended, about 30 seconds. Add nuts and/or seeds and the cassava flour mixture. Mix with the paddle attachment until thoroughly combined but not overmixed. Pour the mixture into the prepared pan.

6. Place the pan in the oven and bake until a sharp knife inserted in the center comes out clean, about 50 to 55 minutes. Remove the pan from the oven and let the bread cool completely before removing it from the pan and slicing.

7. Store in a sealed plastic bag at room temperature for 3 to 4 days or in the freezer for up to 2 months. If you preslice your bread before freezing, you're more likely to be able to fit it in gallon-sizes (liter-sized) freezer bag(s), plus you can easily toast as many slices you need to quickly thaw them instead of having to thaw the entire load.

Recipe Notes:

Using a bread knife or serrated knife, slice the bread into ½-inch to ¾-inch (1.25 to 2cm) slices. You can slice the entire loaf at once, but it will stay fresh longer if you only slice what you need.

* You can soak all your nuts and/or seeds together. The wet nuts and seeds are what make this bread so irresistible.

** To make chia seeds meal, blend 2 cups of chia seeds in a high-powered blender on medium speed for 10 seconds. Measure after blending.

Pizza Recipes

For many years, our family has had weekly pizza nights. I usually prebake the crust in the morning, then right before dinner, I prepare toppings so we can just pop our pizzas in the oven nearly as easily as reheating a frozen boxed pizza. I also often use any of the crust recipes that follow and make personal pan pizza crusts (about 6 inches [15.25cm] wide) so family members can make pizzas for themselves with the toppings they love best. We often have extras of these personal crusts in the freezer to make pizzas for a quick lunch or dinner, using leftovers as toppings.

Kefir Sourdough Pizza Crust

This chewy, thick, sweet-and-sour pizza crust will melt in your mouth. For a crispy crust, prebake the crust for 8 minutes before adding the toppings. Then slide the crust (with toppings) off the sheet and right onto an oven rack to finish baking.

Yield:	Prep time:	Ferment time:	Ferment type:
2 crusts	20 minutes	2 to 3 days	lacto

1 cup Basic Water Kefir (page 140) or Dairy Kefir (page 250)

5 cups whole wheat or whole grain flour, divided, plus more

1 tsp sea salt

⅓ cup extra-virgin olive oil, plus more

1 cup warm water, plus more

1. In a wide-mouth quart (liter) jar, combine the kefir and 1 cup of flour. Mix to make a smooth paste. Cover with a clean tea towel and leave at room temperature until it doubles in volume, about 1 to 3 days. Stir once daily. (Regular stirring helps prevent mold from forming.) When done, the mixture should be bubbly and have a sweet-sour yeasty aroma. This is the kefir starter.

2. In a medium bowl, combine the kefir starter, salt, olive oil, water, and the remaining 4 cups of flour. Add more water as needed to make it mixable. Mix with a wooden spoon or your hands until the dough is moist and elastic.

3. Grease two 10- to 12-inch (25 to 30.5cm) cookie sheets or pizza stones with olive oil. Rub your hands with more olive oil. Make two round balls from the dough. Place a ball on each cookie sheet and use your fingers to press and stretch the dough into a ¾-inch-thick (2cm) layer over all the pan—right up to the edges. Lightly brush olive oil over the top of the dough. Place the pans in a warm location to let the unbaked crusts rise until they're almost double in height, about 2 to 8 hours.

4. Preheat the oven to 450°F (235°C). Place your desired toppings on each pizza.

5. Place the pans in the oven and bake until the crusts are golden brown and the toppings are heated or melted thoroughly, about 15 to 20 minutes. Remove the pans from the oven, Cut the pizzas into 8 wedges and serve immediately. Store in the fridge for up to 1 to 2 days.

Variation: Suggested toppings include homemade pesto, red onions, garlic, bell peppers, cherry tomatoes, fresh basil and thyme, and mozzarella and goat cheeses with olive oil drizzled over the top. Don't forget to sprinkle sea salt and ground black pepper over the top!

Sourdough Mediterranean Pizza

My Middle Eastern heritage inspired me to make this healthy homemade pizza. With a fragrant sourdough crust from the ancient wheat einkorn, crumbled goat cheese, Kalamata olives, and many more toppings, this Mediterranean pizza is a FEAST of savory vegetables and herbs for even the most avid pizza lover.

Yield:	Prep time:	Ferment time:	Ferment type:
2 crusts	1 to 1½ hours	8 to 12 hours	lacto

For the crust

1½ cups Sourdough Starter (page 204), fed 12 hours before

1½ tbsp extra-virgin olive oil

1 tsp sea salt

1 to 1½ cups flour of choice (such as einkorn, spelt, or whole wheat), plus more

For the pizza

3 tbsp extra-virgin olive oil

1 tsp dried thyme

1 tsp dried oregano

3 cups mozzarella cheese

goat cheese, crumbled

¼ red onion, thinly sliced

10 cherry or grape tomatoes, quartered

16 Kalamata or black olives, sliced

¾ bell pepper (any color), thinly sliced

10oz (285g) artichoke hearts, halved

ground black pepper

For the crust:

1. In a medium bowl, combine the sourdough starter, oil, and salt. Add the flour and mix well.

2. Sprinkle a countertop with flour. Place the dough mixture on the flour and begin kneading. Add flour as necessary and knead the dough until all the ingredients are combined. You're looking for a dough that's soft and not sticky. If it's too wet, add more flour. If it's too dry, add more water or starter or add whey. (See Basic Whey recipe on page 39.)

3. Return the dough back to the medium bowl. Cover with a plate and leave until evening. Or let the dough rest for 30 minutes, then roll it out and leave it to sour as an unbaked crust ready to go. Cover with plastic wrap to keep it from drying out.

4. Preheat the oven to 450°F (220°C) or hotter for the prebake. (If you have pizza stones, preheat that now.)

5. Separate the dough into two pieces. Roll out each piece into a 10- to 12-inch (25 to 30.5cm) circle about ½ inch (1.25cm) thick. Poke each several times with a fork. Place the dough circles on 10- to 12-inch (25 to 30.5cm) baking pans if not using pizza stones.

6. Place the pans in the oven (or place the pizzas on the stones). Bake for 5 minutes, but check the crust often to make sure it doesn't get too dark.

7. Remove the pans or pizza stones from the oven and let the crusts cool. Store in plastic wrap in the freezer for up to 4 weeks for not-immediate baking. To bake, first thaw for 1 hour or at room temperature. Then brush with olive oil and proceed with the pizza recipe.

8. If you're using the crusts immediately, brush with olive oil and proceed with the pizza recipe.

For the pizza:

1. In a small dish, combine the olive oil, thyme, and oregano. Brush this over the prebaked pizza crusts.

2. Sprinkle ⅓ cup of mozzarella over each pizza. This will help the toppings stick to the crust.

3. Add the remaining ingredients—goat cheese, red onion, cherry or grape tomatoes, black olives, bell pepper, and artichoke hearts—to each crust in whatever combination you desire. Sprinkle an equal amount of the remaining 2⅓ cup of mozzarella over each pizza. Sprinkle black pepper over the top of each pizza.

4. Place the pans or pizza stones in the oven and bake until the cheese is crispy in places and bubbly, about 10 to 15 minutes.

5. Remove the pans or pizza stones from the oven. Let the pizzas cool slightly before slicing into 8 wedges. Store in the fridge for up to 1 to 2 days.

Other Grain Recipes

In this selection of recipes, I'm introducing you to more breads that are just that much more nutritious and delicious when made with sourdough. Enjoy!

Einkorn Sourdough Chapatis

Chapatis are traditional Indian flatbread—perfect for dipping into soups and stews or eating alongside salads. This recipe is a super-nourishing and easy version with ancient einkorn and sourdough starter.

Yield:	Prep time:	Ferment time:	Ferment type:
6 chapatis	30 minutes	8 hours	lacto

2½ cups einkorn flour (or spelt or emmer), plus more

1 tsp sea salt

2 tbsp extra-virgin olive oil

¼ cup Sourdough Starter (page 204)

¾ cup warm purified water

grass-fed butter or coconut oil for dairy-free

1. In a medium bowl, combine the flour, salt, olive oil, sourdough starter, and water. Stir to get all the flour wet. At the end, when it gets harder to handle, you can switch to your hands. You should have a shaggy dough—don't worry about it being smooth.

2. Cover with a tea towel and leave at room temperature until the flour absorbs the water, about 5 to 15 minutes .

3. Sprinkle a little flour on a countertop. Place the dough on the flour and start kneading. It should be a little sticky, but if it's too sticky to work with, you can sprinkle a little more flour on the countertop. Knead until you have a smooth dough, about 5 minutes.

4. Drizzle a little olive oil in the medium bowl. Return the dough to the bowl and turn the ball over to coat with oil. Cover with plastic wrap and leave at room temperature for 8 hours or overnight.

5. On the stovetop, heat one or two cast-iron skillets over medium heat. (You'll adjust the heat as you go. You want the skillets to stay hot but not smoking.)

6. Pull the dough apart into 6 pieces. A good way to do this is to break the dough in half and then pull each half into 3 equal-sized balls. Place the balls back in the bowl and keep lightly covered to prevent them from drying out.

7. Sprinkle a little flour on a clean countertop. Roll each ball of dough into a smooth ball. Press each ball into a flat disc in the flour, turn it over, and coat the other side with a little flour. You're going to continue pressing out the dough while other discs cook.

8. Once the skillet is hot and almost smoking, it's ready. Place 1 flattened ball in the skillet and cook until it begins to bubble up, about 1 to 2 minutes. Flip, then spread butter or coconut oil on the cooked side. Cook the bottom side for 1 to 2 minutes more. Transfer the chapati to a baking tray while flipping it over again and spread butter or coconut oil on the side that's now facing up. Repeat with the remaining dough.

9. If you're not quite ready to serve the chapatis, place them in a warm oven (or you can use a clay tortilla keeper). They're best served fresh. Stack them on a platter before serving.

10. Store leftovers in an airtight container at room temperature for up to 3 to 4 days. Reheat by warming up each side in a dry skillet over medium-low heat. Or freeze in a resealable plastic bag for up to 2 months, then toast or wrap in a clean towel on a tray in a warm oven to gently reheat. This recipe easily doubles or triples.

Dehydrated Dosa Crackers

You can leave these crispy crackers plain to highlight your favorite dip's flavor or you can accent them with items from your spice rack for a flavor boost.

Yield:	Prep time:	Ferment time:	Ferment type:
varies	5 minutes	1 to 2 days	lacto

2 cups leftover cooked grains and/or beans

½ cup water, plus more

¼ cup starter culture (Appendix B)

½ tsp sea salt, plus more

⅛ tsp ground black pepper

1. In a food processor or blender, combine the grains and/or beans, water, starter culture, salt, and pepper. Pulse until smooth. Add water 1 tablespoon at a time until the mixture has a thick, pancake-batter consistency. Taste and add more salt if desired.

2. Transfer the mixture to a 1-quart (1-liter) or ½-gallon (2-liter) jar, leaving 1 inch (2.5cm) from the jar's rim. Cover with a lid or an airlock. Leave at room temperature for 1 day.

3. Line dehydrator tray(s) with parchment paper or liners. Spread the batter in a layer about ¼ inch (0.5cm) thick in small circles or in a continuous layer.

4. Place the tray(s) in a dehydrator at 115°F (50°C) and dehydrate until dry and crispy, about 12 to 24 hours. Turn over as needed. Remove the tray(s) from the dehydrator and allow the crackers to cool. Store in an airtight container at room temperature for up to 1 week.

Variation: Feel free to add other spices, such as cumin, garlic powder, onion powder, paprika, or cayenne, to these crackers. Blending sun-dried tomatoes into the batter would also be very good!

Injera

Everyone needs a spongy and sour flatbread that complements the food or juices being scooped up. This is it. Functioning as bread and eating utensil, *injera* is the classic flatbread of Ethiopia. Usually, one injera is placed on a plate and then the food is served on top of that. Additional breads are served on the side. Making injera is a two- to three-day process. Traditionally, Ethiopians have made their injera entirely with teff flour, while more modern versions are made with a blend of wheat and teff. Because teff has no gluten, it doesn't rise, making it well suited for creating flatbreads.

Yield:	Prep time:	Ferment time:	Ferment type:
varies	20 minutes	2 to 3 days	lacto

1½ cups teff flour

2 cups water

butter, tallow, or lard

sea salt, to taste

1. In a medium bowl, combine the flour and water. Mix until it forms a thin pancake-batter consistency. Cover with a clean tea towel and leave at room temperature until bubbly and sour, about 2 to 3 days.

2. On the stovetop, heat an 8- or 10-inch (20 to 25cm) skillet over medium heat. Grease the skillet with butter, tallow, or lard.

3. Sprinkle the salt into the batter. Pour the batter into the skillet to thinly coat the entire bottom—thicker than a crêpe but thinner than a pancake. Hold the handle of the pan and immediately swirl the pan to evenly spread the batter.

4. Cook until holes form and the bread lifts up at the edges, not sticking to the skillet, about 3 to 5 minutes. It should firm up entirely and cook through from just the one side.

5. Transfer the bread to a plate, separating each slice with layers of paper towel or napkin to avoid sticking. Repeat with the remaining batter. This bread is best served warm, but you can store it in a resealable plastic bag in the fridge for up to 2 days or in the freezer for up to 1 month.

Variation: Save some of your fermented injera batter and combine it with your next batch to speed up that batch's fermentation.

Sourdough Cold Cereal

My friend Tracey had fun tackling the cereal challenge, discovering her family's preferences and searching for the perfect crunchy texture.

Yield:	Prep time:	Ferment time:	Ferment type:
6 cups	10 minutes	12 to 24 hours	lacto

For the sponge

3 cups sprouted flour or whole grain flour

3 cups rolled oats (not quick-cooking)

½ cup Sourdough Starter (page 204)

3 cups soured milk or yogurt (or use unsoured milk)

For the cereal

⅔ cup coconut oil

¾ cup raw honey, maple syrup, or Rapadura

1½ tsp sea salt

2 tsp baking soda

1 tsp pure vanilla extract

For the sponge:

1. In a large glass bowl, mix together all the sponge ingredients. Leave a little extra space because the grains will rise some during the souring process.

2. Cover and leave at room temperature for at least 12 to 24 hours.

For the cereal:

1. Preheat the oven to 325°F (165°C).

2. In a medium bowl, mix together all the cereal ingredients, including the sponge. Add any desirable flavors. (See Variations.)

3. Transfer the mixture to a glass baking dish, filling it about two-thirds. You might need to use another baking dish.

4. Place the dish in the oven and bake until a toothpick inserted in the center comes out clean, about 40 minutes. Remove the dish from the oven and allow the cereal to cool.

5. Crumble the cereal into small pieces, spread them on a dehydrator sheet, and dry them at 115°F (50°C). I normally start mine in the evening, turn it a few times before bed, and get up in the morning to find it at the perfect texture. However, feel free to tweak the timing based on your preferences. Remove the sheet from the dehydrator and let the cereal dry. (If you don't have a dehydrator, spread the cereal pieces out on cookie sheets and bake them in your oven on the lowest heat possible. I prop my oven open with a knife to decrease the temperature even further. Because this method will probably be quicker than with a dehydrator, be sure to keep an eye on the cereal. Turn the sheets every few hours.)

6. Transfer the cereal to bowls and pour milk over the top before serving. Store in an airtight container at room temperature for up to 2 weeks.

Variations:

• **Peanut Butter Cereal:** 1 cup of peanut butter and 1 teaspoon of organic maple flavoring

• **Apple Cinnamon Cereal:** 2 diced Fuji or other sweet apples and 1 tablespoon of ground cinnamon

• **Walnut & Banana Cereal:** ¾ cup of soaked walnuts, 2 medium bananas, and 1 tablespoon of ground cinnamon

• **Maple Cereal:** 1 teaspoon of organic maple flavoring and 1 teaspoon of ground cinnamon

Impossible Salmon & Spinach Pie

A chewy and flaky biscuit top baked over dill-flavored layers of cheese, spinach, and salmon. Top too dark? Consider tenting this casserole with foil during the last 10 minutes of baking (step 6), then remove the cover while the cheese melts.

Yield:	Prep time:	Ferment time:	Ferment type:
1 pie	5 minutes	none	lacto

¼ cup melted plus 2 tbsp unmelted salted butter, divided, plus more

4 cups coarsely chopped spinach

1 medium yellow onion, diced

3 garlic cloves, crushed

1 (14oz [400g] can of wild red salmon, drained

2 tsp dried dill, divided

1¼ tsp sea salt, divided

⅛ tsp ground black pepper

2 cups shredded cheddar cheese, divided

1½ cups Sourdough Starter (page 204), fed within the last 12 hours

4 large eggs

½ cup whole milk

1 tsp baking soda

1. Preheat the oven to 425°F (220°C). Grease a 9- x 13-inch (23 x 33cm) baking dish with butter.

2. In a small pot on the stovetop over medium heat, place a small amount of water. Place a steamer basket in the pot and place the spinach in the basket. Steam the spinach until wilted but still bright green, about 2 minutes. Drain and set aside.

3. In an 8-inch (20cm) skillet on the stovetop over medium heat, combine the onion, garlic, and 2 tablespoons of unmelted butter. Sauté until soft. Add the salmon and 1 teaspoon of dill. Mix gently to leave chunky while all the ingredients warm. Add the spinach and toss gently. Sprinkle ¼ teaspoon of salt and the pepper over the top. Toss gently.

4. Spread the mixture in the bottom of the prepared dish. Sprinkle 1½ cups of cheese over the top.

5. In a medium bowl, whisk together the sourdough starter, eggs, milk, the remaining ¼ cup of melted butter, the remaining 1 teaspoon of dill, and the remaining 1 teaspoon of salt. Add the baking soda and whisk briskly. When the mixture starts to bubble up, pour immediately over the salmon.

6. Place the dish in the oven and bake until well browned and a toothpick inserted in the center comes out clean, about 30 minutes.

7. Remove the dish from the oven. Sprinkle the remaining ½ cup of cheese and the remaining 1 teaspoon of dill over the top. Return the dish to the oven for 5 minutes to melt the cheese.

8. Remove the dish from the oven. Allow the pie to rest for 10 to 30 minutes before serving. Store in an airtight container in the fridge for up to 2 days.

Variation: Use other preferred meats or vegetables for an unlimited variety of sourdough pies.

Surf to Turf Fermenting

Now that you know the basics of fermenting, you can learn how to ferment animal foods. This section starts with fermenting dairy. You'll get a basic understanding of the particulars of fermenting dairy and what makes it different from other fermenting. Then you'll try fermenting dairy through many recipes. This part concludes with an exploration of fermenting meats and fish. Again, you'll read the pertinent details of fermenting those food groups and then you'll wind up with a collection of delicious recipes.

Noncheese Cultured Dairy

In this first chapter focusing on fermenting the foods of animals, we'll start exploring the kinds of foods you can create when fermenting milk. Fermenting dairy is different from fermenting other types of food, and in this chapter, we'll talk about the special ingredients, techniques, and storage considerations that are unique to fermenting dairy. This chapter includes lots of noncheese cultured dairy recipes that are sure to become staples in your kitchen. In Chapter 13, we'll dive into fermenting simple cheeses.

The Basics of Fermented Dairy

When milk is fermented or cultured, you get all manner of dairy foods: buttermilk, yogurt, sour cream, cream cheese, and all kinds of hard and soft cheeses. They're all cultured dairy. Which one you get is determined by how the dairy is cultured (with what organisms) and how the curds are formed (by acids or through the addition of rennet or both). *Rennet*, or rennin, is an enzyme that causes the protein in milk to coagulate into curds. We'll talk more about rennet later in this chapter.

In this book and out in the world, I and others often use the words "culture" and "ferment" interchangeably, especially when talking about dairy. Most dairy foods in a mainstream grocery store are no longer fermented. The craft of culturing dairy experienced the same fate as the old-fashioned pickles I mentioned in Chapter 1. Modern food production methods replaced traditional fermenting to allow for the production of shelf-stable foods with consistent flavors and results. Also, industrial dairy-farming methods—overcrowding, unnatural feed choices, unhealthy animals, and unsanitary conditions—created contaminated and unhealthy milk, which is one of the main reasons the dairy industry adopted pasteurization in the early 20th century. These changes had a profound impact on which truly cultured dairy foods were available for sale.

To create similar foods rather quickly that would last a long time on the shelf, producers started using fake flavors, fake colors, preservatives, and additives when making sour cream, buttermilk, cheeses, and other dairy foods. Sometimes, producers culture dairy in the beginning but then pasteurize the end product before shipping it to you. This destroys beneficial organisms. There are exceptions, such as yogurt, sour cream, or kefir (similar to yogurt but thinner, tarter, and more effervescent)—many brands of which are marked as containing active cultures. If you read labels, many commercial yogurts or kefirs include significant amounts of sugar as well as other non-whole-food ingredients, such as nonfat dry milk powder. No matter where you fall on the subject of whether those additional ingredients are any good, I'm happy to tell you that what you'll learn in this book are tried-and-true old-fashioned methods of culturing dairy at home to create the most healthful and supremely delicious foods—without additives.

Homemade kefir can include up to 50 different strains of organisms—5 to 10 times more than yogurt. But when kefir first hit the market, trouble hit. Containers on grocery store shelves would explode or significantly expand because of the built-up gases given off by the fermenting organisms. Thus, kefir-makers removed the most effervescent strains from the mother culture to create a more shelf-stable kefir for the mass market. Even though some kefirs contain significant amounts of added sugar, it's still a relatively untouched cultured dairy food on the market.

Just like fermenting other foods, culturing dairy involves beneficial organisms. You can ferment dairy with yeasts, bacteria, or molds—or all or some of them. And just like in other ferments, the organisms can work alone or together. These beneficial organisms feast on milk sugar, called "lactose," and produce carbon dioxide, lactic acid, enzymes, and sometimes other things. The carbon dioxide can make the fermented dairy bubbly, but it really depends on what cultured dairy is in question. For example, kefir can be very bubbly. Some of the organisms fermenting it are excellent bubble-makers!

All other arguments aside, the best-tasting cultured dairy and cheeses come from the raw milk of dairy animals feasting on diverse and lush pastures. If not pasteurized, this milk enables artisan and home cheese-makers to create cultured dairy foods with subtle and complex flavors.

Fermentation of Dairy: A Process All Its Own

Fermenting dairy looks different from the fermentation process of other foods. Let's go over the main differences.

Acid Curdling

Dairy does a funny thing when it fills up with the fermenting organisms' acids: It coagulates into curds, and if the fermentation keeps going, it separates into curds and whey. Other foods don't do this. It's a pretty cool thing because if it didn't, we wouldn't have beautiful and tasty fermented dairy foods, such as sour cream, buttermilk, yogurt, or kefir. All these foods are thickened or set up over time entirely because fermenting organisms produced acids.

We can stimulate quicker milk curdling through the addition of rennet, an enzyme that has the same effect as adding an acid. You'll need rennet in a few recipes in this book. Avoid rennet known as "junket rennet," which is really no good and doesn't perform well. See Appendix B for sources from which to purchase quality rennet. Rennet comes from animal and vegetable sources as well as in liquid, powder, and tablet form. Personally, I keep multiple forms of rennet on hand because I culture a lot of dairy and this gives me maximum flexibility to follow varied recipes.

Starter Cultures

Starter cultures aren't essential when culturing raw milk or cream because this raw dairy contains naturally present beneficial organisms. The organisms can culture the dairy on their own. When the milk or cream is left out at room temperature and loosely covered, the native beneficial organisms thrive and proliferate.

However, certain flavors and results are desirable, which is why cheese-makers often use specific starter cultures. Also, some people can't access or don't wish to use raw milk, in which case using a starter culture is absolutely necessary. Pasteurized milk doesn't contain naturally present beneficial organisms to get the dairy fermenting on its own.

For that starter culture, we can't use whey as you've seen in other types of fermentation. It's too acidic and would curdle milk when we don't want it curdled. It might also change flavors from mild to too sour. So we use special starter cultures for fermenting dairy.

Unless otherwise specified, all fermented dairy recipes in this book call for an all-purpose mesophilic starter culture. *Mesophilic* comes from "meso," meaning middle, and "philia," meaning love, which describes well how the organisms in a mesophilic starter love middle temperatures. They work well right around room temperature up to around 86°F (29°C). I use and recommend the Danisco 4002 and Abiasa Mesophilic III starter cultures (see Appendix B for sources). You can use them interchangeably.

Keep cultures and rennet stored in the fridge or freezer, where they'll last up to a year. It's also a good idea to place the packages inside an airtight container to prevent moisture from getting inside them.

Airflow

The fermenting organisms in dairy work without oxygen inside the milk. But closing off the culturing container isn't usually as important when fermenting dairy as it is with other foods. What we do in most cases is cover a fermenting container that contains dairy with a cloth napkin or paper towel, then secure that to the jar with a rubber band. This way, the ferment can breathe out, but it's protected from dust particles and other contaminants. When the dairy goes into the fridge or cold storage, we cover it more securely with a lid or another airtight seal.

Storage

Fermented dairy foods, like most fermented foods, should be stored in cold storage—either the fridge or cellar. Cheeses that benefit from aging should be waxed and kept in an environment with good airflow, between 40°F and 50°F (4°C to 10°C), and in at least 50% humidity. Controlling these conditions is why many cheese-makers opt to set up a separate cheese-aging area called a "cheese cave." This book doesn't contain any cheese recipes that require this kind of aging, but I thought I'd mention it so you can see the bigger picture.

You can expect the fermented dairy you make to sour more over time rather than spoil. Jars of fermented dairy (such as buttermilk, sour cream, kefir, or yogurt) that are kept in the fridge for many weeks might become very ripe. By that I mean quite sour. However, they're not necessarily spoiled. You might not want to eat them at that point—I grant you that. I'm not sure I do either. For the best results, I'd suggest consuming fermented dairy within 2 to 4 weeks when stored in the refrigerator. You can freeze cheeses in airtight containers for up to 1 to 2 months.

If mold has accumulated on the surface, as it tends to do in the portion exposed to the air, you can skim it away. Often, what's underneath is fine. What to do with very ripe fermented dairy? It makes good food for chickens, you can add it to recipes calling for cultured dairy, such as sour cream or yogurt, or you can use it diluted in salad dressings. No need to waste it.

Nutrition of Cultured Dairy

Before we dig into the recipes in this chapter and the next, let's quickly discuss the nutrition of cultured dairy. You might be lactose-intolerant or you might know someone who is. Remember that lactose is milk sugar. People with certain genetic heritages produce less or no lactase (the enzyme required to digest lactose). For them, eating dairy can cause quite a bit of digestive discomfort or other symptoms. Also, as some people age, they tend to produce fewer digestive enzymes, also leading to lower amounts of lactase available to digest milk sugar. Fermented dairy can help with this quite a bit—and here's how.

Remember that the organisms eat lactose as they ferment it. This means that by the time the dairy passes our lips, there's much less lactose present or none at all. The longer dairy ferments, the more lactose is consumed by the organisms. That's pretty cool, but here's something even better: The organisms produce lactase to help them consume the milk sugar. Now enzymes don't get used up. They're only destroyed by heat. So if we eat the cultured dairy food without heating it up, we're taking in a bunch of lactase to help digest whatever lactose is left. This is marvelous. (And if the dairy were raw in the beginning, lactase is naturally present before any culturing even occurs.)

Fermented dairy contains high levels of vitamins B and C. If the milk came from animals feasting on rapidly growing green grass (and wasn't heated), the fermented dairy also contains significant amounts of essential fat-soluble vitamins: A, D, E, and K. Plus, fermentation makes the calcium in dairy more available to our bodies.

What Milk to Choose

When you're choosing milk (or cream) to use for culturing, it just so happens that the dairy that performs best for culturing also happens to be the most healthful. That makes the choices simple—at least theoretically. I'm going to give you a list of milk choices from best to worst. They're ranked by two qualities: the dairy animals' diet and how the milk is processed.

I should define the terms in the following list. With regard to diet, dairy animals are either "pastured" or "grain-fed." *Pastured* means the animal eats mostly pasture (and quality hay during the off-season) and it might or might not receive a small amount of grain supplementation. On the other hand, *grain-fed* means the animal is fed mostly grain, with very little pasture or hay.

With regard to milk processing, these terms come into play: pasteurized, raw, and homogenized. We talked about *pasteurization* earlier in this book: It's the heating of milk (or any food) to kill all organisms—whether beneficial or spoiling. *Raw milk* is just the opposite: It hasn't been heated and retains all its naturally present organisms and enzymes. *Homogenization* is the process used to prevent the cream from rising to the top in milks that would do this naturally. (Goat and some cow milks don't separate much or at all.) A discussion of why pasteurization and homogenization are unhealthful is beyond the scope of this book, but see Appendix B for recommended websites and books on that topic.

And here are your choices—from best to worst. The best choices produce consistently better results when cultured, not to mention more complex and gourmet flavors in the end result.

1. Raw whole milk from a pastured animal

2. Nonhomogenized pasteurized whole milk from a pastured animal

3. Nonhomogenized pasteurized whole milk from a grain-fed animal

4. Homogenized pasteurized milk (whole is better than skimmed)

5. Ultra-pasteurized milk (whole or skimmed)

The last choice (ultra-pasteurized) *shouldn't* be used for culturing or at least not reliably. The processing denatures the milk components so severely that you can't rely on it to support a culture. However, many recipes call for calcium chloride, an optional ingredient that assists rennet to form curds where rennet might fail by itself. In this way, one can successfully culture ultra-pasteurized milk.

The modern breed of cow, the Holstein, gives milk with more water and less nutrition than milk from the older Jersey breed. You have to drink 1⅔ glasses of Holstein milk to get the same amount of milk fat, protein, calcium, phosphorous, magnesium, and vitamins A, D, E, and K that one glass of Jersey milk contains.

You might be limited in what milk choices are available to you. I suggest searching for local, quality milk sources through the website www.realmilk.com. Options are organized by state. Also, you can ask around to see if anyone you know has a local milk source or raises a dairy animal with extra milk for sale. Otherwise, scour the grocery and health food stores for the very best you can find. No matter what, regardless what milk you choose, you're making it better by culturing it.

And now I think we're ready to try some simple cultured dairy recipes. (Simple cultured dairy cheeses are in Chapter 13.) When you're thinking about how to eat your fermented dairy foods, keep in mind that you'll get the most nutrition from them if they're not heated much past 100°F (38°C). Heat destroys beneficial organisms, vitamins, and enzymes. The first set of recipes are primary ferments, where milk is cultured to create unique and varied ferments. The second set of recipes in this chapter helps you use the fermented dairy foods in various dishes.

Primary Fermentation Recipes

This first assortment of cultured dairy recipes includes all the most familiar, such as buttermilk and yogurt, as well as some that might surprise you, such as cultured butter made from cream that's soured first. Enjoy!

Clabber

This is a mild-tasting, yogurt-like cultured dairy that requires no starter and is delicious when added to smoothies or used in dressings and dips. Clabber, or spontaneously cultured milk, is very similar to what the traveling nomad of legend found in his animal-stomach canteen after a long day's journey. Most people say the enzyme rennin in the lining of his canteen probably curdled the milk, but I believe it's equally likely that acids from the organisms curdled the milk. And that's what clabber is—milk soured and thickened by the acids produced by naturally present and proliferating organisms.

When our family had a Jersey milk cow, Gracie, she gave between 4 and 5 gallons (15 to 18 liters) of milk a day. From that milk, I could make butter, sour cream, cheese, ice cream, kefir and yogurt, and more. But I still couldn't keep up! So I'd take a few gallons (liters) every few days and skim off the cream for butter, sour cream, and ice cream. Then I 'd clabber the skimmed milk. The clabber made nutritious, high-protein, and tasty food for the chickens and dog!

Yield:	Prep time:	Ferment time:	Ferment type:
2 cups	15 minutes	2 to 3 days	lacto

½ gallon (2 liters) raw whole milk
  (cow or goat)

1. Add the milk to a ½-gallon (2-liter) jar. Cover with a cloth napkin or paper towel. Secure with a rubber band. Leave at room temperature until the milk sets up like yogurt, about 2 days. If you're using cow's milk, there will be a layer of sour cream at the top and thickened milk below.

2. Cover with a lid. Transfer to cool storage for up to several weeks. Use in dressings or smoothies. Or use it to make Clabber Cheese (page 272).

Buttermilk

Whole milk buttermilk is rich, sweet, and creamy, and it makes a wonderful substitute for yogurt or sour cream in salad dressings. There are two kinds of buttermilk, not including the fake store-bought kinds. The first is whole milk cultured with middle-temperature-loving bacteria, as seen in this recipe. The second kind of buttermilk is what spills out from fresh sweet cream or cultured cream when butter is made. (See the recipe for Cultured Butter [page 248].)

Yield:	Prep time:	Ferment time:	Ferment type:
4 cups	15 minutes	2 to 3 days	lacto

Use either:

3 cups raw or pasteurized whole milk (cow or goat)

1 cup buttermilk with active cultures

4 cups raw or pasteurized whole milk (cow or goat)

1/16 tsp mesophilic cheese starter culture

1. In a wide-mouth quart (liter) jar, combine either the milk and buttermilk or the milk and mesophilic starter. Stir well.

2. Cover with a cloth napkin or paper towel. Secure with a rubber band. Leave at room temperature until it sets up like yogurt, about 12 to 24 hours.

3. Cover with a lid and chill for at least 6 hours before using. Store in the fridge for up to several weeks.

Cultured Butter

With its complex blend of sweet and sour flavors, cultured butter (made from cream that's allowed to sour) is delicious on toast, pancakes, waffles, muffins, and more. Yellow butter comes from yellow cream—and yellow cream comes from animals feasting on the carotenes in rapidly growing green grass. Yellow butter is a seasonal food of the green grass season and a significant source of essential vitamin A—so eat up!

Yield:	Prep time:	Ferment time:	Ferment type:
1 pound (450 grams)	30 minutes	24 hours	lacto

⅛ tsp mesophilic cheese starter culture or 4 tbsp buttermilk with active cultures

1 quart (liter) raw or pasteurized heavy cream

¼ to ½ tsp sea salt

1. In a wide-mouth quart (liter) jar, combine the mesophilic culture or buttermilk and the cream. Stir well.

2. Cover with a cloth napkin or paper towel. Secure with a rubber band. Leave at room temperature for about 24 hours.

3. Cover with a lid and refrigerate for at least 6 hours to chill thoroughly.

4. Transfer the cream to a food processor, mixer, or blender. Blend the cream through these stages: whipped cream to chunky cream to where butter solids form. Blend for about 30 seconds more to release all the butter solids.

5. Drain the butter using a strainer, catching the buttermilk in a medium bowl. Save this for baking or salad dressings.

6. Place the butter solids in a separate medium bowl. Add cold water to cover. Use a wooden spoon or your hands to repeatedly fold and press the butter into the sides of the bowl. Drain and discard the water.

7. Add fresh cold water and repeat folding and draining until the water stays clear. Drain a final time. Press the butter against the sides of the bowl several times without adding water. Drain any water that releases.

8. Add the salt to taste. Shape the butter into patties or logs on wax paper or use a butter mold. Close up the ends of the wax paper. Store in the fridge for up to a few weeks or in the freezer for many months.

Cultured Butter

Dairy Kefir

Kefir is a dairy ferment similar to yogurt. However, the differences are significant. Kefir is thinner, more tart, more effervescent, and contains a small amount of alcohol (1% according to most sources). It can contain up to 10 times more varieties of beneficial organisms than yogurt. In addition, where yogurt is fermented through bacteria, the kefir mother culture is a cooperative colony of bacteria and yeast. This mother culture is a soft and spongy cauliflower-like clump of grains, aptly called "kefir grains." With care, you can maintain your kefir grains for years and years and years—and even better, they'll have babies you can share with friends.

Yield:	Prep time:	Ferment time:	Ferment type:
1 quart (1 liter)	5 minutes	24 to 48 hours	lacto

1 quart (liter) raw or pasteurized whole milk (cow or goat), plus more

1 tbsp active kefir grains (see Appendix B for sources)

1. In a wide-mouth quart (liter) jar, combine the milk and kefir grains. Swirl lightly. Cover with a cloth napkin or paper towel. Secure with a rubber band.

2. Leave at room temperature for 24 to 48 hours or even 18 hours in warmer weather. It's done when thickened to your liking. You might see ribbons of whey curling up the sides of the jar as an indicator that the kefir is done.

3. Some grains will float to the top. If this occurs, scoop them out and transfer them to a fresh quart (liter) of whole milk to make more kefir, repeating the process. If grains aren't floating to the top or have become separated, transfer the kefir through a plastic or stainless steel strainer to a clean jar. Tap the strainer lightly to help the kefir fall through, leaving the grains in the strainer. Transfer the grains to a fresh quart (liter) of whole milk to make more kefir (no need to rinse), repeating the process. If you don't want to make more kefir, store the kefir grains covered with milk in a small jar in the fridge for up to 1 week. Change the milk weekly—you can use the grains indefinitely.

4. Cover and store in the fridge for up to many weeks, where it will get more sour over time.

Variation: If you're using nonhomogenized whole milk, the cream will rise to the top and thicken like the milk below it. Whisk it all together if desired. Or skim the kefir cream to use like sour cream.

Dairy Kefir

Coconut Milk Kefir

A dairy-free alternative to milk kefir, coconut milk kefir turns out sweeter, thicker, and smoother. The only downside to making coconut milk kefir is that because the kefir grains won't grow in coconut milk, you won't end up with kefir babies to share with others.

Yield:	Prep time:	Ferment time:	Ferment type:
1 quart (1 liter)	5 minutes	24 to 48 hours	lacto

1 quart (liter) coconut milk, whisked with water to make a drinkable consistency, plus more

1 tbsp active kefir grains (see Appendix B for sources), rinsed if from other recipes

1. In a wide-mouth quart (liter) jar, combine the coconut milk and active kefir grains. Swirl lightly. Cover with a cloth napkin or paper towel. Secure with a rubber band.

2. Leave at room temperature for 24 to 48 hours or even 18 hours in warmer weather. It's done when thickened to your liking. You might see ribbons of whey curling up the sides of the jar as an indicator that the kefir is done.

3. Some grains will float to the top. If this occurs, scoop them out and transfer them to a fresh quart (liter) of coconut milk to make more kefir, repeating the process. If grains aren't floating at the top or have become separated, transfer the kefir through a plastic or stainless steel strainer to a clean jar. Tap the strainer lightly to help the kefir fall through, leaving the grains in the strainer.

4. Transfer the grains to a fresh quart (liter) of coconut milk to make more kefir (no need to rinse), repeating the process. If you don't want to make more kefir, store the kefir grains covered with any type of milk in a small jar in the fridge for up to 1 week. Change the milk weekly—you can use the grains indefinitely.

5. Cover and store in the fridge for up to many weeks, where it will get more sour over time.

Kefir Cream

To make a cream that's tangier than your regular sour cream, culturing with a kefir grain adds another dimension when you drizzle the cream on eggs, baked potatoes, or soup or you eat it with raw honey and fruit. If you get a soft, thin layer of white fuzz at the top of your kefir ferments, typically when you allow a longer fermentation, don't be alarmed. This is a yeast in the air that grows right at the top of ferments and is very common with dairy fermentation because we allow airflow. It isn't one of the beneficial desirable yeasts, but then again, it isn't harmful either. To prevent it from changing the flavor of your ferment, skim it off the top rather than stir it in. Next time, try using fewer kefir grains or fermenting for a shorter amount of time.

Yield:	Prep time:	Ferment time:	Ferment type:
2 cups	2 minutes	12 to 24 hours	lacto

1 to 2 tsp kefir grains

2 cups raw or pasteurized heavy cream, plus more

1. In a wide-mouth 1-pint (½-liter) jar, gently combine the kefir grains and cream. Let the grains float freely. Cover with a cloth napkin or paper towel. Secure with a rubber band.

2. Leave at room temperature until the mixture sets up like firm yogurt, about 12 to 24 hours.

3. Scoop out the grains and transfer them to a fresh 1-pint (½-liter) jar of cream to make more kefir cream, repeating the process (no need to rinse the grains. If you don't wish to make more, store the kefir grains covered with milk in a small jar in the fridge for up to 1 week. Change the milk weekly—you can use the grains indefinitely.

4. Cover with a lid and refrigerate for at least 6 hours before using. Store in the fridge for up to several weeks.

Variation: Substitute half the cream in your favorite chocolate ice cream recipe with kefir cream for tangy sweetness.

Instant Pot Yogurt

Is it possible to make thick, raw milk yogurt in an Instant Pot? In other words, can you skip the pasteurizing step, retaining all the raw goodness of your milk and still end up with thick yogurt? Absolutely!

Yield:	Prep time:	Ferment time:	Ferment type:
1 gallon (4 liters)	5 minutes	24 hours	lacto

1 gallon (4 liters) raw and/or whole milk*

2½ tbsp sustainably sourced gelatin (glyphosate-free recommended)**

1/64 tsp LyoPro Y+ yogurt culture***

1. In a 6- or 8-quart (5.5- or 7.5-liter) Instant Pot with the Yogurt function, whisk together 4 cups of milk and the gelatin. Press the Yogurt button. Then press the Adjust button so the display reads Boil.

2. While stirring constantly, let the milk heat just enough to melt the gelatin. You can tell it's ready when no more flakes of gelatin are visible in the milk. (Scoop up a spoonful to check visually). Press the Cancel button.

3. Add the remaining 12 cups of milk and the yogurt culture. Stir well.

4. Put the lid on the Instant Pot and turn the venting knob to the sealing position. Press the Yogurt button. Use the Adjust button if necessary for the Normal setting.

5. Use the -/+ buttons to adjust the time: at least 6 to 8 hours and up to 24 hours for GAPS (Gut and Psychology Syndrome) or THM (Trim Healthy Mama).

6. Place the Instant Pot in a corner of the kitchen to culture undisturbed. (You can periodically open the Instant Pot to check the yogurt if you'd like.)

7. When the time ends, place a glass or silicone lid on the insert pot and transfer that to the fridge for 24 hours to set up fully. This is an IMPORTANT step.

8. Skim the cream that rose to the top for sour cream or making cultured butter if desired. Divide the yogurt into smaller jars or serve the yogurt directly from the insert pot. Store in the fridge for up to 1 month.

* Scale this up to 5 quarts (4.75 liters) for a 6-quart (5.5-liter) Instant Pot or to 7 quarts (6.5 liters) for an 8-quart (7.5-liter) Instant Pot.

** The formula is 1 to 3 teaspoons per quart (liter) of yogurt you're making. Scale up or down accordingly.

*** If you use this culture, you'll need 1/64 teaspoon per quart (liter). For example, 1/64 teaspoon x 4 for 4 quarts (4 liters). Measure using mini measuring spoons. Scale up or down accordingly.

Villi Yogurt

Typically thinner than grocery-store yogurt, this mild yet tart yogurt is delicious on top of pancakes or mixed with fresh fruit and honey. Villi is a traditional yogurt that cultures at room temperature. Yogurt you usually find in grocery stores is cultured at higher temperatures simply because the organisms involved need a higher temperature. With villi—and around a dozen similar strains— the organisms work best right around room temperature. See Appendix B for information about where to buy villi or other similar yogurt starter cultures.

Yield:	Prep time:	Ferment time:	Ferment type:
1 quart (1 liter)	5 minutes	12 to 24 hours	lacto

8½ cups raw or pasteurized whole milk (cow or goat), divided, plus more to keep the starter going

villi powdered yogurt starter (see Appendix B for sources)

1. If using raw milk, heat ½ cup milk in a small pot on the stovetop over medium-low heat to 160°F (70°C). Let cool to room temperature.

2. In a wide-mouth 1-pint (½-liter) jar, combine this milk (or ½ cup pasteurized milk if that's your milk choice) and ½ teaspoon of yogurt starter. Stir well. Cover with a cloth napkin or paper towel. Secure with a rubber band.

3. Leave at room temperature until the yogurt is set and doesn't run up the sides of the jar when tipped, about 24 to 48 hours. Cover with a lid and refrigerate for 6 hours. This is the mother culture.

4. If using raw milk, reserve 1 tablespoon of mother culture. In a ½-gallon (2-liter) jar, combine 7 teaspoons of mother culture and 7 cups of whole milk. Stir well.

5. If using pasteurized milk, in a ½-gallon (2-liter) jar, combine 8 tablespoons of mother culture and the remaining 8 cups of whole milk. Stir well.

6. Cover with a cloth napkin or paper towel. Secure with a rubber band. Leave at room temperature until it has a thin yogurt-like consistency, about 12 to 24 hours. Cover with a lid and refrigerate for 6 hours. This is the villi yogurt, which you can eat as is or strain through cheesecloth to achieve a thicker yogurt. Store in the fridge for up to 1 week, where it gets more sour over time.

7. If using raw milk, in a wide-mouth 1-pint (½-liter) jar, combine the reserved 1 tablespoon of mother culture and the remaining 1 cup of whole milk (heated and cooled as in step 1) to make more mother culture as described in step 1. Use this for additional batches. Store in the fridge for up to 1 week. If not used to make more yogurt within 1 week, use it to make another pure mother culture as described in step 1 and store in the fridge.

8. If using pasteurized milk, reserve enough villi yogurt to make a new batch of yogurt. You need 1 tablespoon of yogurt per cup of milk for future batches, repeating steps 2 and 3 as needed. As a starter, villi yogurt from pasteurized milk keeps in the fridge for up to 1 week. Use within 1 week for a new starter or a new batch of yogurt or else it will lose its culturing strength.

Variation: To achieve a thicker yogurt, strain the finished yogurt through two layers of 90-thread-count cheesecloth.

Dairy-Free Yogurt

When my friend Andrea gave up dairy, she thought her days of eating creamy, delicious yogurt were over. Then she discovered how easy it was to make her own dairy-free yogurt.

Yield:	Prep time:	Ferment time:	Ferment type:
About 3½ cups	30 minutes	12 hours	lacto

3½ cups dairy-free milk of choice (such as 2 (14oz [400g]) cans of coconut milk, divided

2 tbsp tapioca flour or another thickener (see Recipe Notes)

1 packet of dairy-free yogurt starter, ¼ cup plain dairy-free yogurt, or 4 probiotic capsules

1 tbsp raw honey, maple syrup, or evaporated cane juice

1. Add 3¼ cups of dairy-free milk to a medium saucepan on the stovetop over medium-low heat. In a small bowl, whisk together the remaining ¼ cup of dairy-free milk and the tapioca flour. Whisk this mixture into the milk. Cook until bubbling and thickened, about 3 to 5 minutes.

2. Remove the saucepan from the heat and let the milk cool to about 100°F (38°C) or look for the specific temperature for milk given in the yogurt starter instructions (if using).

3. Add the yogurt starter or dairy-free yogurt (whichever you're using) to the milk. Or open the probiotic capsules and sprinkle their contents into the milk. Whisk until combined. Transfer the milk to seven ½-pint (¼-liter) jars or two 1-pint (½-liter) jars.

4. Place the jars in a yogurt maker and culture for 12 hours. If you like a sour yogurt, you might want to culture for longer. If you don't have a yogurt maker, there are many other ways to incubate the yogurt. (See Recipe Notes.)

5. Once the culturing time is complete, cover the jars with lids and place them in the fridge to stop the culturing process and cool.

6. Once cooled, add the honey, maple syrup, or cane juice before serving.

Recipe Notes:

• If you use gelatin, use about 2 teaspoons per quart (liter) of yogurt.

• If you use chia seeds, add 8 tablespoons per quart (liter) of yogurt after culturing but before refrigerating the yogurt.

• If you use agar, because the amount needed depends on the kind purchased, feel free to experiment!

• Use the Instant Pot on the sauté function to prepare the milk mixture. Leaving the milk mixture in the Instant Pot, choose the Yogurt function on "normal" (not low or high) and incubate with the lid on for 12 hours. When done, separate the yogurt into jars and chill thoroughly for 12 to 24 hours.

• In step 4, in a medium or large pot without a long handle, boil a pot of water and cover. Line a cooler with bath towels. Put the pot in the cooler on top of the towels. Also put the jars of milk in the cooler next to the pot and on the towels. Close the cooler lid and let the yogurt incubate in the warmth for 12 hours. When done, transfer the jars to the refrigerator to chill thoroughly.

Variation: To achieve a thicker yogurt, strain the finished yogurt through two layers of 90-thread-count cheesecloth.

Sour Cream

This condiment is sour, sweet, and creamy—providing the perfect excuse to serve more vegetables when you can top them with this! If your cream is raw, you can let it culture spontaneously by eliminating the starter culture and letting the naturally present organisms do the thickening. They might take a little longer. However, even when using raw cream, I find that adding a culture guarantees a mild, consistent, and appealing sour flavor.

Yield:	Prep time:	Ferment time:	Ferment type:
2 cups	5 minutes	12 to 24 hours	lacto

2 tbsp sour cream with active cultures or 1/16 tsp mesophilic cheese culture

2 cups heavy or whipping cream

1. In a wide-mouth quart (liter) jar, combine the sour cream or mesophilic culture and the heavy or whipping cream. Mix well. Cover with a cloth napkin or paper towel. Secure with a rubber band.

2. Leave at room temperature until the mixture sets up like firm yogurt, about 12 to 24 hours.

3. Cover with a lid and refrigerate for at least 6 hours before using. Store in the fridge for up to several weeks.

Variation: Heavy cream or whipping cream yields a thick sour cream, as does a longer culturing time. Lighter cream yields thinner crème fraîche, as does a shorter culturing time.

Fermented Dairy Recipes

Now that you've got all these fermented dairy foods, what do you do with them? I've done my best to give you ideas within the recipes themselves, but here are some more recipes using fermented dairy foods.

Herb, Honey & Mustard Kefir Salad Dressing

Honey, mustard, and fresh herbs complement the fresh and tangy kefir in this dressing. Toss with diced summer vegetables or drizzle over a green salad.

Yield:	Prep time:	Ferment time:	Ferment type:
2 cups	5 minutes	none	lacto

2 cups Dairy Kefir (page 250)

4 tbsp extra-virgin olive oil or toasted sesame oil

1 tsp sea salt

1 tbsp chopped fresh parsley

1 tbsp chopped fresh chives

1 tbsp chopped fresh basil

1 tbsp chopped fresh cilantro

2 tsp freshly squeezed lemon juice

2 tsp raw honey

2 tsp prepared mustard (any type)

1. In a 1-pint (½-liter) jar, whisk together all the ingredients until smooth.

2. Cover and store in the fridge for up to a few weeks.

Variation: Use yogurt or buttermilk or a combination of the two for this dressing. You can also add any other herbs you like.

Creamy Herbed Salad Dressing

This simple dressing will make fresh, vegetable-loaded salads sing! It's rich and filled with herbal goodness—and there's no mayo, making it perfect for anyone with egg allergies.

Yield:	Prep time:	Ferment time:	Ferment type:
about 3 cups	8 minutes	varies	lacto

1 cup soft cheese (chèvre [goat cheese], cream cheese, yogurt cheese, or kefir cheese) or 1½ to 2 cups sour cream

1 cup raw whole milk, plus more (omit if using sour cream)

¼ cup apple cider vinegar

2 tsp herbed seasoning salt or 1 tsp sea salt, plus more

1 tbsp dried dill

1 tbsp dried parsley

pinch of ground black pepper

1. In a food processor or blender (or by hand), whisk together all the ingredients. Add more milk as needed for consistency. Adjust seasonings to taste.

2. Transfer to an airtight container. Store in the fridge for up to 1 week.

Recipe Notes:

• Because yogurt and kefir cheese are tangy, feel free to add a little honey or another natural sweetener. Trim Healthy Mama (THM) plan followers, use stevia or another on-plan sweetening option.

• The flavors develop more as the dressing sits. You might want to give it a couple hours before serving. Taste and adjust as needed.

• If you think you want more of a seasoning, taste the dressing first to make sure.

• Did you add too much of an herb or seasoning? Just add more base ingredients and adjust seasonings to taste.

• Want to use fresh herbs instead? Remember the 3:1 ratio rule: You'll need three times as much fresh herbs as dried.

Radish Raita

Although this is typically made with yogurt, I prefer to use kefir for a bit more tang. Serve this with sandwiches for a delicious, cool spring or summer lunch.

Yield:	Prep time:	Ferment time:	Ferment type:
3 cups	5 minutes	none	lacto

1½ cups Dairy Kefir (page 250)

2 cups thinly sliced radishes

12 mint leaves, finely chopped

1. In a small serving bowl, combine the kefir, radishes, and mint leaves.

2. Refrigerate for 30 minutes to let the flavors meld before serving. Store in an airtight container in the fridge for up to 1 day.

Cucumber & Kefir Salad

I make the traditional Arabic cucumber and yogurt salad with kefir instead because I guess I like things a little more sour and bubbly! In Arabic, this salad is called *khyar bi laban*, which means "cucumber with yogurt."

Yield:	Prep time:	Ferment time:	Ferment type:
6 cups	5 minutes	none	lacto

2 to 3 garlic cloves, peeled

½ to 1 tsp sea salt, plus more

2 to 3 large cucumbers, peeled and diced

1 quart (1 liter) Dairy Kefir (page 250)

1 tsp dried mint

1. Use a mortar and pestle to mash together the garlic and salt.

2. In a medium bowl, combine the garlic mixture, cucumbers, and kefir. Gently mix. Taste and adjust seasoning. Gently stir in the mint.

3. Chill the salad before serving or serve immediately. Store in an airtight container in the fridge for up to 1 day.

Cold Cucumber Soup

This light and refreshing creamy cucumber soup pairs well with sandwiches, grilled meats, and fish.

Yield:	Prep time:	Ferment time:	Ferment type:
6 cups	5 minutes	none	lacto

5 medium cucumbers, divided

4 cups buttermilk

¼ tsp sea salt, plus more

pinch of ground black pepper, plus more

extra-virgin olive oil

1. Peel, seed, and coarsely chop 3 cucumbers. In a blender, combine the cucumbers and buttermilk. Blend until smooth.

2. Transfer the mixture to a storage container. Stir in the salt and pepper. Taste and adjust seasonings.

3. Peel, seed, and dice 1 cucumber. Stir into the cucumber and buttermilk mixture. Cover and chill for a few hours or up to 1 day.

4. Peel and slice the remaining 1 cucumber. Transfer the soup to bowls and drizzle olive oil over the top of each. Top with cucumber slices and more pepper to taste before serving. Store in an airtight container in the fridge for up to 1 day.

Kefir or Yogurt Parfait

Kids love these bowls of honey-sweetened and spiced kefir or yogurt tossed with crunchy nuts and coconut.

Yield:	Prep time:	Ferment time:	Ferment type:
2 cups	5 minutes	none	lacto

1 cup Dairy Kefir (page 250) or Villi Yogurt (page 256)

¼ cup chopped fresh seasonal fruit

1 tbsp dried fruits (such as raisins, chopped dates, or chopped figs)

¼ cup chopped nuts (such as walnuts or pecans)

1 tbsp unsweetened shredded coconut

2 tsp raw honey

pinch of ground cinnamon

pinch of ground nutmeg

1. Add the kefir or yogurt to a small serving bowl. Top with the fresh and dried fruits, nuts, and coconut.

2. Drizzle the honey over the top. Sprinkle the cinnamon and nutmeg over the top. Serve immediately.

Vanilla, Almond & Kefir Ice Cream

Vanilla and almond meet cold, sweet, and tangy to help you beat the heat on a hot day—or any day!

Yield:	Prep time:	Ferment time:	Ferment type:
1 quart (1 liter)	5 minutes	none	lacto

4 cups Dairy Kefir (page 250) or Villi Yogurt (page 256)

3 large eggs from local, pastured chickens (don't use store-bought, factory-farmed eggs), yolks only

⅓ cup raw honey

1 tbsp pure vanilla extract

1 tbsp almond extract

1. In a blender, combine the kefir or yogurt, egg yolks, honey, vanilla extract, and almond extract. Blend until smooth. Chill the mixture thoroughly for a few hours.

2. Transfer the mixture to an ice cream maker and freeze according to the manufacturer's directions.

3. Transfer the ice cream to a serving bowl and freeze for 1 to 3 hours to harden more. Serve when ready. Store leftovers tightly covered in the freezer for up to 1 week. Let soften at room temperature for 5 to 10 minutes before scooping.

Variations: If this is a little too sour for your taste, feel free to substitute sweet cream or whole milk for up to half the kefir or yogurt. To make Chocolate & Almond Ice Cream, omit the vanilla extract and add ½ cup of cocoa powder.

Chocolate & Honey Sour Cream Ice Cream

Like the Chocolate Sourdough Cake (page 212), this ice cream is perfectly tangy and chocolaty. Is your ice cream too hard? Using liquid sweeteners, such as honey, can help the ice cream harden quite a bit when frozen. Then let the ice cream thaw at room temperature for 15 to 20 minutes to soften before serving.

Yield:	Prep time:	Ferment time:	Ferment type:
1 quart (1 liter)	5 minutes	none	lacto

4 cups Sour Cream (page 260)

3 large eggs from local, pastured chickens (don't use store-bought, factory-farmed eggs), yolks only

½ cup cocoa powder

⅓ cup raw honey

1 tbsp pure vanilla extract

1. In a blender, combine the sour cream, egg yolks, cocoa powder, honey, and vanilla extract. Blend until smooth, although not so much as to make whipped cream. Chill the mixture thoroughly for a few hours.

2. Transfer the mixture to an ice cream maker and freeze according to the manufacturer's directions.

4. Transfer the ice cream to a serving bowl and freeze for 1 to 3 hours to harden more. Serve when ready. Store leftovers tightly covered in the freezer for up to 1 week. Let soften at room temperature for 5 to 10 minutes before scooping.

Variation: Omit the chocolate if you'd like a simple Honey Sour Cream Ice Cream.

Summer Berry & Kefir Smoothie

Sweetened with summer berries and dates, this smoothie is loved by those who think kefir is normally too tart.

Yield:	Prep time:	Ferment time:	Ferment type:
8 cups	5 minutes	none	lacto

10 pitted whole dates

4 cups frozen summer berries

4 cups Dairy Kefir (page 250)

1 tbsp pure vanilla extract (optional)

1. In a blender, combine the dates, berries, kefir, and vanilla extract (if using). Blend until smooth.

2. Transfer the mixture to 32-ounce (950-gram) glasses. Serve immediately or store in the fridge for up to 1 day.

Variation: Use Villi Yogurt (page 256) instead of Dairy Kefir for an even milder, less sour smoothie. Or freeze as popsicles for probiotic summer treats.

Orange Cream & Kefir Smoothie

Like the orange creamsicle of my childhood summers, this citrusy, creamy smoothie satisfies my summer cravings in a healthy way.

Yield:	Prep time:	Ferment time:	Ferment type:
5 cups	5 minutes	none	lacto

2 cups Dairy Kefir (page 250) or Villi Yogurt (page 256)

1 cup heavy or whipping cream

3 oranges, peeled and quartered, seeds removed

2 large eggs from local, pastured chickens (don't use store-bought, factory-farmed eggs), yolks only

¼ cup raw honey

1 tsp pure vanilla extract

10 ice cubes

1. In a blender, combine the kefir or yogurt, cream, oranges, egg yolks, honey, vanilla extract, and ice cubes. Blend until smooth.

2. Transfer the mixture to 32-ounce (950-gram) glasses. Serve immediately or store in the fridge for up to 1 day.

Simple Cheeses

In this second chapter on dairy, we're going to focus on basic cheese-making. Follow the guidelines in Chapter 12. You won't need a cheese press or any other fancy equipment to complete these simple recipes. Here's all you'll need: two pieces of 90-thread-count cheesecloth, a stainless steel colander, a 2½-gallon (10-liter) stainless steel pot, and a thermometer that reads up to 88°F (31°C).

You'll also need rennet, which coagulates curds through the action of the enzyme rennin (as opposed to the acid curdling you saw in Chapter 12). I don't recommend junket rennet. See Appendix B for places to purchase good rennet.

Finally, because you'll be using a lot of cheesecloth, here's how to clean it:

1. Rinse in cool water.

2. Sterilize by boiling for 2 minutes or using the sterile cycle of your washing machine.

3. Hang to dry.

4. Fold up and store in a clean place.

Cheese Recipes

What follows is an assortment of my family's favorite cheeses. We rotate through these cheeses and usually at least one of them can be found our fridge or freezer. I hope you love them too. Enjoy!

Clabber Cheese

Turn your sweet, mild clabber into a delicious cheese to spread on toast, muffins, or pancakes.

Yield:	Prep time:	Ferment time:	Ferment type:
2 cups	15 minutes	2 to 3 days	lacto

½ gallon (2 liters) raw milk   ½ tsp sea salt (optional)

1. Add the milk to a ½-gallon (2-liter) jar. Cover with a cloth napkin or paper towel. Secure with a rubber band. Leave at room temperature until the milk sets up like yogurt, about 2 days.

2. Place a colander in a container that fits it. Line the colander with two layers of 90-thread-count cheesecloth. Pour the sour milk into the cheesecloth. Tie the ends and place them inside the colander.

3. Let the whey drip for 1 or 2 days. Hang the bag to speed up the process.

4. Untie the cheesecloth. Scrape out the cheese and transfer to an airtight container. Mix in the salt (if using).

5. Store in the fridge for up 2 weeks.

Variations: You can use clabber cheese wherever you'd use cream cheese. Add herbs and salt for a fantastic vegetable dip. Or sprinkle the cheese with cinnamon and drizzle with honey, then eat it with fresh fruit.

Hanging a Bag of Curds Using a Stick

Preserving Dry Cheeseballs in Olive Oil

Cream Cheese

You'll never go back to store-bought cream cheese after making your own. Flavor it up to match the little tubs of flavored cream cheese—only better. You'll also save money!

Yield:	Prep time:	Ferment time:	Ferment type:
2 cups	2 minutes	36 hours	lacto

1 quart (1 liter) raw or pasteurized cream (not heavy)

⅛ tsp mesophilic cheese starter culture or 4 tbsp buttermilk with active cultures

1. In a wide-mouth quart (liter) jar, combine the cream and mesophilic culture or buttermilk. Stir well. Cover with a cloth napkin or paper towel. Secure with a rubber band. Leave at room temperature until the mixture sets up like firm yogurt, about 8 to 15 hours.

2. Line a colander with two layers of 90-thread-count cheesecloth. Place the colander in a bigger bowl or pot. Pour the cultured cream into the cheesecloth. Tie the ends and place them inside the colander.

3. Let the whey drip for 12 to 18 hours or until the cheese is as dry as you'd like. Hang the bag to speed up the process.

4. Untie the cheesecloth and transfer the cheese to an airtight container. If desired, add any of the flavor combinations listed in Variations. Store in the fridge for up to 2 weeks.

Variations:

• **Onion & Chives Cream Cheese:** In a large bowl, combine 1 cup of cream cheese, ¼ cup of finely diced red onions, 2 tablespoons of chopped fresh chives, and ¼ to ½ teaspoon of sea salt.

• **Cinnamon & Walnut Cream Cheese:** In a large bowl, combine 1 cup of cream cheese, ¼ cup of chopped walnuts, ½ teaspoon of ground cinnamon, and 3 tablespoons of sweetener (Sucanat, rapadura, raw honey, or maple syrup).

• **Fruit Cream Cheese:** In a small bowl, combine 1 cup of cream cheese and 2 to 4 tablespoons of your favorite jam.

• **Garlic & Herb Cream Cheese:** In a medium bowl, combine 1 cup of cream cheese, 1½ teaspoons of dried herbs or 1 tablespoon of chopped fresh herbs, 1½ teaspoon of crushed fresh garlic, and sea salt to taste.

Kefir Cheese

More tart than other soft cheeses, kefir cheese has many uses: Add herbs and salt for dips or dressings; combine with honey and spices for a quick and delicious topping; or spread on toast or pancakes like cream cheese.

Yield:	Prep time:	Ferment time:	Ferment type:
2 cups	5 minutes	1 day	lacto

1 quart (1 liter) plain Dairy Kefir (page 250)   ¼ to ½ tsp sea salt (optional)

1. Place a colander in a container that fits it. Line it with two layers of 90-thread-count cheesecloth. Pour the kefir into the cheesecloth. Tie the ends and place them inside the colander.

2. Let the whey drip for 1 day. Hang the bag to speed up the process.

3. Untie the cheesecloth. Scrape out the cheese and transfer to an airtight container. Mix in the salt (if using).

4. Store in the fridge for up 2 weeks.

Variation: If you hang the bag of cheese longer (for 2 to 3 days), you'll end up with a drier cheese you can form into balls and store submerged in extra-virgin olive oil in a cool, dark pantry indefinitely. Keep in mind that the longer the cheese hangs, the more sour it gets.

Blossom Cheese

This is the easiest cheese to make, requiring little time and effort. The biggest requirement: one to two days of patiently waiting! Once the basic cheeseball is done, flavor as desired. Be sure to check Variations for two of my favorites.

Yield:	Prep time:	Ferment time:	Ferment type:
1 cheeseball	5 minutes	24 to 48 hours	lacto

2 quarts (2 liters) yogurt or dairy kefir

1. Tuck 90-count cheesecloth into a ½-gallon (2-liter) glass canning jar to create a net that reaches about one-fourth to one-third of the way down. Secure the cheesecloth to the jar's rim with a rubber band.

2. Slowly pour as much yogurt or kefir as you can into the cheesecloth. The whey will drip into the bottom of the jar. Check the yogurt or kefir in about an hour. (By then, it will have descended a bit into the jar.)

3. Keep adding yogurt or kefir until the entire 2 quarts (2 liters) are in the cheesecloth. Flip the loose ends of the cheesecloth up and over the top of the jar to keep dust and bugs off while the whey continues to drip.

4. Patiently wait 1 to 2 days for the whey to be extracted and a pliable yogurt cheeseball to form. To avoid the cheese from getting more sour than you prefer, you can transfer it to the fridge.

5. Once the cheese forms a ball, transfer to an airtight container. Store in the fridge for up to 2 weeks. See Variations for flavor additions you can make.

Variations:

• **Honey Hazelnut Yogurt Cheeseball:** In a small skillet on the stovetop over medium-low heat, melt 2 to 3 tablespoons of butter. Add ¾ cup of finely chopped hazelnuts. Toast the hazelnuts for 5 to 10 minutes, stirring constantly, but don't let them burn! Remove the skillet from the heat and salt the hazelnuts to taste. Let cool a bit, then add 1 to 2 tablespoons of raw honey. Mix well. Refrigerate until cool. Spread the nut mixture on a plate, then roll the cold cheeseball in the nuts to evenly coat.

• **Onion & Garlic Yogurt Cheeseball:** In a small skillet on the stovetop over medium heat, melt 2 tablespoons of butter. Add ½ finely chopped red onion and 2 garlic cloves minced. Sauté until soft. Remove the skillet from the heat and let the onion and garlic cool. Gently mix them into the cheese. Add sea salt to taste. Form the cheese into a ball.

Smierkase

Enjoy this traditional Dutch cottage cheese with fresh fruit for breakfast or dessert. It's creamy and moist from the added raw milk

Yield:	Prep time:	Ferment time:	Ferment type:
1 cup	15 minutes	2 to 3 days	lacto

1 quart (1 liter) raw milk

¼ to ½ cup light cream

¼ tsp sea salt

1. Add the milk to a wide-mouth quart (liter) jar. Cover with a cloth napkin or paper towel. Secure with a rubber band. Leave at room temperature until the milk sets up like yogurt, about 2 days.

2. Place a colander in a container that fits it. Line the colander with two layers of 90-thread-count cheesecloth. Pour the soured milk into the cheesecloth. Tie the ends and place them inside the colander.

3. Let the whey drip for 12 or 24 hours or until the cheese is dry. Hang the bag to speed up the process.

4. Untie the cheesecloth. Scrape out the cheese and transfer to a medium bowl.

5. Add the cream and mix until a spreadable consistency forms. Stir in the salt. Transfer to an airtight container. Store in the fridge for up to 3 weeks.

Fromage Blanc

Quite tasty, mild, and useful, this whole milk cheese resembles cream cheese in texture, although it's made from whole milk rather than cream. Use this cheese where you'd normally use cream cheese or ricotta. As an inoculant for other ferments, this whey works just as well as that from kefir or yogurt—so save it!

Yield:	Prep time:	Ferment time:	Ferment type:
2 cups	10 minutes	2 days	lacto

½ gallon (2 liters) raw or pasteurized whole milk (cow or goat)

⅛ tsp mesophilic cheese starter culture

¼ cup water

1 drop of regular- or double-strength vegetable rennet

½ tsp sea salt

1. In a ½-gallon (2-liter) jar, combine the milk and mesophilic culture. Stir well with a wooden spoon.

2. In a small bowl, combine the water and rennet. Stir well. If the rennet is regular strength, add 2 tablespoons of this mixture to the jar. If the rennet is double strength, add 1 tablespoon of this mixture to the jar. Stir well. Discard or save the rest of the mixture, which you can store for up to 1 week and will begin to smell bad when it can no longer be used.

3. Cover the jar with a cloth napkin or paper towel. Secure with a rubber band. Leave at room temperature until the mixture sets up like firm yogurt, about 24 hours.

4. Line a colander with two layers of 90-thread-count cheesecloth. Place the colander in a bigger bowl or pot. Pour the cultured milk into the cheesecloth. Tie the ends and place them inside the colander. Let the whey drip for 24 hours or until the cheese is as dry as you'd like it.

5. Untie the cheesecloth and transfer the cheese to an airtight container. Mix in the salt. Adjust to taste. Store in the fridge for up to 2 weeks or in the freezer for up to 2 months.

Feta

This is absolutely amazing and incredibly easy to make. I urge you to try to wait the full month while it ages. It's worth it! If the feta falls apart during aging or storage, the blocks were too soft. If this happens, remove them from the brine and store them in the fridge or freezer. You'll need to eat the blocks in the fridge within a few weeks. They'll taste great but will lack somewhat in texture.

Yield:	Prep time:	Ferment time:	Ferment type:
½ gallon (2 liters)	2 minutes	1 month & 4 days	lacto

½ gallon (2 liters) plus ¼ cup water, divided, room temperature

2 gallons (8 liters) raw or pasteurized whole milk (cow or goat)

¼ tsp mesophilic cheese starter culture

¼ tsp lipase

1 rennet tablet, 30 drops of regular-strength liquid rennet, or 15 drops of double-strength liquid rennet

1 tsp calcium chloride (optional but helpful if milk is homogenized)

½ cup sea salt or kosher salt, plus more

1. Add the milk to a 2½-gallon (10-liter) stainless steel pot on the stovetop over medium-low heat. (Use a double boiler for a water bath if room temperature is very cool.) Sprinkle the mesophilic culture and lipase over the top. Let them dissolve for a few seconds, then stir in very well. Bring the mixture to 86°F to 88°F (30°C to 31°C) while keeping the pot covered and stirring infrequently to avoid hot spots.

2. Maintain the same temperature while keeping the pot covered for 1 hour. Don't stir.

3. Fifteen minutes before the hour is up, add the ¼ cup of water to a small bowl. Crush the rennet tablet or add the drops to the water. Let dissolve fully. If you're using homogenized milk, mix the calcium chloride with the remaining ¼ cup of water in a small bowl.

4. While stirring the milk, add the rennet mixture. While continuing to stir, add the calcium chloride mixture (if using) to the milk. Stir very well.

5. Cover and let the milk mixture sit for about 1 hour. Monitor the temperature to maintain 86°F to 88°F (30°C to 31°C). Don't disturb the forming curds with any stirring or moving of the thermometer.

6. Test for a clean break by sliding a knife into the curds at an angle. The curds will cut cleanly and whey will pour into the cut made by the knife if it's ready. If it's not set up yet, give it more time, about 5 minutes after each check.

7. Cut the curd into ½-inch (1.25cm) cubes. (See Recipe Notes for instructions.) Leave undisturbed for 5 to 10 minutes for cow's milk and 10 to 15 minutes for goat's milk.

8. Stir the curds gently, using a slotted spoon to cut any you missed. Monitor the temperature and use a towel over the lid of the pot to keep the curds at 86°F to 88°F (30°C to 31°C) for another 45 minutes. Stir gently every 10 minutes to keep the curds from sticking.

9. Place a colander inside a bowl or pot. Spread one piece of 90-thread-count cheesecloth inside the colander. Transfer the curds to the colander. Tie the ends and place them inside the colander. Let the whey drip for 2 or 4 hours. Hang the bag to speed up the process.

10. Take down the bag, undo the cheesecloth, and flip the cheese over. Retie the cheesecloth and rehang the bag until the total time reaches 24 hours. The lipase will make the cheese smell very strong during this period.

11. Take down the bag and undo the cheesecloth. Cut the ball into 2- to 3-inch (5 to 7.5cm) chunks. Salt all sides of each chunk and place them in an airtight container in a single layer, making sure they don't touch. Tightly cover and leave at room temperature for 2 to 3 days. During this time, they'll spill out more whey and firm up.

12. In a large bowl, combine the salt and the remaining ½ gallon (2 liters) of water. This is the salt brine

13. Transfer the cheese to a 1-gallon (4-liter) or ½-gallon (2-liter) jar. Pour the salt brine over the cheese. Cover tightly. Add a layer of plastic wrap under the lid if it's not airtight.

14. Age in cool storage for 1 month before eating. This will keep indefinitely.

Recipe Notes: To cut cheese curds: (1) Make a series of parallel cuts straight down into the curds—as far apart as the recipe specifies. (2) Rotate the pot 90 degrees. Make another set of parallel cuts that are perpendicular to the first set of cuts— as far apart as the recipe specifies. (3) Tip the knife 45 degrees and make a set of parallel cuts along the same lines as the cuts in step 2. Reach as far as you can with the knife. (4) Rotate the pot 90 degrees. Tip the knife 45 degrees and make a set of parallel cuts along the same lines as the cuts in step 1. Reach as far as you can with the knife. (5 and 6) Rotate the pot 90 degrees and repeat steps 3 and 4.

Feta

Middle Eastern Hard Cheese

Middle Eastern Hard Cheese

Mild and salty, this Middle Eastern cheese is fantastic paired with extra-virgin olive oil on hummus or eaten with fresh pocket bread. Because this authentic recipe doesn't call for a starter culture, you must use raw milk that comes with its own colony of beneficial organisms. You can use raw milk from any animal. I've made this cheese from raw cow's milk and raw goat's milk. This is the cheese of my growing-up years. I love how low-tech it is, requiring neither heat nor culture nor press. I make this cheese with fresh milk from the morning milking, which is the perfect temperature for culturing. The best times of year to make this cheese are spring and fall. Because of the lengthy aging time at room temperature without having been inoculated with a starter colony, it usually spoils in temperatures above 80°F (27°C).

Yield:	Prep time:	Ferment time:	Ferment type:
1 pint (½ liter)	30 minutes	3 to 4 days	lacto

1 gallon (4 liters) raw whole milk (cow or goat)

1 rennet tablet, 20 drops of regular-strength liquid rennet, or 10 drops of double-strength liquid rennet

¼ cup cool water

½ cup sea salt

½ gallon (2 liters) water, room temperature

1. Add the milk to a 2-gallon (8-liter) stainless steel pot over medium-low heat. Let the milk come to slightly warmer than room temperature. (When you insert a clean finger, it will feel comfortable to touch.)

2. In a small bowl, combine the rennet and water. Stir until the rennet dissolves. Add the mixture to the milk while stirring. Cover and let the milk mixture sit undisturbed for about 1 hour.

3. Test for a clean break by sliding a knife into the curds at an angle. If they're ready, they should cut cleanly and whey will pour into the cut made by the knife. If it's not set up yet, give it more time, about 5 minutes after each check.

4. Cut the curds into ½- to ¾-inch (1.25 to 2cm) cubes. Leave them undisturbed and covered for 15 minutes.

5. Gently stir the curds, using a slotted spoon to cut any you missed.

6. Place a colander inside a bowl or pot. Place one layer of 90-thread-count cheesecloth inside the colander. Transfer the curds to the colander. Tie the ends and hang the cheesecloth for 24 hours.

7. After about 8 to 12 hours, take the ball down, undo the cheesecloth, and flip the cheese over. Be gentle because the cheeseball will probably be soft, wet, and fragile. Retie the cheesecloth and rehang the bag to complete the 24-hour hanging period.

8. Take down the bag. Untie the cheesecloth and cut the cheese into ¾-inch-thick (2cm) slices. Because they'll be pretty soft and wet inside, be gentle. Cut each slice into 2- to 3-inch-wide (5 to 7.5cm) pieces.

9. Line a tray or an airtight container with three to four layers of paper towels (or absorbent cloths). Place an absorbent cloth under the tray to absorb whey that will drip off. Sprinkle salt on all sides of each piece and place them on the tray in a single layer, making sure the pieces don't touch. Cover tightly with plastic wrap or an airtight lid if you have one that fits the tray.

10. Leave at room temperature for 3 days. Every 24 hours, resalt each piece of cheese on all sides. Every 24 hours, remove the wet paper towels and replace them with fresh ones. Make sure to re-cover the tray or container. During this time, more whey will spill out while the cheese will dry out and firm up significantly. On the second day, the salt level is just about right for eating. By the third day, the cheese will taste too salty.

11. During the 3 days of aging, inspect the cheese for spoiling. If it develops moldy or slimy areas, trim these areas off and smell the cheese. If it regains its fresh, pleasant, cheese smell, it's fine. If it still smells bad, the spoiling has likely spread to the entire piece of cheese and it should be discarded.

12. In a large bowl, combine the salt and water. This is the salt brine.

13. The cheese is done when the blocks are firm and have shrunk to about ½-inch (1.25cm) thick. They'll still break and crumble, but they're no longer like custard and more like less-crumbly feta. Transfer the cheese pieces to a ½-gallon (2-liter) or quart (liter) storage jar. Pour the brine over the cheese. Keep the brined cheese in cold storage for up to 1 year.

Cheddar Cheese Curds

Want to make cheddar cheese but don't have a cheese press or cave? Maybe the thought of pressing cheese or aging cheese sounds too complicated? I've got an idea for you: Make cheddar cheese curds! You might wonder why they don't turn out deep orange like grocery store cheddar. Yellow grass-season cream will yield softly yellow cream cheese because the rapidly growing green grass is rich in beta-carotene that ends up in the milk of animals eating it. This gives cream (and cheeses made with it) a yellow or even mildly orange color. The taste is more rich and grassy—in a good way. Other times of year, cream and cheese are more pale and less complexly flavored.

Yield:	Prep time:	Ferment time:	Ferment type:
1 pound (450 grams)	2 hours	4½ hours	lacto

2 to 4 gallons (8 to 15 liters) raw and/or whole milk

¼ tsp mesophilic cheese starter culture (Danisco MA19 recommended or use MA4001)

¾ tbsp good-quality vegetable rennet

¼ cup water

1 to 2 tbsp fine sea salt

1. Add the milk to a large pot on the stovetop over medium-low heat. Over a couple hours, slowly warm it to 86°F (30°C), stirring occasionally. Keep the pot covered to preserve the heat.

2. Sprinkle the mesophilic culture over the milk. Stir in very well. Cover and let culture or "ripen" for 45 minutes to 1 hour, keeping the temperature at 86°F (30°C). During the summer, turn the burner off and cover the lid with a bath towel to keep the milk at temperature. This is the ripening time.

3. In a small bowl, combine the rennet and water. Stir until the rennet dissolves. Add this mixture to the milk. Stir well. After the ripening time, add the rennet mixture to the milk. Stir well. Cover again and let the milk set until a firm curd forms, about 30 to 45 minutes. If you cut into the curd with a knife, it should make a "clean break"—where the curd splits and whey pours into the crack.

4. Cut the curd into ½-inch (1.25cm) cubes. Be very gentle with the curds at this point. In fact, after cutting them, leave them undisturbed in the pot for 5 minutes. Keep the cover on to keep them warm.

5. Turn on the burner and heat the curds to 102°F (39°C) for 40 minutes. During this time, stir gently every 5 or 10 minutes to keep the curds from sticking and to make them smaller. Keep the curds at 102°F (39°C) for 30 minutes more. Stir occasionally. The curds should be firm and a bit stretchy, surrounded with lots of whey. They should hold together if pressed. Let the curds settle at the bottom of the pot.

6. Transfer about two-thirds of the whey to another pot or container. You can keep this raw, cultured whey for lacto-ferments or soaking where a stronger flavor works well (such as for fermenting vegetables). Transfer the curds to a colander, leaving the remaining whey in the pot.

7. Nest the colander inside the pot to suspend the curds over the whey. This begins the "cheddaring process," which gives the cheese its squeaky texture. Let the curds drain for about 1 hour. Cover with a piece of cheesecloth and the pot lid. Keep the burner on low if necessary to keep the whey warm. Turn the curds over a few times to make sure they're draining well.

8. Transfer the curds to a cutting surface. Cut them into chunks, then cut the chunks into slices. Place them in a bowl and toss with fine sea salt until just lightly salted. These curds are ready for eating!

9. Store in an airtight container in the fridge for up to 2 weeks. They'll continue to release whey—just pour it off to prevent the curds from becoming soggy.

Recipe Notes:

Ideas for using cheddar curds:

• Dice the strips for toppings on rice bowls, tacos, burritos, or other main dishes.

• Dice the strips for use in cold grain salads or other salads.

• Place the strips on top of your almost-fried eggs. Cover and let melt.

• Use in grilled cheese sandwiches.

• Use in cold sandwiches.

• Use the strips or large dices for appetizers and serve with crackers and pickles.

Using Cheeses in Other Recipes

In the next few recipes, I'll give you some ideas for incorporating the easy cheeses of this chapter into delicious dishes.

Chocolate Cream Cheese Frosting

This is the perfect frosting to use on the Chocolate Sourdough Cake (page 212) or with any other cake or cupcake for that matter.

Yield:	Prep time:	Ferment time:	Ferment type:
1½ cups	5 minutes	none	lacto

1 cup cream cheese or Fromage Blanc (page 278)

½ stick unsalted butter, room temperature

1 tsp pure vanilla extract

1½ cups unrefined sweetener, powdered by pulsing in a blender or food processor

½ cup cocoa powder

1. In a food processor, combine the cream cheese and butter until smooth.

2. Add the vanilla and sweetener. Cream until smooth.

3. Add the cocoa powder. Cream until smooth.

4. Transfer the frosting to an airtight container. Refrigerate until ready to use. Because it will harden when chilled, let it soften at room temperature for a few minutes before using. Store for up to 1 week.

Variation: Omit the cocoa powder to make a vanilla cream frosting. Unrefined sweeteners tend to be golden-colored, as will your frosting.

Chard & Feta

Easy to put together, this simple side dish goes well with practically anything. Draining the cooking water is another way besides fermentation to reduce oxalic acid in dark, leafy greens and vegetables of the cabbage family. By adding the cheese after the chard has cooled, you retain the probiotic benefits.

Yield:	Prep time:	Ferment time:	Ferment type:
2 cups	5 minutes	none	lacto

2 cups water

7 to 9 large leaves of rainbow chard, washed, dried, and cut into 1-inch (2.5cm) strips and pieces, including the stems

¼ cup melted salted butter

sea salt

ground black pepper

powdered or granulated garlic

¼ cup crumbled Feta (page 279)

1. Add the water to a medium saucepan and place a steamer basket in the saucepan. Place the saucepan on the stovetop over medium heat. Add the chard to the basket and steam until just wilted yet still colorful, about 2 to 3 minutes. Discard the cooking water.

2. Transfer the chard to a small serving bowl. Drizzle the butter over the top. Season with the salt, pepper, and garlic. Toss and adjust seasonings to taste. Once the chard has cooled, toss with the feta. Store leftovers in the fridge for up to 1 day.

Variation: Use kale, beet greens, spinach, or other dark greens in this recipe. You can also switch out the feta for Middle Eastern Hard Cheese (page 282).

Recipe Notes: Granulated garlic is dried garlic with a coarser texture than garlic powder. I like it because it doesn't poof up and fill the air when I sprinkle it on foods. Because granulated garlic has half the strength of powdered garlic, use twice as much granulated garlic. You should be able to find it in your grocery store's bulk spice section.

Chard & Feta

Creamy Herb Salad Dressing

Herbs and salt dress up slightly sour soft cheese for a wonderful, versatile salad dressing (or dip!).

Yield:	Prep time:	Ferment time:	Ferment type:
2 to 3 cups	5 minutes	none	lacto

1 cup Instant Pot Yogurt (page 254), Clabber Cheese (page 272), Kefir Cheese (page 275), or another soft cheese

½ to 1 cup raw or pasteurized whole milk (cow or goat), plus more

¼ cup apple cider vinegar

1 tbsp dried dill

1 tbsp dried parsley

1 tbsp dried chives

½ tsp garlic powder

½ to 1 tsp sea salt

⅛ tsp ground black pepper

1. In a 1-quart (1-liter) jar or small bowl, whisk together all the ingredients. Add more milk to reach your desired consistency.

2. Transfer to an airtight container and store in the fridge for up to 2 weeks.

Smoked Salmon & Cheese on Toast

This is delicious with scrambled eggs for a refreshing breakfast. It also makes a great snack!

Yield:	Prep time:	Ferment time:	Ferment type:
1 piece of toast	5 minutes	none	lacto

1 to 2 tbsp Clabber Cheese (page 272), Cream Cheese (page 274), Kefir Cheese (page 275), or another soft cheese

1 slice of buttered whole grain toast

2oz (60g) smoked salmon, room temperature

1. Spread the cheese on the toast and top with the salmon. Serve immediately.

Two-Cheese Egg Salad

You'll enjoy this light, flavorful, and tasty salad, which you can serve on English Muffins (page 209).

Yield:	Prep time:	Ferment time:	Ferment type:
3 cups	15 minutes	none	lacto

12 large hard-boiled eggs, peeled, chilled, and diced

½ medium onion (any type), diced

¼ cup crumbled Feta (page 279)

⅓ cup diced cheddar cheese

1 tsp dried dill

½ tsp sea salt

¼ tsp ground black pepper

1. In a medium bowl, combine all the ingredients. Toss until the eggs are coated.

2. Transfer the salad to an airtight container and refrigerate until ready to serve. Store for up to 3 to 5 days.

Probiotic Potato Salad

This is a definite crowd-pleaser and kefir cheese adds just the tang a perfect potato salad needs.

Yield:	Prep time:	Ferment time:	Ferment type:
6 cups	30 minutes	none	lacto

1 cup Kefir Cheese (page 275)

raw or pasteurized whole milk (cow or goat)

1 to 2 tsp homemade herb seasoning salt (see Recipe Notes for instructions), plus more

⅛ tsp ground black pepper

1 tbsp chopped fresh parsley

1 tbsp chopped fresh dill

12 medium red potatoes, boiled, cooled, and diced

4 large hard-boiled eggs, peeled and diced

½ medium onion (any type), diced

2 celery stalks, diced

2 garlic cloves, crushed

1. In a small bowl, whisk together the kefir cheese and 1 tablespoon of milk at a time until you get a salad dressing consistency. Add the seasoning salt, pepper, parsley, and dill. Stir well.

2. In a medium bowl, combine the potatoes, eggs, onion, celery, and garlic. Toss to mix well. Add the kefir cheese mixture. Toss well. Adjust seasonings to taste. Chill until ready to serve. Store for up to 1 week.

Recipe Notes: To make the herbed seasoning salt, in a small bowl, combine 1 cup of sea salt; 1 teaspoon each of dried oregano, dried thyme, dried basil, dried dill, dried garlic, dried chives, dried sage, celery seeds, and marjoram; 2 teaspoons of dried onion powder; ½ teaspoon of ground rosemary; ½ cup of dried parsley; 2 teaspoons of dried ground kelp (optional); and ¼ cup of nutritional yeast. Store in a glass jar or saltshaker in a cool, dry place.

Sprouted Lentil Salad

Sprouted lentils are filling and refreshing. In this recipe, they combine with salad vegetables, cheese, and an herbed dressing for a satisfying main dish meal.

Yield:	Prep time:	Ferment time:	Ferment type:
9 cups	5 minutes	none	lacto

1 cup dry brown or green lentils

4 cups water, plus more

1 cup shredded carrots

1 cup diced Roma or other slicing tomatoes

1 bell pepper (any color), diced

1 medium cucumber, peeled and diced

1 avocado, peeled, seeded, and diced

½ cup sliced black olives

¼ cup crumbled Feta (page 279)

2 tbsp chopped fresh parsley

2 tbsp chopped fresh cilantro

1 cup Creamy Herb Salad Dressing (page 288), plus more

1. Sort through the lentils and remove any pebbles. In a ½-gallon (2-liter) jar, combine the lentils and water. Place a sprout screen on the jar. (See Appendix B for sources.) Let soak for 12 hours or overnight.

2. Drain the lentils. Rinse with cool water until the water runs clear.

3. Return the lentils to the jar. On a towel, place the jar on its side or with its bottom slightly elevated. Place the towel and jar in a cool room temperature location. Twice daily, rinse and drain the lentils until the water runs clear and the lentils have ¼-inch (0.5cm) sprouts.

4. Transfer the lentils to an airtight container and refrigerate until needed, rinsing and draining the lentils every other day to keep them fresh. (Store for up to 1 week.)

5. Add 5 cups of sprouted lentils to a medium salad bowl. Add the carrots, tomatoes, bell pepper, cucumber, avocado, olives, feta, parsley, and cilantro. Toss well. Pour 1 cup of the dressing over the top and toss to incorporate. Add more salad dressing as needed for your desired consistency.

6. Chill until ready to serve. Store for up to 3 days, although it's best served fresh or within a few hours of making.

Beet, Mint & Feta Salad

Mint and salty feta crumbles accent the earthy and sweet beets in this Mediterranean-inspired cold salad.

Yield:	Prep time:	Ferment time:	Ferment type:
4 cups	5 minutes	none	lacto

5 to 6 medium beets, unpeeled, greens cut off

¼ cup extra-virgin olive oil, plus more

¼ cup crumbled Feta (page 279)

2 tbsp chopped fresh mint or 1 tsp dried mint

½ tsp sea salt

⅛ tsp ground black pepper

1. Preheat the oven to 375°F (190°C). Place the beets in a single layer on a baking sheet.

2. Place the sheet in the oven and bake until fork-tender, about 25 minutes to 1 hour. Remove the sheet from the oven. Let the beets cool.

3. Use your fingers to rub the peels off the beets. (They should release easily.) Dice the beets.

4. In a medium salad bowl, combine the beets, olive oil, feta, mint, salt, and pepper. Taste and adjust seasonings.

5. Serve at room temperature or chilled. Store in an airtight container in the fridge for up to 3 days.

Mediterranean Carrot Salad

The sweetness of carrots and balsamic vinegar combine with the smokiness of cumin, salty feta, and fresh parsley for a winning side salad.

Yield:	Prep time:	Ferment time:	Ferment type:
4 cups	5 minutes	none	lacto

2 cups water

4 medium carrots, thinly sliced

¼ cup crumbled Feta (page 279)

¼ tsp ground cumin

1 garlic clove, crushed

3 tbsp extra-virgin olive oil

2 tsp balsamic vinegar

1 tbsp chopped fresh parsley

¼ to ½ tsp sea salt

pinch of ground black pepper

1. Add the water to a small saucepan. Place a steamer basket in the saucepan. Place the saucepan on the stovetop over medium heat. Add the carrots to the basket and steam until tender but not too soft, about 5 minutes. Drain. Transfer the carrots to a medium bowl and let cool for about 10 minutes.

2. Add the feta, cumin, garlic, olive oil, balsamic vinegar, parsley, salt, and pepper. Toss well. Adjust seasonings to taste.

3. Chill thoroughly before serving. Store in an airtight container in the fridge for up to 1 week.

Mediterranean Quinoa Garden Salad

With pearly, chewy quinoa dressed up with garden vegetables, cheese, and chicken, this salad is hearty enough to be a main dish yet light enough not to leave you feeling heavy.

Yield:	Prep time:	Ferment time:	Ferment type:
6 cups	5 minutes	none	lacto

2 cups dry quinoa

4 cups water, plus more

4 tbsp apple cider vinegar

½ to 1 cup plus 2 tbsp extra-virgin olive oil, divided, plus more

2 tsp sea salt, divided

½ cup diced Middle Eastern Hard Cheese (page 282)

2 cups diced cooked chicken

1 medium cucumber, peeled and diced

2 bell peppers (any color), diced

2 medium plum or Roma tomatoes, diced

2 medium carrots, shredded

½ medium red onion, diced

2 garlic cloves, crushed

1 tbsp chopped fresh basil or 1 tsp dried basil

1 tbsp chopped fresh parsley or 1 tsp dried parsley

2 tbsp toasted sesame oil

2 to 4 tbsp balsamic vinegar

¼ tsp ground black pepper

1. Place the quinoa in a fine mesh strainer. Rinse the quinoa under cold running water for 2 minutes. Transfer the quinoa to a medium saucepan. Add the water and apple cider vinegar. Cover and let soak for 12 hours or overnight.

2. Place a fine mesh strainer over a medium bowl. Drain the quinoa through the strainer. Measure the drained water, then discard. Rinse the quinoa with cool water for 2 minutes.

3. Return the quinoa to the saucepan. Add the same amount of fresh water that was drained in step 2. Add 2 tablespoons of olive oil and 1 teaspoon of salt.

4. Place the saucepan on the stovetop over medium-high heat. Bring to a boil, then reduce the heat and simmer covered until all the water is absorbed and the quinoa is tender, about 15 to 20 minutes. Remove the saucepan from the heat and let the quinoa cool to room temperature or transfer to the fridge to cool quickly.

5. In a large bowl, combine the quinoa, cheese, chicken, cucumber, bell peppers, tomatoes, carrots, onion, garlic, basil, and parsley. Toss well. Add the sesame oil, balsamic vinegar, and the remaining ½ to 1 cup of olive oil. Add the black pepper and the remaining 1 teaspoon of salt. Toss well. Adjust seasonings to taste.

6. Cover and refrigerate for 3 hours to let the flavors mingle. Serve. Store for up to a 3 days.

Mint, Cucumber, Tomato & Feta Salad

In the height of summer garden season, dress up your tomatoes and cucumbers with fresh mint, feta, and olive oil for a fantastic Mediterranean salad.

Yield:	Prep time:	Ferment time:	Ferment type:
6 cups	10 minutes	none	lacto

2 medium cucumbers, peeled and diced

2 large tomatoes, diced

½ medium red or yellow onion, diced

1 garlic clove, crushed

¼ cup Feta (page 279)

¼ cup extra-virgin olive oil

1 tbsp balsamic vinegar or freshly squeezed lemon juice

2 tbsp chopped fresh mint or 1 tsp dried mint

¼ to ½ tsp sea salt

⅛ tsp ground black pepper

1. In a medium bowl, combine all the ingredients. Toss well. Adjust seasonings to taste.

2. Serve at room temperature or chilled. Store in an airtight container in the fridge for up to 1 day. This is best served within a few hours.

Meats & Fish

Chapter
14

In this chapter, I'll share a brief history of meat and fish preservation. Then you'll find out how to safely ferment meats and fish as well as master the art of making fermented sausages. Finally, I'll share a selection of tasty recipes that are ideal for getting experience with meat and fish fermentation.

History of Meat Preservation

Before refrigerators and freezers became commonplace, people had very few options for preserving the meat of animals and fish. Basically, they could eat it fresh and avoid the whole issue or they could salt it.

An early discovery was how salt drew water out of animal flesh, with the result that the salted, dried meat wasn't nearly as susceptible to decay, spoiling, or infestation. Such methods are called "salt curing" and are applied by soaking meat in a very salty brine or by layering salt on the outside of the meat to do two things: draw out water so the inside will be protected from spoiling and protect the outside of the meat from infestation by airborne contaminants. With the latter, salt would be reapplied almost daily because as it drew off water, it became wet.

Such curing methods aren't methods of fermentation because the salt levels are so high, they inhibit beneficial organisms along with spoiling organisms. Also, the amount of salt is so significant that the meat tastes very salty.

I suppose fermentation came about part accidentally and part purposefully. Someone might have created a preserved meat that was less salty but bursting with complex, pleasing, and sour flavors. To recount how all this could have happened isn't nearly as important as sharing what people learned about how to achieve it regularly. Basically, they discovered that good things happen to the meat when they create conditions that favor the fermenting organisms and restrict the others.

We now know that lactic-acid-producing bacteria eat carbohydrates (sugars) and produce lactic acid. (Interestingly, meats don't contain sugar, so sugar is sometimes added to fermenting meat mixtures as a food source for the cultures.) Under the right conditions, this fermentation by beneficial organisms creates safe fermented foods. Let's talk about how to do this.

Ensuring Safe Fermentation

To safely ferment meats and fish, you need to restrict the growth of spoiling or pathogenic organisms. When meat is fresh, it's like a vacant lot: Who's going to set up shop? We hope the good guys will win and we'll help ensure that by setting up protections. What are they?

First, we control the time and temperature. Given enough time in warm enough temperatures, spoiling organisms multiply rapidly. Therefore, good recipes have you working quickly with cold meat and then proceeding with the fermentation at optimum temperatures for the beneficial organisms. Most recipes include a short fermentation time at warmer temperatures so the lactic-acid-producing bacteria can get established. Then you transfer the mixture to cooler temperatures for storage or a longer fermentation. Always follow a recipe's specific temperature guidelines for each stage. In addition to the other factors that follow, the fermenting times and temperatures depend largely on the style of fermentation (fast, medium, or slow) and the organisms being cultured.

Second, we increase acidity. Or in other words, we want to lower the pH to at least 5.0 but ideally 4.6. Spoiling and pathogenic organisms are severely restricted or even stopped at such acid levels. You can add acids to a fermenting mixture or you can let the acids be produced by fermenting organisms. You get more complex, gourmet flavors from the latter scenario, but that takes longer and the results are less certain because of the extra time. Additionally, you can nurture wild, beneficial organisms into a strong colony or you can use a starter culture to establish a colony from the beginning.

And finally, you can control salt and moisture levels. Adding salt to a meat mixture or a brine makes water unavailable to spoiling organisms and therefore most can't survive. You have to be careful, though, because with 4% salt or higher, the beneficial organisms can't survive either. (Most fresh meat recipes call for 1.5% to 2% salt for good flavor, but that isn't enough to ensure safe meat fermentation. Good fermented meat recipes call for 2.3% to 3%.)

Some harmful organisms can survive high-salt and low-moisture levels, which is why the recipes call for sodium nitrates or sodium nitrites (chemical salts) to be introduced into the meat mixture. These salts are the only sure protection against *Clostridium botulinum*, the organism that causes botulism by producing toxins that build up in the meat. Nitrates/nitrites also suppress salmonella. Quicker fermentation recipes call for nitrites (called pink salt or Cure #1; see Appendix B for sources), while longer fermentations call for nitrates (called Cure #2; also see Appendix B for sources). Nitrates are converted to nitrites during fermentation. In a ferment, nitrates act much like slow-releasing nitrites. Don't eliminate nitrites or nitrates in any recipes unless the recipe tells you it's optional.

Traditionally, people used saltpeter (potassium nitrate) to keep cured meats pink and to inhibit toxins. Today, we use sodium nitrate or sodium nitrite for the same purpose. Nitrites are controversial: In some conditions, they can produce cancer-causing compounds called "nitrosamines." But evidence suggests that vitamin C in the presence of nitrites *prohibits* production of the nitrosamines.

Today, we consume far fewer nitrates or nitrites than people of history because we eat fewer cured meats and recipes are more carefully formulated. Also, keep in mind that nitrites are found naturally in vegetables—and some argue they're present in greater concentrations than in cured meats!

Because nitrates and nitrites provide the only sure protection against botulism, I can't recommend eliminating them from any long-fermented meat recipes. All this talk of botulism and pathogens might make you uncomfortable. Please take heart that under the right conditions (which good recipes provide), the beneficial organisms have the upper hand. They're stronger competitors and they can better tolerate salty and less moist conditions.

About the Fermented Meat & Fish Recipes

In this chapter, we'll explore fermenting meat in three ways: First, I'll share a set of simple brined meat recipes. They're easy and quick. You'll need nothing more than what you've been using for other recipes in this book. However, for best results, don't use open-air containers or jars. No nitrates or nitrites are required because these recipes are either quick or salty enough already.

Second, the recipe for fermented sausage is a transition recipe—great for beginners or those who don't have the tools for making sausage (grinding and stuffing and casings and all that). You'll get your sausages made at the butcher shop in any style you love (the recipe is written for German sausage) and then bring them home to ferment in brine and to cold-smoke. There are basically two types of sausages: dry, long-fermented sausages and semi-dry, medium- or fast-fermented sausages. Dry sausages are ready in about three months, while semi-dry are ready in one to three weeks. You can smoke any sausage type. You'll have to set up a smoker of some sort. (See Appendix B for a book recommendation for doing this.)

Finally, the last four recipes come from fermented-sausage-making experts. In fact, the father and son team of Stanley and Adam Marianski wrote the book on it: *The Art of Making Fermented Sausages*. They've given me permission to share four of their carefully formulated fermented sausage recipes with you—to ensure safety and tasty results. You'll need a meat grinder and sausage stuffer for these recipes. You'll also have to get casings from your local butcher shop as well as be able to control humidity and temperature.

Ingredients

The same principles I shared in Chapter 4 apply here—only they get a little tighter.

Meat & Fat

Only the best and freshest meats and fish will do. You'll get the best results and you'll get a safe, uncontaminated start. Remove blood clots and glands, which might harbor undesirable bacteria. Trim away gristle and sinews.

The sausage recipes in this book don't call for additional fat, but choosing meats with about 10% fat is a great idea. Pork back fat is best when a recipe asks for additional fat because it's white and firmer, and it has a higher melting point. The higher melting point is important because even a few minutes of working with a sausage can warm it up considerably. If the fat melts, it can smear and block holes in the sausage casing and therefore prevent even drying.

Pink Salt (or Cure #1)

Also called by other names—usually some form of Cure #1—this is a source of nitrates for fast- to medium-fermented sausages or other meat dishes. It's salt with nitrates added and colored pink so you don't mistake it for anything else. Keep it away from children and store it where it can't be used accidentally. It would be harmful should someone use it like table salt. See Appendix B for sources.

Cure #2

This salt provides a source of nitrates, which convert to nitrites over time, for long-term meat curing. It also goes by various names—usually with "#2" in the name. Keep away from children or accidental use. No recipe in this book uses Cure #2.

Starter Cultures

The sausage recipes later in this chapter mention specific starter cultures that work well at the temperatures and amounts of sugar specified in the recipes and produce particular flavors. You shouldn't alter the starter cultures unless you're prepared to adjust the other factors to account for it. See Appendix B for sources.

Sausage Casings

You can find or special-order sausage casings through your local butcher or ethnic shop or even the meat department of the grocery store. You can use natural (the inner lining of animals' intestines) or synthetic. Many prefer the better flavor and result of using natural casings. Natural casings come packed in dry salt or salt brine. Synthetic casings keep for a year refrigerated, while the natural casings keep for a month. Either way, before use, you must soak them in fresh water for an hour or a few days to de-salt them. You should also rinse the insides (by holding the casings open under running water) and inspect for holes. You need about 2 feet (0.5 meters) of hog casing or 4 feet (1.25 meters) of sheep casing for each 1 pound (450 grams) of sausage. Casings from other animals, such as beef cow or goat, can also be used. You can change the size of the casing in a recipe if you want bigger or smaller sausages, but keep in mind this will affect smoking and drying times accordingly. Still, this is a substitution you can feel free to make.

Sugar

Some brined meat recipes might call for additional sugar. Feel free to substitute any natural sweetener. The sausage recipes call for dextrose in addition to granulated sugar. Please don't substitute for these until you get more experienced. Dextrose is a form of corn sugar with readily available sugar for the fermenting organisms. The organisms don't have to do any work to convert it, which means as a food source, because it's ready to go, the organisms can get stronger sooner. You'll see it more often in fast-fermented sausages than long-fermented ones.

Spices

Always use dry spices because fresh might carry undesirable bacteria. Organic spices are preferred to avoid pesticides that might interfere with the fermentation.

Sausage-Making Techniques

Before we get into the recipes, let's talk about some sausage-making techniques that might be unfamiliar to you. The techniques involved aren't hard, but they'll likely take some practice. Every kitchen, set of tools, and user are likely different. Some people like to work in pairs to keep up a good pace, while others find they work faster and more efficiently alone. Here are the basic steps of sausage-making.

Grinding

You'll have to do this or have it done for you. The recipes specify the size of grinder plate to use and the amount of meat and fat. If you're doing it yourself, make sure your meat and fat are partially frozen to prevent the fat from melting and smearing the mixture (and to prevent growth of unwanted organisms). Keep your equipment and work area clean. Keep your knives and grinding plates sharp. It's helpful to chill equipment before using and to grind the meat and fat into a bowl set in ice. Just think about keeping everything cold and working quickly.

Mixing

Mix ingredients together until they're sticky and hold together. Once the starter culture is added, try to start stuffing as soon as possible. You can test whether your mixture is sticky enough by forming a patty in your hand. If you're working with large amounts, refrigerate the bulk of the mixture and stuff in small portions.

Stuffing

Use de-salted casings of the size specified in the recipe or your desired size and follow the instructions provided with your sausage-stuffer appliance or attachment. Here more than anywhere else, practice and experience will be your best guides. A wet surface below the stuffer will help your sausages slide easily. Twist lengths of sausages in alternating directions to the specified lengths. Use a sterilized pin or knife tip to prick any air pockets. Then use your fingers to squeeze out the air.

Fermenting

Follow the recipe's guidelines for time, temperature, and humidity levels of the fermentation period. Home sausage-makers usually set up a devoted room or chamber (even an emptied-out fridge) with an adjustable humidifier, a hydrometer (to measure humidity), and a thermometer. You'll need a way to hang the sausages so they get good airflow and aren't crowded. This stage is skipped when making fresh sausages—those meant to be eaten right away or refrigerated for a short time or frozen for longer. (Therefore, cures and starter cultures aren't needed either.)

Smoking

Smoking is an old method of flavoring and keeping mold off sausages. You can cold-smoke or warm-smoke. Cold-smoking lets fermentation continue while drying out is accomplished. During cold-smoking, you should include some periods of no smoke to avoid a bitter-tasting sausage. Follow a recipe's guidelines for the temperature and humidity of smoking. Commercial smokers are available or you can make a homemade smoker chamber. (See Appendix B for a resource.)

Drying

Sausages dry from the inside out. If drying occurs too quickly, the outsides will harden and the insides can't dry out. Also, the sausages might develop an unsightly gray ring on the outside. Monitor how well your sausages are drying by checking on them frequently. Higher humidity slows drying, while higher temperatures quicken drying. Adjust those factors to slow down or speed up drying. You can also make a salt brine mixture (1 tablespoon of sea salt and 1 cup of water) to spray on the sausages periodically if they're drying too fast on the outside.

Storing

Sausages are best stored in a dark, cool room (50°F to 59°F [10°C to 15°C]) with just a minimum airflow and low humidity (65 to 75%). If mold develops (an indicator that the temperature or humidity are high), wipe it off with a vinegar-water solution or cold-smoke it for a few hours more. If the sausages were fermented, smoked, and dried well, the mold is likely only on the surface. Such sausages have a shelf life of many months to several years, and during storage, their flavor will continue to develop—less acidic and milder.

Brined Meat & Fish Recipes

Pickled Salmon

This makes a great appetizer to serve with crackers, other pickled or sliced vegetables, and cheese.

Yield:	Prep time:	Ferment time:	Ferment type:
1 quart (1 liter)	5 minutes	1 day	lacto

1 tbsp sea salt

1 cup water, room temperature

¼ cup starter culture (Appendix B)

1 tbsp raw honey

½lb (225g) boneless, skinless, raw wild salmon, cut into ½-inch (1.25cm) pieces

2 small onions (any type), coarsely chopped

1 medium lemon, scrubbed, thinly sliced

1 tbsp mustard seeds

½ tsp ground black pepper

1 dried bay leaf

1 tbsp dried dill seeds or 3 tbsp chopped fresh dill

1. In a small bowl, make the brine by combining the salt and water. Add the starter culture and honey. Mix until the honey dissolves.

2. In a wide-mouth quart (liter) jar, combine the salmon, onions, lemon, mustard seeds, pepper, bay leaf, and dill. Pour the brine to 1 inch (2.5cm) from the jar's rim. Add more water to cover if necessary.

3. Place a clean regular-mouth jar lid on top of the mixture to hold the ingredients below the liquid. Cover with a lid or an airlock.

4. Leave at room temperature for 1 day. Transfer to cool storage for up to 2 weeks.

Pickled Mustard Herring or Mackerel

Mustard, red pepper flakes, and coriander make this fish smoky and spicy. It's delicious with toast for breakfast or as an appetizer with crackers.

Yield:	Prep time:	Ferment time:	Ferment type:
1 quart (1 liter)	5 minutes	1 day	lacto

1 tbsp sea salt

1 cup water, room temperature

¼ cup starter culture (Appendix B)

1 tbsp mustard seeds or 2 tbsp prepared mustard

1½ lb (680g) skinless, raw herring or mackerel, cut into ½-inch (1.25cm) pieces

2 small onions (any type), coarsely chopped

1 tsp coriander seeds

½ tsp ground black pepper

1 dried bay leaf

⅛ tsp red pepper flakes

1. In a small bowl, make the brine by combining the salt and water. Add the starter culture. If you're using prepared mustard, add this now. Mix well.

2. In a wide-mouth quart (liter) jar, combine the herring or mackerel, onions, mustard seeds (if using), coriander, pepper, bay leaf, and red pepper flakes. Pour the brine to 1 inch (2.5cm) from the jar's rim. Add more water to cover if necessary.

3. Place a clean regular-mouth jar lid on top of the mixture to hold the ingredients below the liquid. Cover with a lid or an airlock.

4. Leave at room temperature for 1 day. Transfer to cool storage for up to 2 weeks.

Fermented Tuna

This fish dish is great as an anytime snack or as part of a smorgasbord-style lunch. Splash some vinegar over the fish before serving to give it that traditional Scandinavian bite.

Yield:	Prep time:	Ferment time:	Ferment type:
1 quart (1 liter)	5 minutes	1 day	lacto

1 tbsp sea salt

1 cup water, room temperature

¼ cup starter culture (Appendix B)

1 tbsp raw honey

1lb (450g) tuna loins, skinned, boned, and cut into bite-sized pieces

two ¼-inch (0.5cm) lemon slices

1 small onion (any type), thinly sliced

1 bunch of freshly snipped dill

1 dried bay leaf

8 crushed black peppercorns

5 crushed whole allspice or juniper berries

1. In a small bowl, make the brine by combining the salt and water. Add the starter culture and honey. Stir until the honey dissolves.

2. Into a wide-mouth quart (liter) jar, pack the tuna, lemon, onion, dill, bay leaf, peppercorns, and allspice or juniper berries. Pour the brine to 1 inch (2.5cm) from the jar's rim. Add more water to cover if necessary. Cover with a lid or an airlock.

3. Leave at room temperature for 1 day. Transfer to cool storage for up to 2 weeks.

Cured Meat Recipes

Corned Beef

Salty and gray (rather than pink), this traditional recipe will yield tender beef for sandwiches or a main dish roast. Because this is beef meant to be cooked, use the Corned Beef Dinner (page 308) recipe for cooking your corned beef.

Yield:	Prep time:	Ferment time:	Ferment type:
½ gallon (2 liters)	10 minutes	10 to 12 days	lacto

½ cup plus 2 tbsp sea salt

1 tbsp unrefined sweetener (such as Sucanat, rapadura, or maple syrup)

4 cups water

3 to 4lb (1.4 to 1.8kg) grass-fed beef brisket or another tough roast cut (such as chuck, round, or shank), rinsed, then cut into 2- to 3-inch (5 to 7.5cm) chunks

1. In a medium saucepan on the stovetop over medium-low heat, make the brine by combining the salt, sweetener, and water. Stir until the salt dissolves. Remove the saucepan from heat and let the brine cool to room temperature.

2. Into a ½-gallon (2-liter) airlock container, pack the beef. Add the brine. Place a lid or some other clean, flat, disc-shaped object on top of the meat to hold it below the brine. Place an airlock on the jar.

3. Leave at room temperature for 8 hours, preferably in a dark location. Transfer to the fridge for up to 7 to 10 days. Check the brine level daily and add more as needed to keep the meat covered.

Corned Beef Dinner

Amazingly tender after curing and simmering, the slightly salty and tasty corned beef works great on bread for sandwiches or served in chunks with potatoes and steamed cabbage.

Yield:	Prep time:	Ferment time:	Ferment type:
3 to 4 pounds (1.4 to 1.8 kilograms)	10 minutes	none	none

Corned Beef (page 307)

½ large yellow onion, quartered

½ tbsp pickling spice

2 bay leaves

1 tbsp dried thyme

6 garlic cloves

½ tsp sea salt

1. Drain the beef and rinse well under cold running water. Discard the brine.

2. In a medium to large stockpot on the stovetop over medium-low heat, combine the beef, onion, pickling spice, bay leaves, thyme, garlic, and salt. Add enough water to cover. Bring to a boil, then reduce the heat to a simmer. Cover and let simmer until tender, about 1½ to 2 hours.

3. Transfer the beef to a covered serving dish. Shred or serve in chunks. Discard the brine when cool (because it will be too salty to eat).

4. Store in the fridge for up to 3 to 5 days.

Corned Beef

Pepperoni

Peppery, smoky, and a little spicy, this pepperoni will be ready for pizza in 24 hours. Traditional pepperoni isn't smoked. For this and the next three recipes (all four from *The Art of Making Fermented Sausages* by Stanley and Adam Marianski), you'll need specialty sausage starter cultures called T-SPX and F-LC. T-SPX is a culture for slow fermentation at temperatures not higher than 75°F (24°C). F-LC is a set of fermenting bacteria that works in a wide temperature range. It produces acids quickly as well as prevents pathogenic bacteria growth. See Appendix B for where to buy these and other cultures.

Yield:	Prep time:	Ferment time:	Ferment type:
11 pounds (5 kilograms)	1 hour	5 days	lacto

7.7lb (3.5kg) pork

3.3lb (1.5kg) beef

6 tbsp plus 1 tsp fine sea salt

2 tsp Cure #1 (see Appendix B)

¼ cup dextrose

¼ cup granulated sugar

2 tbsp plus 1 tsp ground black pepper

4 tbsp plus 1 tsp paprika

2 tbsp cracked anise seeds or 2½ tbsp cracked fennel seeds

2 tbsp plus 2 tsp ground cayenne

½ tsp F-LC culture (see Appendix B)

2¼-inch (6cm) beef casings

1. Use a ³⁄₁₆-inch (5mm) meat grinder plate to grind the pork and beef.

2. In a large bowl, combine the pork, beef, salt, Cure #1, dextrose, sugar, pepper, paprika, anise or fennel seeds, cayenne, and F-LC culture. Stuff the mixture into the casings.

3. Leave for 24 hours at 100°F (38°C) and with 85 to 90% humidity. You can also warm-smoke for 6 hours at 110°F (43°C) and with 70% humidity. Gradually increase the smoke temperature until the internal meat temperature reaches 140°F (60°C). For drier sausages, dry the sausages for 2 days more at 60°F to 70°F (16°C to 21°C) and with 65 to 75% humidity.

4. Store the sausages at 50°F to 59°F (10°C to 15°C) and with 75% humidity. These will keep for up to 5 to 6 months.

Summer Sausage

This popular and tasty American sausage is a fabulous addition to a gift basket of homemade jams and cheeses.

Yield:	Prep time:	Ferment time:	Ferment type:
11 pounds (5 kilograms)	1 hour	1 to 3 days	lacto

7.7lb (3.5kg) pork

3.3lb (1.5kg) beef

6 tbsp plus 1 tsp fine sea salt

2 tsp Cure #1 (see Appendix B)

¼ cup dextrose

⅛ cup granulated sugar

1 tbsp plus 2¾ tsp ground black pepper

1 tbsp plus scant 1 tsp ground coriander

1 tbsp plus 2 tsp whole mustard seeds

1 tbsp plus scant 1 tsp ground allspice

1⅓ tsp ground nutmeg

1 tbsp plus scant 1 tsp garlic powder

½ tsp F-LC culture (see Appendix B)

2¼-inch (60mm) beef casings

1. Use a ³⁄₁₆-inch (5mm) meat grinder plate to grind the pork and beef.

2. In a large bowl, combine the pork, beef, salt, Cure #1, dextrose, sugar, pepper, coriander, mustard seeds, allspice, nutmeg, garlic powder, and F-LC culture. Stuff the mixture into the casings.

3. Leave for 24 hours at 86°F (30°C) and with 85 to 90% humidity.

4. Warm-smoke for 6 hours at 100°F (38°C) and with 70% humidity. Gradually increase the smoke temperature until the internal meat temperature reaches 140°F (60°C).

5. For drier sausages, dry for 32 days more at 60°F to 70°F (16°C to 21°C) and with 65 to 75% humidity.

6. Store the sausages at 50°F to 59°F (10°C to 15°C) and with 75% humidity. These will keep for up to 5 to 6 months.

Variation: Use all beef for these sausages.

Lebanon Bologna

Not traditionally cooked, this is a moist, stable, heavily smoked sausage from Lebanon, Pennsylvania.

Yield:	Prep time:	Ferment time:	Ferment type:
11 pounds (5 kilograms)	varies	5 days	lacto

11lb (5kg) lean beef (no extra fat)

6 tbsp plus 1 tsp fine sea salt

2 tsp Cure #1 (see Appendix B)

¾ cup granulated sugar

¼ cup dextrose

2 tbsp plus 1 tsp ground black pepper

1 tbsp plus scant 1 tsp ground allspice

1 tbsp plus scant 1 tsp ground cinnamon

3½ tsp ground cloves

5½ tsp ground ginger

¼ tsp T-SPX culture (see Appendix B)

1⅝- to 4¾-inch (4 to 12mm) natural or collagen casings

1. Use a ⅛- to ³⁄₁₆-inch (3mm to 5mm) meat grinder plate to grind the beef.

2. In a large bowl, combine the beef, salt, Cure #1, sugar, dextrose, pepper, allspice, cinnamon, cloves, ginger, and T-SPX culture. Stuff the mixture into the casings. With larger casings, because these are heavy, you'll have to support them with butcher's twine when hanging them.

3. Leave for 72 hours at 75°F (24°C) and with 85 to 90% humidity.

4. Cold-smoke for 2 days at 72°F (22°C) and with 85% humidity.

5. For drier sausages, dry for 2 days more at 54°F to 60°F (12°C to 16°C) and with 80 to 85% humidity.

6. Store the sausages at 50°F to 59°F (10°C to 15°C) and with 75% humidity. These will keep for up to 5 to 6 months.

Merguez

This spicy, short lamb or beef sausage from North Africa is delicious when fried in olive oil.

Yield:	Prep time:	Ferment time:	Ferment type:
11 pounds (5 kilograms)	1 hour	5 days	lacto

11lb (5kg) lamb

6 tbsp plus 1 tsp fine sea salt

2 tsp Cure #1 (see Appendix B)

¼ cup dextrose

scant ¼ cup ground black pepper

3½ tbsp garlic powder

4 tbsp plus 2 tsp ground cayenne

3 tbsp plus 2 tsp paprika

1 tbsp plus 2 tsp ground cumin

1 tbsp plus scant 1 tsp ground coriander

6 tbsp olive oil

½ tsp F-LC culture (see Appendix B)

¾- to 1¹⁄₁₆-inch (19 to 27mm) sheep casings

1. Use a ³⁄₁₆-inch (5mm) meat grinder plate to grind the lamb.

2. In a large bowl, combine the lamb, salt, Cure #1, dextrose, pepper, garlic powder, cayenne, paprika, cumin, coriander, olive oil, and F-LC culture. Firmly stuff the mixture into the casings. Form the casings into 5- to 6-inch (12.5 to 15.25cm) links or leave the casings in one continuous rope.

3. Leave for 48 hours at 75°F (24°C) and with 85 to 90% humidity.

4. For drier sausages, dry for 18 days more at 54°F to 60°F (12°C to 16°C) and with 80 to 85% humidity.

5. Store the sausages at 50°F to 59°F (10°C to 15°C) and with 75% humidity. These will keep for up to 5 to 6 months.

Variation: Use beef instead of lamb.

Easy Brined & Smoked German Sausage

This is delicious eaten like jerky or thinly sliced and served with cheese and crackers. This recipe is from author and homesteader Michael Bunker. He keeps sausages handy in his office to eat while writing. He says you can store these sausages in bags, boxes, or burlap. Lower humidity during storage will cause the sausages to dry out more. (This is okay, but it results in a tougher, drier sausage.) Higher humidity might cause mold. His family often vacuum-packs their sausages to store them in warmer or more humid locations, such as root cellars.

Yield:	Prep time:	Ferment time:	Ferment type:
10 to 12 pounds (4.5 to 5.4 kilograms)	1 hour	6 days	lacto

1 gallon (4 liters) water

1¾ cups fine sea salt or kosher salt

3 tsp Cure #1 (see Appendix B)

5 garlic cloves, peeled and halved

1 tbsp ground black pepper

1 cup apple cider vinegar

10 to 12lb (4.5 to 5.4kg) fresh German sausages in casings from butcher, refrigerated but not frozen

1. In a medium pot on the stovetop over medium-high heat, make the brine by combining the water, salt, Cure #1, garlic, pepper, and apple cider vinegar. Bring to a boil, then remove the pot from the heat. Let the brine cool to room temperature. Transfer to a sterilized 5-gallon (18-liter) food-grade bucket.

2. Use a toothpick to poke holes about 1 inch (2.5cm) apart all over the sausage casings. Add the sausages to the bucket, making sure they're all submerged. Use a weight if necessary to keep the sausages submerged. Place a lid on the bucket. Place the bucket in a cool location (between 40°F and 50°F [4°C to 10°C]) for 24 hours.

3. Drain and rinse the sausages. Pat dry with paper towels. You can leave them in a cool location—unsubmerged and spread out for good airflow—for another 24 hours if you'd like a more sour taste or you can proceed with step 4.

4. Refill the bucket with fresh water. Submerge the sausages in the water. Use a weight if necessary to keep the sausages submerged. Place a lid on the bucket. Leave in a cool location for 12 hours to draw the salt out.

5. Drain the bucket. Remove the sausages and pat dry with paper towels. Place the sausages on clean paper towels to air dry for 10 to 15 minutes.

6. Cold-smoke the meat for 5 days at less than 80°F (27°C) and with 75% humidity. If the outside is drying too quickly, make a small amount of brine and periodically spray the outsides of the sausages. Cut open some sausages to make sure they're dry on the insides. Keep smoking until they are.

7. Store the sausages at 50°F to 59°F (10°C to 15°C) and with 75% humidity. These will keep for up to 5 to 6 months.

Variation: Use any variety of sausage you like.

Glossary

aerobic A biological process that requires oxygen.

airlock A special lid for a vessel that uses a water barrier to let fermenting gases escape while preventing outside air from getting in.

ale Beer that's fermented at warmer temperatures for shorter periods of time and the yeasts ferment at the top of the carboy.

anaerobic A biological process that doesn't require oxygen.

antinutrients Natural or synthetic substances that interfere with the absorption of nutrients.

bacteria Single-celled microscopic organisms that have a cell wall but lack organelles and an organized nucleus. They eat starches and sugars in foods.

BPA-free Plastic containers or metal cans that don't contain bisphenol A, or BPA. BPA is a chemical compound linked to certain health conditions, such as infertility, cardiovascular problems, and diabetes.

brine A water and salt mixture, with a high concentration of salt.

carcinogens Substances capable of causing cancer in living tissue.

culture To ferment.

enzymes Substances, usually proteins, which act as catalysts to bring about specific actions in the body, such as the digestion of particular nutrients.

ethyl alcohol The intoxicating component of wine, beer, and other alcoholic beverages. It's also known as "ethanol."

fermentation What happens when bacteria, yeasts, or other microorganisms break down food, giving off gases.

gut A casual term for the intestines.

gut flora A colony of microscopic organisms living within the intestines.

homogenize The process by which fat molecules in milk are forced to become the same size as other molecules in the milk to prevent the cream from rising to the top.

kefir   A yogurt-like fermented dairy beverage that can contain up to 50 beneficial organism strains.

lactic acid   The main acid produced in most fermentations. It's a natural food preserver because it makes food too acidic for spoiling organisms. Beneficial organisms love its acidity and exist quite happily in its presence—whether in the food or when entering the digestive system.

lacto-fermentation   The type of fermentation that occurs when yeasts and bacteria convert starches and sugars in foods into lactic acid.

lager   A beer that's fermented at cold temperatures for long periods of time with yeasts that work at the bottom of the fermenting container.

minerals   Inorganic substances essential for good health and nutrition that our diet must supply. When we don't get enough, we suffer from nutritional deficiencies.

molds   Multicellular fungi that grow in moist environments, such as on food. They produce enzymes that break down food for them to eat.

pasteurization   The process of heating foods to kill disease-causing bacteria or microorganisms. It also kills beneficial organisms, destroys heat-sensitive vitamins, and denatures fragile proteins.

probiotics   Microorganisms consumed by the body for their benefits. Also known as beneficial organisms, beneficial bacteria, beneficial microbes, beneficial yeasts, or beneficial bacteria.

raw food   A food that isn't heated beyond 115°F (46°C) and thus retains any naturally present beneficial organisms and enzymes that would otherwise perish during heating.

sake   A Japanese alcoholic drink made from fermented rice, traditionally drunk warm in small porcelain cups.

starter cultures   A set of desirable fermenting organisms (bacteria, yeast, or molds) you can use to help ensure a successful fermentation.

vitamins   Organic substances that are essential for good health and nutrition that our diet must supply. When we don't get enough, we suffer from nutritional deficiencies.

whey   The acidic, watery part of milk that remains after the curds form. Uncooked whey might be added to ferments as a starter culture.

yeasts   Single-celled microscopic fungi that convert sugar into water, alcohol, acids, and carbon dioxide. Scientists know of about 1,500 species of yeasts.

Great Resources

Books

Bentley, Nancy Lee. *Truly Cultured: Rejuvenating Taste, Health and Community With Naturally Fermented Foods: A Cookbook and Nourishment Guide.* Two Pie Radians Foundation. 2007.

Buhner, Stephen Harrod. *Sacred and Herbal Healing Beers: The Secrets of Ancient Fermentation.* Brewers Publications. 1998.

Campbell-McBride, Natasha. *Gut and Psychology Syndrome: Natural Treatment for Autism, Dyspraxia, A.D.D., Dyslexia, A.D.H.D., Depression, Schizophrenia.* Medinform Publishing. 2010.

Fallon, Sally, and Mary G. Enig. *Nourishing Traditions: The Cookbook That Challenges Politically Correct Nutrition and the Diet Dictocrats.* NewTrends Publishing. 2001.

Harmon, Wardeh, Erin Vander Lugt, Sara Kay Michalski, Katie Kimball, and Christina Dickson. *Sourdough A to Z.* Traditional Cooking School by GNOWFGLINS. 2011.

Katz, Sandor Ellix. *Wild Fermentation: The Flavor, Nutrition, and Craft of Live-Culture Foods.* Chelsea Green Publishing. 2003.

Leverentz, James R. *The Complete Idiot's Guide to Cheese Making.* Alpha. 2010.

Madison, Deborah. *Preserving Food Without Freezing or Canning: Traditional Techniques Using Salt, Oil, Sugar, Alcohol, Vinegar, Drying, Cold Storage, and Lactic Fermentation.* Chelsea Green Publishing. 2007.

Marianski, Stanley, Adam Marianski, and Robert Marianski. *Meat Smoking and Smokehouse Design.* Bookmagic. 2009.

Marianski, Stanley, and Adam Marianski. *The Art of Making Fermented Sausages.* Bookmagic. 2009.

Morris, Margaret P. *The Cheesemaker's Manual.* Glengarry Cheesemaking & Dairy Supply. 2003.

Papazian, Charlie. *The Complete Joy of Home Brewing.* Collins Living. 2003.

Ruhlman, Michael, and Brian Polcyn. *Charcuterie: The Craft of Salting, Smoking, and Curing.* W.W. Norton. 2005.

Schmid, Ronald F. *The Untold Story of Milk: The History, Politics and Science of Nature's Perfect Food: Raw Milk From Pasture-Fed Cows.* NewTrends Publishing. 2009.

Ziedrich, Linda. *The Joy of Pickling: 200 Flavor-Packed Recipes for All Kinds of Produce From Garden or Market.* Harvard Common Press. 1998.

Websites & Classes

Campaign for Real Milk
www.realmilk.com

DIY Airlock Instructions
www.traditionalcookingschool.com/DIYairlock

Traditional Cooking School by GNOWFGLINS: my blog
www.TraditionalCookingSchool.com

Bible-based cooking program: my online classes in sourdough, cultured dairy, cheese, lacto-fermentation, the fundamentals of traditional cooking, and more
www.TraditionalCookingSchool.com/enroll

Weston A. Price Foundation: wise traditions in food, farming, and the healing arts
www.westonaprice.org

Cultures & Supplies

Chaffin Family Orchards: olives, olive oil, and more from Oroville, California
www.ChaffinFamilyOrchards.com

Cultures for Health: fermentation vessels, Grolsch-style bottles, nondairy starter cultures, water kefir grains, dairy kefir grains, muslin bags for cultures, cheesecloth, cheese cultures, rennet, yogurt starters, cheese-making tools, kombucha SCOBY, soy cultures, sourdough starters, gluten-free sourdough starters, sprout screens, glass fermenting weights, and books
www.CulturesForHealth.com

Five Star Chemicals & Supply: Star-San sterilizer
www.FiveStarChemicals.com

Homesteader Supply: fermentation vessels, Grolsch-style bottles, starter cultures, cheesecloth, cheese cultures, rennet, Prepper Pro (kraut pounder), Pickle Pro (fermenting lids), and cheese-making tools
www.HomesteaderSupply.com

Lead-Safe Mama: information on heavy metals in kitchenware
www.tamararubin.com

Perfect Supplements: cod liver oil and glyphosate-free gelatin; use coupon code TCS10 to get 10% off your order
www.PerfectSupplements.com

Pomona's Pectin: non-sugar-based thickener for jams, jellies, and more
www.PomonaPectin.com

Radiant Life: purification systems or countertop filters that don't strip minerals
www.radiantlifecatalog.com

The Sausage Maker: starter cultures, pink salt, Cure #1, and Cure #2
www.SausageMaker.com

SweetLeaf: stevia
www.SweetLeaf.com

Trace Minerals Research: mineral drops
www.TraceMinerals.com

Wyeast Laboratories: traditional yeast for home brewing
www.wyeastlab.com

Index